Michigan Legal Studies

SOVIET LEGAL INSTITUTIONS

A publication from
The University of Michigan Law School

Soviet
Legal
Institutions

DOCTRINES AND SOCIAL FUNCTIONS

by
Kazimierz Grzybowski

ANN ARBOR

THE UNIVERSITY OF MICHIGAN PRESS

To zżk

FOREWORD

This book represents the highlight of a career of scholarship by its author and a most significant contribution to the literature, which will bring to those who seek it an understanding of the role law plays in Soviet Russia. More important, it will bring that understanding in a comparative context which sharpens the impact and compels a careful analysis of the social function legal institutions perform in both systems. Though Soviet jurists may deny the validity of comparative methodology as applied to the Soviet legal order, the analysis which is here presented proves not only that comparisons are possible but also that they can be most illuminating.

In some respects it is a grim story which unfolds in this perceptive work. The Western mind is not unfamiliar with governmental efforts to shape human conduct through the creation or manipulation of legal institutions. We are not unmindful that the monopoly of force reserved to government can be turned, through the imposition of penal sanctions, to deter human conduct which would otherwise emerge as a result of other social pressures. But the Western mind will find the chapter on Homo Sovieticus extremely disquieting as the author traces the means by which and the extent to which the compulsive force of law is directed toward reshaping the ideas, the attitudes, the minds of the Soviet citizens. To read, from the Judicature Act of 1933, that courts of law "shall educate the citizens of the USSR in the spirit of devotion to the country and the cause of socialism . . ." cannot but evoke in the Western mind a response of shock, when one recalls the power of the court to enforce its dictates. To watch the concept of "public official" being expanded through legal manipulation to include practically an entire population, while simultaneously observing that the state is imposing a stringent liability upon public officials who deviate from current political or economic views, will not be restful. To learn that libel suits have disappeared from the dockets of socialist courts because the press now represents functionally the best way to attack problem spots in the social and economic life and must not be impeded by individual interests from pursuing social action, will not appeal to those who champion freedom of the press.

But this book is not written to shock the reader. It is written to bring him enlightenment concerning the realities of legal order in Russia. Not many persons could write it. To do so requires a deep understanding of several legal systems, a capacity to translate the verbal doctrine into terms of social function, and an ability to perceive those points of comparison which will permit the reader to understand the human meaning of legal institutions. The distinguished author, Dr. Kazimierz Grzybowski, has all these qualifications and he has brought them to bear in full measure to produce this volume.

We at the Michigan Law School were privileged to assist the late Vladimir Gsovski in publishing, in 1948, his vitally important work on the Soviet Civil Code. We are proud to have assisted also in making possible this current exposition of the Soviet legal order which should stand as a monument to the values of scholarly research.

Allan F. Smith
Dean, University of Michigan Law School

Ann Arbor, Michigan
May, 1962

ACKNOWLEDGMENTS

My thanks go first to Dean Allan F. Smith and the faculty of the University of Michigan Law School for the fellowship which made this book possible. The year spent in Ann Arbor as an Edson R. Sunderland Senior Research Fellow permitted me to concentrate on the task of writing and made me a member of that community of jurists oriented toward legal research, who were always generous with their time, advice, and suggestions.

I am especially grateful to Professors Alfred F. Conard, Eric Stein, and Whitmore Gray for reading parts of the manuscript in various phases of its preparation, and to Dr. Vera Bolgar of the *American Journal of Comparative Law* for long hours spent with me discussing various problems and issues treated in the present study. I am also indebted to Professor Hobart Coffey, director of the Law Library, and to his staff for extending to me the magnificent facilities of the Law Library, and for their innumerable courtesies in anticipating my needs and requests. In particular I have exploited the extensive knowledge of foreign law and foreign literature of Mrs. Lilly Roberts, bibliographer of the Law Library, who generously devoted much of her time to my project. Finally, I wish to thank Mr. Bernie Burrus of the Legislative Research Center and Miss Alice Russell, assistant editor of the Michigan Legal Publications, for editing and preparing the manuscript for publication.

CONTENTS

ABBREVIATIONS

B.O.	Buletinul Oficial (Rumanian Official Law Gazette) March 1, 1949—
DU	Dziennik Ustaw (Polish Official Law Gazette) 1919—
D.V.	Durzhaven Vestnik (Bulgarian Official Law Gazette) 1879–1950
G.Z.	Gazeta Zyrtare (Albanian Official Law Gazette) 1944—
Highlights	Highlights of Current Legislation and Activities in Mid-Europe, 1953–1959
I.P.N.S.	Izvestia na Prezidiuma na Narodnoto Subranie (Bulgarian Official Law Gazette) 1950—
M.O.	Monitorul Oficial (Rumanian Official Law Gazette) 1860–1949
OGDDR	Entscheidungen des Obersten Gerichts der Deutschen Demokratischen Republik, 1951—
PiP	Państwo i Prawo (State and Law) 1946—
PiZ	Prawo i Zycie (Law and Life) 1956—
Sbirka	Sbirka zakonu republiki Ceskoslovenske (Collection of Laws of the Czechoslovak Republic) 1918—
SGP	Sovetskoe gosudarstvo i pravo (Soviet State and Law) 1931—
Sl. L.	Sluzbeni List Demokratske Federativne Jugoslavje (Yugoslav Official Law Gazette) 1946—
Sob. uzak.	Sobranie uzakonenii i rasporiazhenii raboche-krestianskogo pravitelstva RSFSR (Collection of Laws and Decrees of the Workers' and Peasants' Government of the RSFSR) 1917–1938
Sob. zak. SSSR	Sobranie zakonov i razporiazhenii raboche-krestianskogo pravitelstva SSSR (Collection of Laws and Decrees of the Government of the USSR) 1924–1938
Sots. zak.	Sotsialisticheskaia zakonnost (Socialist Legality) 1931—

Sov. iust.   Sovetskaia iustitsia (Soviet Justice) 1922–1941

Vedomosti   Vedomosti Verkhovnogo Soveta SSSR (Journal of the Supreme Soviet of the USSR) 1938—

ZOIC   Zbiór Orzeczeń Sądu Najwyzszego, Izba Cyvilna (Collections of Decisions of the Polish Supreme Court, Civil Bench) 1945—

ZOIK   Zbiór Orzeczeń Sądu Najwyzszego, Izba Karna (Collections of Decisions of the Polish Supreme Court, Criminal Bench) 1945—

Chapter I

TERMS OF REFERENCE

PARALLELS AND ANALOGIES

The present social and economic order of the Soviet Union, with its emphasis upon industrial economy and the urban mode of life, is only a phase of that general process of change which has produced modern industrial society. The principal instrument of change occurred in the mastering of the new technological processes and in the application of modern science to the satisfaction of social needs. In the Soviet Union, as well as in the Western societies where the process of change originally started, industrial and social revolutions made it necessary to redefine certain basic legal concepts, with the result of a veritable jural revolution. In the Soviet Union, no less than in the West, the role of the state and the concept of public order have been reformulated as the control and management of the national economy became the central problem of public concern. Thus, in new social conditions the concept of public function has acquired a new meaning.

The purpose of the present chapter is to lay ground for a systematic examination of Soviet reality in terms of the social functions of Soviet legal institutions. Soviet jurists, preoccupied with the political aspects of their legal order, reject the idea of the comparative method regarding the Soviet legal order. In spite of the formal similarities between socialist and capitalist legal institutions, Soviet professors alleged that the different political content precludes analogy between socialist and capitalist law, for:

Terms of bourgeois legislation are found in separate articles of Soviet statutes and in the statutes in their entirety. That, however, is not the point. The heart of the matter is that Soviet character of . . . the law is expressed in its political character . . . in its socialist content.[1]

1 Yudin, "Socialism and Law," in Soviet Legal Philosophy 294 (1951).

Admittedly, the political motivation behind a legal rule is an important element in the determination of its purpose and of its function. It is equally true, however, that governmental policies do not account for all aspects of the social function of the enacted rules of law. Legal institutions live their lives and are inspired by their own policies. And these are broader than the actual policies of the regime. In order to obviate overemphasis on the political aspects of social ordering in the Soviet polity, the present inquiry is less concerned with the general theories of the function of the Soviet legal system than with the social role of the institutions of Soviet law, including all aspects of their influence on the course of human affairs.

In order to provide a general framework for the comparative treatment of the institutions of Soviet law, the reader's attention is drawn to some of the main features of the modern legal systems in Western Europe. New social conditions tend to emphasize the role of public law. The final result has been the creation of a new branch of legal regulation, administrative law, while private law has declined as a regulator of basic social functions. New avenues are thus opened for action by the public authority in the promotion of the interests of the polity and of the social welfare. The shape and systematic arrangement of the rule of law have been seriously affected by the increased flow of legal regulations. Finally, the expansion of administrative action has called for the redefinition of the tasks and scope of judicial control.

In the field of legal theory, two trends of jurisprudence have been outlined as important for the understanding of Soviet legal ideas; though never fully acknowledged by Soviet jurists, they reflect the evolution of ideas which resulted from the social changes of the nineteenth century. The positivistic school, in linking legal order with the institution of the state, sees in the latter the most important element in the preservation of social order. The sociological school, emphasizing the role of the social milieu, on the other hand, relegates the state to a less important place.

The central idea inspiring the policies of social reform in the Soviet Union is the theory of the progress of human society toward higher forms of social organization as it was formulated by Karl Marx. This theory was conceived as a process of social evolution under the impact of the changing, ever more efficient and more collective production techniques. Soviet policy has supported the action of social agents by the action of the state in enforcing Soviet law. Thus, a new legislative technique has been evolved. Aiming at the achievement of social reform through the enforcement of the rule of law, it is an idea not only non-Marxian, but in addition, has been borrowed from the sociological ideas of the West.

THE IDEA OF PROGRESS

After a period of initial doubt as to the place of legal regulation in the socialist society, Soviet leadership determined to accord it a role in the realization of the aims of the Soviet state. The law, it was concluded, offered a useful mechanism for coordinating the activities of social organizations, for reorganizing economic life, and for instilling new ideas on the purpose of social action in the minds of the people. In the words of Vyshinskii, who was called on to perform the act of faith in the name of the Soviet legal profession, the state and the law serve to "eradicate completely and finally the remnants of capitalism in the economic system, to develop the class conscience of the people and to create the Communist society." [2]

A Soviet jurist, writing in the post-World War II period for the benefit of his less experienced Polish brethren, stated that:

Socialist legality . . . is defined by the policy of the Soviet state. . . . The policy of industrialization, of collectivization, required a number of legal measures, which ensured historical achievements of socialist construction in the USSR. Stalin's five-year plans are laws strictly executed. . . . Here the correlation between politics, legal regulations and socialist legality is direct and immediate.

Thus, the idea of planned progress toward higher forms of social and economic organization provides the ethos for the legislative embodiments of Soviet policy. In addition, it constitutes the foundation for the Soviet claim that socialist law is a higher type of law. As the Soviet scholar continued:

At the present time, countries of people's democracy having liquidated the capitalist order, are achieving in the development of their new law,

2 Vyshinskii, Materialy pervoi konferentsii nauchnykh rabotnikov prava, May 16–19, 1938, at 183 (1938).

not the reception of Roman law patterns, but of the highest type of law: socialist law.[3]

In spite of its simplicity, however, the idea of irresistible progress toward better forms of social organization, when viewed in the context of the basic assumptions of Marxist world outlook, presented a number of practical difficulties in the promulgation of concrete legal rules. While there was no doubt in the minds of Soviet leaders that transforming the backward economy of Russia required imitation of Western industrial techniques, it was far less certain in which direction to seek the models for reforming the antiquated laws of the country. Since Marxist theory dictated that progress be conceived as a dialectical process, in which higher forms of production were reflected in new social relations, the new laws could not be borrowed nor imitated outright from the bourgeois experience or patterns.[4]

And yet, repeal of prerevolutionary laws did not mean renunciation of the basic convictions of Russian jurists who, though siding with the Revolution, nevertheless sought to correlate their own revolutionary convictions and work for the new order with the teachings of progressive jurists of the bourgeois world. A decade after the outbreak of the October Revolution, a Soviet jurist reporting on trends in legal science in the Soviet Union acknowledged that Soviet legal scholars still adhered to the main current of European jurisprudence.[5] It is not surprising then that a great many ideas and formulations of modern European scholars have been incorporated into Soviet legislation, although on occasion there was involved little more than terminological similarities reflecting, it would appear, habits of thought rather than fundamental convictions.

In view of the intellectual debt owed to Western jurisprudence, it is no wonder that the idea of uniqueness of the Soviet experiment did not appear coterminous with early statutes. The conviction of the Bolshevik leaders that the October Revolution was only the first outbreak in a chain of revolutions which would change the political

3 Mankowski, "Zasady radzieckiej praworządności socialistycznej," 5 PiP 27–28 (1950).
4 Grzybowski, "Continuity of Law in Eastern Europe," 6 Am. J. Comp. L. 48–49 (1957).
5 Stalgevich, Puti razvitia sovetskoi pravoi mysli (1928).

and social face of Western civilization likewise militated against the assertion of uniqueness. To the same effect, Soviet jurists, together with sociologists, poets, artists, and scientists, looked upon the achievements of modern social and scientific thought, and modern trends in art and literature, as a legitimate heritage of revolutionary Russia.

Further, the method of legal reform in revolutionary Russia was the very process of codification, employed in the Western European tradition, and indeed, by prerevolutionary Russian lawyers themselves. Thus, after an initial averment of the revolutionary concept of law, which relied on the theory that revolutionary justice could function without formal legal rules, the Soviet government, in order to implement its policies and provide the foundations for the orderly operation of its institutions, returned to formalized lawmaking, and legislative procedures became the main source of Soviet law.[6]

As a result of the intellectual heritage of the West and the relative indifference of Soviet leaders to socialist aspects of legal form, the Soviet legal system, even after forty years of existence, has not ceased to belong to that broad category of legal tradition which is known as civil law. This is even more remarkable in view of the fact that the Soviet regime, as distinguished from Soviet scholars, has accorded little attention to modern developments and legislative trends in the free world. Hence, in spite of the current claim that the Soviet social system represents a unique achievement, qualitatively different from the institutions of the free world, Soviet legal order nevertheless may be analyzed in terms of response to the challenge of social change, a response which has retained the formal aspects of the modern European law. By no means may the Soviet legal system be called a legal order of the new civilization, for Soviet institutions remain copies of similar institutions in Western Europe.[7]

While the formal similarities represent a valid basis for comparing legal institutions with those of nonsocialist countries, there are other important reasons to justify the comparative treatment. No economist or sociologist would hesitate to compare social and eco-

6 1 Gsovski, Soviet Civil Law 163 ff. and 193 ff. (1948).
7 Hazard, Settling Disputes in Soviet Society 478–79 (1960).

nomic data of socialist countries with those of Western societies. On the contrary, they readily integrate the Soviet experiment into the general pattern of the development of modern industrial societies. Furthermore, the phenomena explored and the terminology employed are entirely compatible with a legalistic analysis of Soviet reality, and particularly is this true regarding the active role of the State in managing and shaping social institutions. Soviet legislative policies, the content of the legal rule, and the doctrines of Soviet legal institutions are related to similar phenomena in the nonsocialist world. The Soviet experiment with the social reconstruction and industrialization of Russia is part and parcel of the general process of the growth of industrial societies, with all that those changes mean to the mode of life of modern man. The structural alterations in Soviet society, the functions of organized social groups in the public life of the socialist countries, the social and moral ills of modern man within the socialist orbit—all bear a striking resemblance to the developments and problems on our side of the world.

At the present moment, Soviet polity represents perhaps the only social milieu in which the idea of inexorable progress provides a motive force for social action. Soviet world outlook expresses unfailing optimism and the promise of the planned achievement of the millennium. Nevertheless, even in this atmosphere of official optimism, the idea of progress has not survived untarnished. Indeed, the very concept of the role of Soviet law would appear the result not so much of the teachings of Marxism as of the Russian national tradition in which action by the central government constituted the principal motor of reform.[8]

This tradition, combined with the influence of prerevolutionary legal education, was characterized by the great concentration on

8 For a recent expression on the role of progress in Soviet thinking, see Doklady i vistuplenia predstavitelei sovetskoi filosofskoi nauki na XII mezhdunarodnom filosofskom kongresse (1958).

"Broad propaganda by the contemporary bourgeois philosophy of scepticism and agnosticism represents one of the forms of struggle against science and dialectical materialism." 39 Bolshaia Sovetskaia Entsiklopedia 223.

"The world outlook of the proletariat, the basis of which is Marxism-Leninism, is permeated by the faith in the brilliant future and the triumph of communism." 32 *id.* 564.

private law problems, which figured high in the plans of the reform of Russian laws. The legal mind of prerevolutionary Russia operated within the framework of the individual collectivity relations, which predicated progress on the influence of the rule of law on the human mind in the position conceived by the French philosophers of the eighteenth century. In this respect, then, Soviet ideas on the function of the legal order in modern society predate the origins of the Marxist doctrines. Scientific achievements of the age of enlightenment were useful in germinating within the individual a new understanding of the surrounding world, in dispelling his prejudices and liberating him from the tyranny of superstition. Social progress was conceived to be a matter of the moral advancement of each individual, which in turn could be advanced by proper legislative policy.

Beccaria, formulating his ideas on modern penal policies, insisted on moderate punishments and efficient administration of justice as the best means of crime prevention, on the ground that swift justice has a greater chance of eradicating criminal inclinations from the human mind. The very idea of nonretroactive justice was rooted in the concept that moral improvement had a decisive part in determining the purpose of criminal law.

To similar effect, Condorcet, in his plans for reforming French society, saw in bad laws the only cause of bad social mores. "To remove bad morals, it is necessary to remove their cause. And there is only one, that is bad laws." [9] And in 1794 Cambacérès, the chief author of the French Civil Code, wrote: "laws are the seeds of mores." [10] His associate, Portalis, who was the author of the *Discours préliminaire,* a first modern example of legislative motives for the consideration of the legislative assembly and for the enlightenment of the public, concluded that a statute's main purpose was to "make people better." [11]

This moralizing role of legal regulation bore directly upon the individual collectivity relations noted above. Thus, the autonomy of

9 Grzybowski, "The Criminal Law of France," in Essays on French Law 47–48 (1958); Condorcet, Réponse à d'Épremesnil (1779).

10 1 Fenet, Recueil complet des travaux préparatoires du Code Civil 108 (1827).

11 *Id.* at 473.

the individual will constitute the main source of laws, although the law itself enjoyed obligatory force only as the dictate of reason. The more reasonable, therefore the more moral, was the individual human being, and the easier it was for society to discover the rule of law by which to establish a balance between individual life and the interests of the collectivity.[12]

This concept of the function of the legal rule in modern society, however, did not survive. A century later Pollock had a less exalted idea as to the function of legal rule: "Law does not aim at perfecting the individual character of men, but at regulating the relations of citizens to the commonwealth and to one another." [13]

Pollock's views summarize a veritable revolution of ideas concerning the nature and mechanism of progress. In revolt against the French concepts of lawmaking, the German historical school, as well as the philosophy of Hegel, was addressed to the social milieu as differing both from the state and the individual. The simple formula of individual collectivity relations was replaced by a scheme of human relations including the individual, society, and the state, each of which was assured separate autonomous existence. Though Hegel focused primary attention upon the state, society as well was endowed with especial function in his analysis of social reality. To the latter, the state was no longer the result of social contract—something consciously created by the compact between individuals for the fulfillment of specific purposes. It was, rather, the organ of the entire community and a historic necessity.

In time the historical school, which ascertained the source of law in the ideas of law and justice crystallized during the course of the historical development of human societies, and in the tenets of the transcendental truth the agent which limited the arbitrary human will, was supplemented by the theory of evolution. This even more perfect motor of progress espoused the view that society was the environmental milieu in which evolutionary changes took place. At-

---

12 Rommen, Die ewige Wiederkehr des Naturrechts 76 ff. (1947); also Rommen, Natural Law, A Study in Legal and Social History and Philosophy, 77, 83–85, 94–96 (1947).
13 Pollock, A First Book of Jurisprudence for Students of the Common Law 46 (2d ed. 1904).

tention was thus directed to society as opposed to the Hegelian pre-occupation with the State.

The idea of society in conjunction with the theory of evolution made possible the studies of Comte, Bagehot, Spencer, and Marx. Comte, the most systematic thinker of this new trend, established a new direction of inquiry into human affairs by laying the foundations for sociology as a separate discipline. Crucial to his theory was the so-called "law of three stages" through which Comte believed sciences and societies have passed: the theological, the metaphysical, and the positive. In the theological stage, imagination played the principal role, and man interpreted his environment in terms of gods and spirits. In the metaphysical stage, universal ideas were used to explain the universe, and the idea of nature was substituted for the idea of God. The third stage, the positive, subordinated both imagination and reason to experience. Truth was said to consist of empirical facts. Thus, he arrived at the concept of sociology, or "social physics," limiting its tasks to the discovery of the laws of social life. Society was, for Comte, an organism subject to evolution. In consequence, it could be explained scientifically by reference to the concept of cause and effect.

In 1859 there appeared Darwin's *Origin of Species*. It was then left to the sociologist to demonstrate that social life obeyed the same general laws of evolution as did nature, and thus to predict scientifically the future development of society. The *Origin* had demonstrated that the evolution of species led to better and more perfect forms of life. Thus, Darwin discovered the laws of the development of the organic world; according to Engels, Marx discovered the laws governing human society.[14]

14 Marx & Engels, 2 Selected Works 153 (1950). *Cf.* also Bury, The Idea of Progress, An Inquiry Into Its Origin and Growth 164–66, 194–95, 205–6, 209, 234–36, 276–77 (1942).

"In the last quarter of the century Darwin's ideas set a fashion for positivist-historical thought. Embryology seemed to give an analogy for history. The development of an institution or of a doctrine was parallel to the development of an organism. A crop of books on the evolution of law followed, expounding legal institutional development in terms of Darwin.... Today, no one thinks in this fashion. Instead, the correct thing is to urge an administrative absolutism." Pound, Fashions in Juristic Thinking 9 (1938).

Of the various trends of socialist theory on the role of the law and the state in social development toward higher forms of existence, Soviet theory is without doubt the farthest removed from the original Marxian doctrine. Only reformist socialists in the West have accepted fully the doctrine of the growth of the socialist forms of life in its pure form. Only they have found it possible to coordinate the growth of socialism with the existence of the modern state, to assure social peace in order to foster the growth of socialism through the work of social processes alone.

Soviet leadership has found it impracticable to implement fully the idea that changes in social structures and in property relations are the result of such social forces, as techniques of production, which are equated with Darwin's environmental causes.

Thus, after more than forty years of the Soviet order, L. Sobolev, chairman of the Writer's Union of the RSFSR, in addressing the plenary session of the Union's Board in May 1960, still clung to Stalinist concepts of the role of the state and of coercion in social engineering. Sobolev visualized progress toward higher forms of social existence in terms of an attack on the prejudices which he believed to constitute an unhappy heritage of capitalism. "We find ourselves," Sobolev asserted, "on approaches to communism. I consciously use this military term, because, in the progress of the assault which our society is mounting, we must still overcome the minefields laid thousands of years ago—the so-called survivals of capitalism in the consciousness of the people." [15]

SOCIAL CHANGE AND THE RULE OF LAW

An additional perspective for the study of Soviet legal institutions may be gleaned from the realization that the fundamental juristic ideas underpinning the legislation of the free world preceded the emergence of the modern industrial society with its concomitant submergence of individual life. Thus, the *Code Civil* of France was the code of an agricultural society. It was conservative and static in its concepts, and was addressed primarily to the various types of property and to the family unit. It was designed to serve the interests

15 Pravda, May 11, 1960.

and life of a society which depended for its existence upon the cultivation and ownership of land.

But even more important was the fact that in the Code culminated the idea of the two kinds of law, public and private. The Code reflected the scheme worked out by Jean Domat (1625–1696) who in his *Traité des lois* had delimited the separate spheres of public and private law with a greater precision than was ever done before him. To the province of private law belonged all matters of property, contracts and other agreements, guardianships, statutes of limitation, mortgages, and successions. In a very real sense, therefore, the Code had its roots in the social order which preceded the Revolution. In their quest for the abolition of medieval society, the philosophers of legal reform in France relied on the idea of individual liberty, whether their specific concern was with the structure of property relations, the economic organization, or with the political order.[16]

The structural changes produced by the Industrial Age in the Western World found expression primarily in the separation of ownership and control of the means of production. Personal ownership of industrial property was replaced by the ownership of stocks and bonds, while physical control of productive processes passed to centralized groups of professional managers. With the management of property in bulk, business concerns frequently acquired the character of public institutions.[17] Increasing urbanization and standardization of life produced the phenomenon of masses, the latter being characterized by identity of interests and similarity of occupation and conditions of existence. In the new conditions, classes and social groups "must be taken account of no less than individuals." [18] This in turn produced a veritable revolution in the content of the legal rule and led to the reform of the basic concepts of the legal order.

Generally speaking, as a response to the legal reform changing conditions of modern life took three forms. The most obvious and

16 Savatier, Du droit civil au droit public (1950).
17 Berle & Means, The Modern Corporation and Private Property 7 (1933). *Cf.* also Friedmann, Legal Theory ch. 31 (1953), and Bolgár, "The Magic of Property and Public Welfare," 2 Inter-Amer. L. Rev. 288 (1960).
18 Pound, The Spirit of the Common Law 31 (1931).

easiest to account for was the increased scope of regulation, the effect of which was to change the role of public authority and of social organizations. The second was the activity of the courts in reshaping and redesigning the rules of positive law.[19] Thirdly, the civil law institutions themselves lost much of their social significance.

In that system of social and economic activity which linked business activity with personal control of the means of production, private law institutions were of central importance. Provisions of civil codes regarding inheritance, community property, and the management of property during the personal incapacity of owners constituted a vital part of a vast social and economic structure of which family and individual entrepreneur were the most important features. The depersonalization of economic activity and the substitution of great corporations for individual enterprise, however, relegated private law with its system of rights to an inferior position in terms of social function.

The place of individual entrepreneurs and family businesses became occupied by enormous corporations and employers' associations. These new bodies were faced at the other end of the social spectrum by the trade unions, together with a host of other organizations representing the related and intermediary interests of consumers, small producers, cooperatives, professions, etc. The resulting complication is compounded by the fact that the modern state has abandoned its exalted position of social umpire protecting the broader interests of the polity. Rather, it has assumed direct responsibility for the management of key branches of the national economy.

The state's intervention is justified by the necessity of assuring the flow of services deemed essential to modern life and its public functions and of adjusting the availability of capital, raw material, and other resources in order to promote industrial activity or consumption.

Furthermore, judicial activity in the adaptation of civil law rules, as well as in the implementation of the modern laws of the welfare state, tends to equalize the burden of risk inherent in such modern

19 *Cf*. Geny, Méthode d'interprétation et sources en droit privé positif (1899).

forms of life as mass transportation, the operation of great industrial factories, and the catastrophic fluctuations in economic activities.[20] Lines of division between what was previously considered as the exclusive realm of the private law and that which pertained to public law have been further blurred by the fact that the state, in order to discharge its responsibilities, has assumed the garb of a private entrepreneur. The result has been a great difficulty in demarcating between government owned or controlled, public or mixed corporations, and economic institutions which are not owned by the state, emphasizing further the fact that modern forms of industrial and economic activity ceased to be wholly encompassed by the rules of private law.

These structural changes in modern societies have confronted the modern state with new problems. Depersonalization of control of the means of production and the corresponding concentration of economic power have created tensions which the state has had to control in order to preserve social peace. Further, the great mass of private entrepreneurs was replaced by a small number of organizations, thus permitting easier identification of social issues with the conflicting interests of economic and social organizations. This, in turn, has permitted a change in the method of social regulation. The state has been enabled to intervene directly in a manner which makes of itself a third party representing broader interests.

Prior to the emergence of great social organizations representing the interests of the masses, the state had been little interested in the internal organization of associations. Only where external interests expressed in the standards of legal commerce and public confidence were concerned did the state intervene. Now, with the mass participation of individuals in associations, the matter of membership has become a matter of public concern. The obvious reason is that inclusion or exclusion may mean very much the same thing as partnership in the national polity itself. Thus, the restriction of contractual freedom and the intervention of public authority in the process of

---

20 *Cf.* Friedmann, Law in a Changing Society 24–25 (1959); also Savatier, *supra* note 16; Savatier, Métamorphoses économiques et sociales du droit civil d'aujourd'hui (1948) specifically in regard to the function of contract.

collective bargaining have been paralleled by government intervention into the internal affairs of great associations representing economic and social interests. Regulation is justified on the ground that, though voluntary in principle, such associations by their very size exercise what amounts to a monopolistic position in their particular spheres of professional or social activity.

An interesting process may be observed in connection with the vast expansion of the social activities of the state and the virtual statification of social and economic institutions which are not state organizations. Regulation by the public authority tends to shape the business and social activities of great organizations into standard forms, which are then presented in uniform terms to the public. Contracts and forms of organizing activity must conform to standards dictated by the needs of public order. At the same time, legal regulation tends to rely less and less on the form of an abstract legal command.

Portalis, the spokesman for the committee which drafted the French Civil Code, asserted that the abstract form of the legal rule constituted its indispensable characteristic: "[T]he law provides the rule for all: it considers men en masse, never as individuals; it should not deal with individual facts, nor with litigations which divide the citizens. . . ." [21] The French society of the Civil Code, however, was a society of individuals. The modern nation, on the other hand, coalesced into great organizations. In consequence, the state has had to readopt the role of the medieval sovereign. It must face broad social interests and powerful groups, joining them in compacts, playing one against the other, and using its influence and control of resources in order to promote cohesion and the orderly operation of social services.[22] The basic difference between the modern state and its medieval antecedent is that the aspect of liberty which was the product of the French Revolution has survived the social crises of modern times. Thus, personal freedom continues to represent a social goal in its abstract formulation and may not be

21 Portalis, Discours préliminaire, Projet de Code Civil présenté par la Commission nommée par le Gouvernement, le 24 Thermidor an 8.

22 Friedmann, *supra* note 20, 74, 101, 109, 286, 297, 309. *Cf.* Pound, *supra* note 18, at 31. Savatier, *supra* note 20, at 9, 64–65, 71, 86–87, 208–9 (2d series 1959).

translated into terms of status with reference to the social and economic ramifications of modern societies.[23]

LEGAL ORDER OF SOCIAL INTERVENTION

The social mechanism envisaged by the Civil Code of France was perhaps best described by the following quotation from Jhering's classical work (1872):

What is sowed in private law is reaped in public law and the law of nations. In the valleys of private law, in the very humble relations of life, must be collected, drop by drop, so to speak, the forces, the moral capital, which the state needs to operate on a large scale, and to attain its end. Private law, not public law, is the real school of the political education of the people, and if we would know how a people, in case of need, will defend their political rights and their place among the nations, let us examine how the separate members of the nation assert their own right in private life.... Law is idealism—paradoxical as this may seem—not the idealism of the fancy, but of character: that is, of the man who looks upon himself as his own end, and esteems all else lightly when he is attacked in his personality.[24]

Thus, the main stream of legal commerce was thought to flow in the bed of private law transactions; and private law litigation, to constitute the principal means to be employed by the public authority in upholding the rule of law. It was in this spirit that West European legal scholarship in the nineteenth century approached the problem of reforming codes of civil procedure. Simplification of court proceedings was sought through the adoption of the principle of immediacy and publicity, by the oral examination of witnesses, and by the direct participation of parties and their legal counsel in court proceedings. But almost simultaneous with the achievement of these goals of simplification and expediency, permitting speedy and cheap disposition of cases, juristic preoccupation with private litigation was superseded by the problems of social change.[25]

23 *Cf.* Grzybowski, "Fundamental Rights of Persons and Social Groups," in 3 (pt. 6) Memoires de l'Académie Internationale de Droit Comparé 15–24; also Rivero, Les droits de l'homme dans le droit constitutionnel français d'aujourd'hui, *id.* at 25–40.

24 Jhering, The Struggle for Law 99–101 (1915).

25 Engelman *et al.*, A History of Continental Civil Procedure 587–615, 628–44, 748–82 (1927).

Gradually, juridical attention became riveted to the forms of the administrative activities of the state.[26]

As social interests could no longer be safeguarded through the enforcement of private rights, state activity assumed new forms. From the role of umpire in private litigations, it now assumed the role of social and economic organizer and administrator of national assets. The creative function of public administration, with its new forms of governmental action, thus became an indispensable feature of the modern state.

The intervention of the state in social and economic affairs, however, raised a number of legal problems requiring solutions which challenged accepted ideas of the role of public authority vis-à-vis the public. The final outcome has been the evolution of administrative law. Its subject matter consists in the attempt to determine the responsibilities of governmental authorities, as well as the rights of citizens and social organizations. It further provides the framework for a partnership between the authority and the citizen either as a private individual or as a member of an organization.

The emergence in Western Europe of the modern welfare state was facilitated by the familiarity of the civil law world with state and territorial corporations acting in the capacity of private persons. And it was due to this tradition that there finally emerged the principle that in all of its activities the state was subject to the rule of law, and to administrative procedures and a system of controls in which the courts performed the important function of preventing the abuse of power.[27]

The appearance of the modern welfare state in its varied aspects called for the reassessment of the criteria of legality of governmental action. Now, it is obvious that, in order to achieve their purposes, administrative authorities must be guided by different and perhaps more lenient rules as to the formal legality of their action than those rules pertaining to courts of justice. In fact, even with regard to the latter, the European tradition contained the seeds of that type of public action which finally became characteristic of the

26 Robson, Justice and Administrative Law 229 (1947).
27 Friedmann, *supra* note 20, 351–52.

life of the modern state. Civil law courts in pursuit of their functions as guardians of minors, of absentee interests, and of those deprived for various reasons of their capacity for legal transactions, and in all nonadversary proceedings, exercise their power with a minimum of attention to form. Discretion is moderated by expediency rather than by formal legality. While public authority acting *qua* public authority has had to adhere to the principle of legality, its criteria have been changed. Thus, when representing the proprietary rights of the state, it is endowed with a certain degree of discretionary power, somewhat similar to that degree of freedom of action enjoyed by a private person or state agency. As French jurisprudence has almost unanimously recognized, freedom of action is essential if the state action is to achieve its purpose:

The mission of public administration cannot be restricted to a slavish execution of the provisions of the public law legislation. Missions of public authority cannot be put in terms of the blind execution of the commands of the legislator, not even in terms of ideas contained in the legal rules. Public authority must examine independently those elements which are left to its decision in the perspective of its proper functions, in accordance with the spirit of the institution.... When an administrative authority applies the law, it does so with certain independence, which is quite considerable at times.[28]

This freedom of action of the administrative authority was further enlarged by the recognition that it could also act as a private person, and could engage thereby the interests of the state in the terms of private law. "The methods of performing public services have the character of administrative action, except when administration voluntarily resorts to the procedures of normal life, or is enjoined by the legal rule to resort to them." This rule, firmly established since 1872 by the French *Conseil d'État,* provides another

28 Walter, Le contrôle juridictionnel de la moralité administrative 34–36 (1929).

"L'administration n'est seulement l'exécutrice servile de la loi ou le rouage de transmission des commandements législatifs; elle est encore un organe autonome et créateur." Alibert, Le contrôle juridictionnel de l'administration au moyen du recours pour l'excès de pouvoir 16 (1926). *Cf.* Renard, Le droit, la logique et le bon sens 362 (1926); Stier-Somlo, Politique 29 (4th French ed. 1919).

basis for the integration of public action with the social and economic pursuits of the citizens.[29]

In the final analysis, however, the character of public action depends not so much upon the form as upon the need for action in the discharge of the duties and functions of the modern state. The tendency has been toward expansion of those activities which cannot be strictly determined by legal regulation. Administrative authority, as some French writers suggest, follows rules of conduct which are not law in the strict sense, but are rather rules of conduct within the framework of legal order. Here standards of public action acquire a coloring which suggests assimilation of the criteria of public action into the standards of ethics controlling the actions of the individual. Realization of the "bien commun" must follow the rules of what is suggestively termed "moralité administrative," "administrative convenances," or "rules of good administration." [30] The analogy between private initiative and the intervention of public authority is further suggested by the fact that ultimately the tasks and responsibilities of the modern state are dictated not so much by the fact that the state alone can undertake to provide social services, as by the fact that these services cannot be provided by private initiative:

Public service exists in all those cases when competent authorities consider that ... private initiative is unable to perform a certain task or cannot perform it in a satisfactory manner, and decide to assume responsibility for the service which seems to them to be of public utility.

This same flexibility applies also to practical measures which the public authority adopts in order to discharge its responsibilities. Such may entail direct action by the public authority itself, a gov-

29 Hauriou, Précis de droit administratif 40 (1927); Fleiner, Über die Umbindung der zivilrechtlichen Institute durch das öffentliche Recht 6 ff. (1906).

30 "Le contrôle jurisdictionnel de la moralité administrative est, avant tout, le moyen d'assujettir l'activité administrative—non à la seule legalité formelle, mais au buts qui lui sont impartis, suivants la disposition de l'ordre administratif, en vue de satisfaction de l'interêt public." Welter, *supra* note 28, at 36. *Cf.* Hauriou, *supra* note 29, at 197; Renard, Le droit, la justice et la volonté 400 (1924); Beurdeley, Le détournement de pouvoir dans l'interêt financier ou patrimonial de l'administration 164–65 (1928).

ernment-organized commercial corporation, or a government inspired private enterprise.[31]

The revolution in the scope of governmental action was followed
by a revolution in the field of concepts regarding judicial control,
as the old precept that court action was restricted to the private law
area alone could no longer be maintained.

The principle of judicial control of administrative authority, and
the problem of the type of judicial control to be employed, called for
the reappraisal of time-sanctioned doctrines as to the existence of
two branches of legal regulation, public and private, over which the
powers of the courts were thought to hold a different compass. Thus,
civil law relations were subject to judicial adjudication even when
the state appeared as a claimant of proprietary rights. Otherwise,
public authority was not subject to judicial control.

Roughly corresponding to the above distinction was the doctrine that only those actions of the state which were covered by the
provisions of the law, i.e., legal interests, were capable of judicial
review according to the general principles of litigation. Eventually,
this latter doctrine was replaced by still another distinction, this time
between government activities which constituted an exercise of power
(*actes de pouvoir, acta imperii*) and those which were the acts of
normal administration (*acta gestionis*). This last division corre-
sponded to the view of an absence of court jurisdiction regarding
those acts of the state which were not a subject of parliamentary
legislation, or which did not involve proprietary rights of the state
in its capacity as a private person (*fisc*). This, in fact, was true quite
irrespective of their impact on the rights of the individual.[32]

The succession of theories and doctrines described above ex-
hibited inexorable progress toward the principle of judicial control
of state action. The only question remaining was that of a proper
distribution of responsibility, according to the specific qualifications
of the two great branches of the judiciary, i.e., courts of general
jurisdiction and the administrative judiciary. Since 1872 in France,

31 Waline, Traité élémentaire de droit administratif 6 ff. (1957); Fleiner,
supra note 29, at 6 ff.

32 Laferrière, Jurisdiction et contentieux (1896); Bahr, Der Rechtsstaat
(1864).

the *Conseil d'État* has made it clear that administration is always accountable at court, and court jurisdiction depends upon the manner of public action.[33]

Today, even on the continent of Europe where the history of administrative law nears the century mark, the accelerated pace of social and economic change has impeded the efforts of administrative law both in the achievement of clarity and of simplicity in legal provisions and in the effectuation of symmetrical and systematic arrangement characteristic of the admirable monuments of legislative technique represented by the modern codes of Europe. The result is that a good deal of uncertainty continues to persist as to the distribution of the border areas of social life and as to their definite assignment to one of the two branches of adjudication. This situation is further complicated by the feeling that new social services call for the participation of the social interests involved, which in turn cause multiplication of special tribunals. The concept of "public service," which replaced other criteria of expediency of administrative action in specific situations, again caused confusion. The problem was that the old distinction between action resulting from special authorization and a transaction of private law was no longer held to be decisive in the assignment of judicial responsibility.[34] This approach was further confused by the emergencies resulting from national catastrophes. After World War II, the need to organize basic services and to undertake social and economic reconstruction, coupled with the mobilization of private enterprises, created another problem of jurisdiction. It was held that private entrepreneurs servicing the public under government contract also could be classified as falling into the category of the agents of public services.[35]

The common feature of the experiences of the two great legal cultures of the world, of the civil law and of the Anglo-American tradition, is that the principle of judicial control dominates juristic thinking in regard to the responsibilities of the modern state. In the

---

33 Hauriou, *supra* note 29, at 40.
34 Appleton, Traité élémentaire du contentieux administratif 114 (1927); Bernatzik, Rechtssprechung und materielle Rechtskraft 36–37 (1886).
35 Durand, "Les fonctions publiques de l'entreprise privée," 8 Droit Social 246–50 (1945).

Anglo-American tradition, the technique was to expand the responsibilities of the general courts, while the tendency in the civil law countries has been toward more specialized tribunals. The result, however, has not been the devaluation of judicial authority. Rather, great administrative tribunals rival in stature and authority the supreme courts of their countries.[36] The emergence of the former was due to the complexity of administrative action and to the unsystematic character of the provisions of administrative law. Public authority could not, in a world of great corporations and mass organizations, assure satisfaction of broader social interests through the formal commands of the law. Even before the period of the great wars, a French jurist, in characterizing the new law which had come to occupy the most important place in the legal systems of modern societies, said:

In its new conception the law no longer assumes to tender absolute commands, it strives at diversity in its practical operation, seeks to guide, to counsel, endeavors to regularize the movements of social life. . . .[37]

And indeed mediation, arbitration, administrative pressure, persuasion, mobilization of public opinion, joint industrial enterprise, use of privilege and exemption from taxation, subsidy and control of standardized contracts, and internal intervention into the life of private associations—all have become legitimate means of administrative action. A distinguished jurist, referring to the circumstances of postwar France, has expressed doubt that the social stresses and conflicts of contemporary society permit orderly law enforcement at all.[38] Indeed, it seems that the "acceleration of history," which appears to be the mark of our time,[39] will not permit modern societies to engage in a labor comparable to that of the Civil Code of France, which aimed at systematic codification of all law into one book. Nevertheless, there are fundamental legal ideas which do con-

36 Tezner, Das Oesterreichische Administrativverfahren 430 ff. (1925); Geny, Science et technique en droit privé positif (1927); Perraux, Technique et jurisprudence en droit privé (1923).

37 Leroy, La loi, essai sur la théorie de l'autorité dans la démocratie 19 (1908). *Cf.* Friedmann, *supra* note 20, at 288–90.

38 Roubier, Théorie générale du droit 279 (1946). *Cf.* Rippert, Le déclin du droit 154 (1949).

39 Halévy, Essai sur l'accéleration de l'histoire (1948).

stitute the core of the administrative law of modern societies. Principal among these is the conviction that public authority has the power to act only with reference to a rule of law. Thus, the attributes of discretion and freedom from judicial control persist only when the law directly and expressly so provides. In this manner, the function of legal order to provide balance between individual life and collective existence has asserted itself anew. In reference to new conditions, law enforcement has changed in form, but not in ultimate purpose.[40]

Structural changes in legal systems and the reappearance of old concepts which stress the idea of relation or function have been sometimes interpreted as per se significant to the acceptance of new ideas regarding social aims and methods of social control. Some authors aver that concepts of function or relation are specific for certain social or national environments.[41] Others claim that jurists' concern with the issue of rights is only a relic of a situation characteristic of the conflict between the exercise of governmental power and the idea of the law.[42]

A mere glance at the history of these ideas should dispel such

---

40 Bernatzik, *supra* note 34, at 36–47; Laun, Das freie Ermesse und seine Grenzen 61–79 (1910); Jellinek, Gesetz, Gesetzanwendung und Zweck-massigkeitserwagung 89 (1913).

41 Guins, Soviet Law and Soviet Society 382 n. 44 (1954).

42 "An opposition has for long existed in Britain between the idea of 'law' and the idea of 'government.' This is a heritage from the conflict in the seventeenth century between, on the one side, a sovereign claiming to rule by the divine right and to exercise an undisputed prerogative in all matters of government, and, on the other side, a nation claiming a supreme law to which the sovereign should be subject. That struggle between King and Commons has become transformed in our own day into a conflict between the Executive on the one hand, and the Judiciary and the legal profession on the other. The lawyers still regard themselves as champions of the popular cause; but there can be little doubt that the great departments of State administering or supervising public health, public education, pension schemes, unemployment and health insurance, housing and all the other modern social services, are not only essential to the well-being of the great mass of people, but also the most significant expressions of democracy in our time. Considerations of this kind, however, could scarcely be expected to weigh with the predominantly upper middle-class legal mind." Robson, *supra* note 26, at 316.

preconceptions. Their employment in juristic constructions to meet the needs of changing times has no ideological significance per se. Similarly, it seems quite futile to endeavor to explain away the issue of rights as no longer providing an insight into the meaning and the function of legal institutions. Only the context of the exercise of rights has been changed, and both the sociologist and the jurist must seek their content within broader human institutions.[43]

DOCTRINES OF THE INSTITUTIONS

Soviet legal theories are predicated upon the idea of progress and are identified with the Soviet policy of transforming, according to a predetermined plan, the economic and social order into that of an industrial civilization. In order to achieve higher material and moral values, Soviet leadership has concentrated all social and official action, including the method of legal regulation, on the task of surpassing the economies of the more advanced industrial nations of the West. Soviet legal order is thus designed to accomplish concrete functions in the program of the transformation of social reality in Russia.

Hence, a comparative study of the Soviet legal system must seek to answer two questions. First, have Soviet jurists been able to develop new techniques in response to the singular tasks faced by the Soviet society and legal order? Second, have the role of the Soviet legal order and concrete social conditions affected the inner meaning and function of Soviet legal institutions, and if so, in what manner? Soviet jurists claim broadly that Soviet law and Soviet legality represent new values, permitting realization of higher standards of personal freedom.

Our inquiry here calls for a sketch, albeit in most general terms, of the impact of the process of social change on the legal institutions of modern societies. Admittedly, in open societies neither the state nor the legal order has entertained ambitions comparable to those advanced by the Soviet polity. However, the planned participation of the state and its legal order in the program of social re-

---

43 Pound, *supra* note 18, at 31. Pound, "Individualization of Justice," 7 Fordham L. Rev. 153 (1938); Bolgár, "The Concept of Public Welfare," 8 Am. J. Comp. L. 44–71 (1959); Bolgár, *supra* note 17, at 283–316.

construction can hardly be considered, from the viewpoint of Western civilization, as a full and complete response to the social needs of any environment. While the law must promote social discipline, its functions cannot be limited to that task alone. It must also preserve human autonomy in forms related to the social techniques of the time.

Doctrines of legal institutions must be distinguished from broad legal theories. Thus, doctrines, as opposed to theories, constitute the premise on which a legal institution operates in a concrete historical situation. They also explain the inner changes generated by social conditions, which find reflection in the institutions themselves. In the light of doctrines, institutions appear as social techniques intended to achieve political aims and in the process to realize eternal values of the law.

To take a concrete example, legislation represents a method of social ordering. In modern times, it operates on the theory that it is a major instrument of democracy in that it constitutes the chief function of the representative institutions. However, changes in the legislative techniques and in the formal aspects of the laws reflect the impact of the times. One of the experiences of our times is the fact that lawmaking is no longer a monopoly of a single governmental institution.

Proceeding further, it would perhaps be well to point out the close kinship between the basic juristic categories which constitute the common background of the Soviet legal order with the legal orders of the free world.

The era of codified statutes in Western Europe, which sought to comprehend within a single book all the various fields of law of a given state, was fathered by the conviction that there exists a system of natural laws, discoverable by reason and legal scholarship. In the course of the nineteenth century, however, the idea of immutable and perfect natural law was replaced by the scholarship of trained lawyers.[44] The Austrian Civil Code of 1811 still referred the judge to principles of natural law when the law could not provide a rule for the solution of a case. Section 9 of the Russian Civil Procedure of 1864 ruled that in such a case the court was to base its decision on

44 Aumann, The Changing American Legal System: Some Selected Phases 30 (1940); Schultz, History of Roman Legal Science 23 (1946).

the "common sense of laws." And Article 1 of the Swiss Civil Code, which was the product of legal scholarship of the twentieth century when the theories of natural law had lost their validity, enjoined the judge, unable to solve a case by application of a written statute or its interpretation, to resort to the customary law as a subsidiary source of legal rule. In the absence of the latter he was to apply a rule such as he would enact if he were a lawmaker, being guided by established doctrine and tradition.

Under the Austrian Code, the judge was called upon to enforce a legal system of which the Code was only a written part. Russian and Swiss provisions for filling lacunae in the laws of the country were the result of century-old experience in codification. The conviction that a legal order was a part of a natural system of law had dimmed by that time, but not so the belief that law was an autonomous discipline. Thus, it was still felt that answers to every legal problem could be found, either in the common sense of law or in doctrine and tradition.

An interesting aspect of the evolution of ideas regarding methods of providing an answer to legal problems where no direct answer is prescribed in the rules of the positive law is that in the main the tradition survived the impact of revolutionary changes. Article 12 of the Italian Civil Code of 1942, which was the product of the Fascist regime, has departed little from the original pattern. It ordained that if "a controversy cannot be solved by the application of the provision which applies directly to the case, regard will be taken of the provisions which apply to similar cases or regulate analogous matters; if the case is still doubtful, it shall be decided according to the general principles of the general legal order of the state."

The general purport of Article 12 of the Civil Code of 1942 leaves little doubt that it is a product of the traditional approach. But it also leaves little doubt that the actual content of the legal rule which the court would establish by following its instructions would be colored in the final analysis by the political nature of the actual regime, and that the real doctrine of the institution is discoverable only by analysis of its function within the social context of the moment. Although no legislator in the past anticipated it, the same applies with equal force to the Austrian, Russian, or Swiss examples.

The teachings of general experience, necessitating the correlation of the formal provision with the actual social and economic order in order to arrive at the proper role of legal rule, apply equally to the legal order of the socialist countries. Particularly is this true where Soviet legislators rely on the experiences of the common historical past. To this end, Section 1 of the Bulgarian law on Obligations and Contracts of 1950 provided that:

This law regulates obligations and contracts in order to support the construction of socialism, fulfillment of the national economic plans, and the realization of the rights of the toilers in the People's Republic of Bulgaria.

According to Section 2 of the same law, if the law contains no direct rule covering the case:

[A] provision which governs a similar case is applicable to the case not provided in it, if this corresponds to the rules of life in the socialist community. If this is not possible the general principles of the socialist law apply.[45]

The Bulgarian formulation added a new element, which qualified the use of the analogy by demanding adherence to the general goals of the legal order. It does not materially differ from the Italian formula, except that it lists specifically the constituent "rules of life in a socialist community." But even this formulation leaves little doubt as to the source of the inspiration for the Bulgarian provisions, and the mere detailed enumeration of social goals to be achieved in the course of law enforcement constitutes no guarantee of performance. In the final analysis, therefore, the technique is a different matter from the political or social content of the legal rule. The former is apparent from the form of the legal rule, the latter from its actual operation in life.

Thus are set forth the scope and the method of the present study.

45 D.V. 275/1950. Bulgarian Civil Procedure as amended in 1930 provided in section 9 as follows: "The courts shall decide according to the exact meaning of the laws in force. If these are incomplete, unclear or contradictory, the courts shall decide according to the general meaning of the laws; in case of a gap in legal provisions with respect to a given matter, they shall decide according to custom, and in the absence of such, according to justice."

The task is to establish, on the basis of external criteria, the origin of Soviet legal institutions and to confront their original purpose with their role and function in the Soviet polity. In a sense, the institutions of Soviet law are treated as part and parcel of the legal tradition of Europe; and the question is, what is their role in a social and economic order which claims to have achieved higher standards of liberty and a more perfect realization of the postulates of social justice?

JURISPRUDENCE OF STATE WORSHIPPERS

The identification of Soviet legal thought with the policies of the regime is achieved in Soviet theory through concentration on the idea of progress, with the latter's postulation of a social environment highly influenced by the state and legal order. The final outcome of state action is to achieve the merger of public institutions with social structures. By some process, the outlines of which are at present the subject of earnest discussion in leading Soviet intellectual circles, society is to emerge finally as the composite of the assumption, by the public institutions, of all the functions of the state, while nevertheless parting with none of their own. Although highly purposive and teleological in their formulations, Soviet jurists, in working out the grand lines of the process of transition to higher forms of social existence, are not concerned with the doctrines of Marxism. Their concern is chiefly with the practical problems of lawmaking as responses to the social needs—such responses being occasioned by commands from the leadership of the Party.[46]

The pattern of Soviet theoretical thinking is thus linked with two main trends of thought in the West, which make either the state or society the frame of reference within which problems of legal order are considered. Hence, in order to provide proper perspective for the problems discussed in this study, some restatement of the principal theoretical propositions concerning the relationship between the state and the operation of the legal order within the social structures appears useful if not essential. In particular should be noted those propositions which have exerted an influence on the theoretical formulations of Soviet scholars.

46 Hazard, "Le droit soviétique et le dépérissement de l'État," in 8 Travaux et conférences, Université Libre de Bruxelles 15 ff. (1960).

In this connection, two trends of thought seem to be of importance. In the first place, the normative school has provided the material for the construction of Soviet legal concepts; and secondly, the modern sociological school has stimulated Soviet theoretical speculations. It would be futile to seek recognition of Soviet indebtedness to the thought of Western European scholars. Soviet thinkers are precluded from such acknowledgment by the theory of the qualitative difference of Soviet institutions from their counterparts in the free world. Nevertheless, Western European legal thought provides a capital guide for the analysis of Soviet reality.

In this context, the idea of the rule of law within the framework of the constitutional government (*Rechtsstaat*) deserves special attention. Such was a logical derivative of the idea of natural law. The function of the *Rechtsstaat* is to administer justice to all. It is not merely to protect individual status, but to establish every individual in his right status. The concept of the rule of law in this form originated with a group of liberal jurists (Gneist, Lorenz von Stein, Bahr, and others). Embracing the legal ideology of the French Revolution, and in particular the doctrines of Montesquieu, they assimilated such theories for the use of German jurisprudence.

In the early formulations of the rule of law, the idea of law was distinct from the idea of the state. The state was governed by law, but it became *Rechtsstaat* when it was governed by the right law. Although differing from the public order described by Montesquieu in his claim of integral governance by the law, it did not differ in nature from the state of the eighteenth century. As a consequence, it had to be controlled. As Otto Bahr put it:

[T]o make the Rechtsstaat come true it is not sufficient that public law be expressed in statutes; there must also be a judiciary qualified to establish what is right in the concrete case and thus give an indisputable foundation for the rehabilitation of law where it has been violated.[47]

In time, the idea of judicial control was supplemented by the idea of the independence of the administrative mechanism of the

47 Bahr, *supra* note 32, at 8; Mohl, "Gesellschaftswissenschaft und Staatswissenschaft," 7 Zeitschrift für die gesammte Staatswissenschaft (1851); Stein, System der Staatswissenschaft (1856); Stein, Der Begriff der Gesellschaft (1855); Gneist, Zur Verwaltungsreform und Verwaltungsrechtspflege in Preussen (1881); Gneist, Der Rechtsstaat (1872).

state from the political elements in the higher echelons of government. An additional supplement was the theory that statutory enactments, although representing the pressure of politics on the system of public authorities, become divorced from their makers. The state in this role was conceived as the supreme association, though but one of many in the social structure. Its primary function was to assure unity of all social elements.

Further in this direction was the identification of integral government by law with the state, as the legal order itself. Thus, the state became only a name for the legal order. Kelsen, who extended this line of thought to its ultimate conclusions, stated the point in truly magisterial terminology:

The state as a legal community is not something apart from its legal order, any more than a corporation is distinct from its constitutive order.... We must admit that the community we call "State" is "its" legal order.[48]

Identification of the state with the law was the last step in the process of rejection of natural law theories. Individual rights could not be conceived otherwise than in relation to the positive legal order. As such they depended on membership in the specific polity. Individuals had rights not as humans but as citizens.

The integral identification of public order with legal order constituted a first step in the direction of the total separation of laws from the transcendental values which constitute the legitimacy of the legal rule. The development of democratic institutions had identified the right law with the idea of the formally right law adopted by the representatives of the people, or rather by their majority. Once this happened, the way was open for all theoretical speculations stressing the formal aspects of legal rule, and for the method which was characterized by the progressive elimination from legal inquiry of all elements of reality which were unsuitable for the employment of the method. Starting with the age of reason, through the historical school and down to the period of positivistic orientation, progress in the techniques of legal method signified a constant narrowing of experience, on which each succeeding generation of learned jurists relied for the materials for their scholarly theories. Juridical speculation was

48 Kelsen, General Theory of Law and State 182 (1945).

finally restricted to the legal rule itself, exclusive of social trends, scientific developments, and technical developments affecting social and economic facts, which in turn affected the meaning and the function of legal institutions. The task which Kelsen envisaged for legal science was the building of a theory "resulting from the comparative analysis of the different positive legal orders." [49]

It was little realized that in the quest for a pure science of law, the very idea of restraint in lawmaking, which after all constitutes the soul of legal order, is lost. Jean Domat, in attempting a systematic arrangement of all the laws of the realm of France, differentiated those which were made by the king from those made by the Church. Simultaneously, he recognized the force of custom, the rules of law found in the *Digesta* or *Codex Justinianus* and also some that were made by the decisions of the courts. Not all of these laws, however, belonged to the same order, as some of the rules were unchangeable, while others were imposed at will. Nevertheless, they could not be contrary to the laws that were unchangeable, and no one could change laws resulting from the nature of things or discoverable by reason.

For Bodin, the supreme authority was subject to the authority of natural and divine law and the law of all nations. While supreme authority was exonerated from following the positive law of the state, owing to its power to enact new positive laws, it could not alter the laws which concerned the state of the realm. The king had to respect the property of his subjects and honor royal contracts. Both Domat and Bodin would have recognized the value of the Kelsenian inquiry, but would not have agreed that it could provide the material to build a general system of legal theory. Social reality, which they contemplated, told them that such was a futile endeavor.

Stammler, who represented another trend in the same general direction, concerned himself exclusively with the normative and formal aspects of law: "The pure forms . . . are conceptual methods of ordering. . . ." In his opinion, any endeavor to establish an ideal legal system with a concrete content was futile. It was not possible to conceive

49 "The general theory, as it is presented in this book, is directed at a structural analysis of positive law rather than at a psychological or economic explanation of its conditions, or a moral or a political evaluation of its ends." Kelsen, *supra* note 48, at xiii–xiv.

of a legal system which would have a content, however limited in its subject matter, which would nevertheless hold good for all times and for all peoples. Only pure forms could claim an absolute validity of conceptions, and this held true in legal questions as well. Experience regarding the normative and formal aspects of the legal rule might be arranged according to a fixed and mandatory plan, valid for all ages and social conditions. "There are certainly," as Stammler asserted, "pure forms of juristic thought which are unconditionally necessary as ordering principles for any content of law." [50]

Along different lines, neo-Kantians argued that legal science differed from sociology, which was a natural science (*Kausalwissenschaft*), since legal theories were directed only to the "ought" and not to the social fact. Their successors, however, abandoned this distinction. Thus, sociologists of the positivist conviction claimed that it was possible to discover by observation and experience absolute mechanical social laws, such having produced all social, political, and legal institutions irrespective of human will.[51]

The positivist sociologist considered the legal norm as a social fact in the same sense that Kelsen regarded sociology, i.e., as natural science. The most extreme among them, the Nordic school, in fact, identified legal analysis with the study of the exercise of power.

The basic principle of the Nordic theories is the categorization of the various phenomena observable in social life into those which really matter for the determination of the nature of law and such as are important for its analysis. These are to be separated from those which constitute legal ideology, sham structure, a figment of imagination, if not a pure superstition. Stripped of those elements, law is but "a link in the chain of cause and effect. It has a place among the facts of the world of time and space." The binding force of law, separate from the process of its enforcement, exists, according to this view, as a reality only as an idea in the human mind. Law is a fact

---

50 Stammler, Theorie der Rechtswissenschaft 17 (1911); Stammler, "Fundamental Tendencies in Modern Jurisprudence," 21 Mich. L. Rev. 862 ff. (1923).

51 Verdross, Abendlandische Rechtsphilosophie 180 (1958); Pound, *supra* note 18, at 161–62; 1 Pound, Jurisprudence 304 (1959); Cohen, "The Place of Logic in Law," 29 Harv. L. Rev. 630 ff. (1914–16); Olivecrona, Law as Fact 16–17 (1939).

only in the form of pressure exercised on the population. This distinction, according to Olivecrona, constitutes a dividing line between realism and metaphysics, scientific method and mysticism.[52]

Somewhat naïvely, Olivecrona announced that "words" printed in the law books were facts, as were ideas evoked in the mind of the reader of these words. But if this is reality, in what sense do these words in the law books differ from other words in other law books, which constitute ideology? In the mind of the judge who renders sentence, opined Olivecrona, printed words of the statute met and merged with the ideology.[53]

Law as social fact, according to the Nordics, is the norm which concerns the application of force. Right and might are not opposites, and the relation between those who decide what is to be law and those who are subject to the law is one of power. Identification of power with the law is complete; power functions through law.[54]

Lundstedt, the most radical of the Nordic school, rejected that "body of concepts properly called legal ideology, under whose continued domination jurisprudence has remained in a deplorable state of prescientific wordmongering." Rather, he identified law with the very life of mankind in organized groups and with the conditions which made social coexistence possible—with the controls which made it possible for man to exist in society. Social control consisted of legislation and of the legal machinery in action. For Lundstedt, legal machinery had one purpose only, and that was "checking the impulses of the people" in following their otherwise natural inclinations to make use of existing commodities within their reach.[55]

Lundstedt rejected the view that law was the result of a conflict between the individual and the collectivity, thus providing a setting for the concept of individual rights as counterpoised by the rights of the community. "It is impossible," said Lundstedt, "except in an imagination entirely divorced from reality, to take the whole and set it up in contrast to its parts." Nevertheless, he admitted that it was

52 Olivecrona, *supra* note 51, at 17.
53 *Id.* at 19–20.
54 Ross, On Law and Justice 52–53, 58 (1959); Olivecrona, *supra* note 51, at 134 ff.
55 Lundstedt, Legal Thinking Revised 9, 86, 301–2 (1956).

possible to speak of "the rights of state against an individual, and vice versa." [56]

The crux of the matter is that even the state of the rule of law is capable of injustice. Such is clearly demonstrated in the fate of the minorities and the ever-recurring phenomenon of exceptional legislation. To give an example from French practice, it is enough to quote the case of the decree law of November 3, 1939, which amended Article 83 of the French Criminal Code, and treated as crimes "all wilfull acts which by their nature could obstruct national defense," if such acts could not be qualified as an offense against the external security of the state. After the liberation of France, Executive Order of December 26, 1944, created a crime of national indignity, which consisted of "wilfull direct or indirect assistance to Germany or her allies, or of an attack on the unity of the nation, or on the liberty of the French or equality between them." Simultaneously, special tribunals were established for trying such offenses. Quite apart from the question of whether these measures were dictated by real expediency, their conflict with the fundamental principles of the French criminal law is evident. One might say that this type of legislation is in conflict with the very idea of the state, which is considered by the positivists to be the legal order itself. However, positivist jurists concede that, according to their criteria, exceptional legislation and retroactive laws constitute valid rules. Thus, a Danish representative of the Nordic school admitted that:

> It has been maintained that Hitler's rule of violence was not a legal order, and juridical "positivism" has been accused of moral treason.... But a descriptive terminology has nothing to do with moral approval or condemnation. While I may classify a certain order as a "legal order," it is possible for me at the same time to consider it my highest moral duty to overthrow that order.[57]

LEGAL THEORIES OF SOCIAL CHANGE

Thus, the theories of the normative school permitted contemplation of the systematic arrangement of legal institutions and rendered thereby great services to academic studies and legal instruction. On

56. *Id.* at 33.
57 Ross, *supra* note 54, at 31–32.

the other hand, practical problems, which were the result of the changing content of the legal rule, called for a new approach, more closely connected with social realities. One of the first questions which had to be answered was where to find a scientific guide for the action of public authority when the social premises of the existing legal order underwent a process of change. The very life of modern society had made obsolete the rules of the Code and required the various organs of the state, the courts and administrative authorities, to discover new meanings and functions for the legal provisions. The guide to such actions had to be found in the social sciences, where the modern jurist was enjoined to seek understanding of the conflicts of interests and to ascertain the purpose of the rule of law. Hence, the new trend in jurisprudence abandoned the pretence that law constituted a self-contained discipline and invoked, by way of supplement, the use of auxiliary disciplines.[58]

From these auxiliary guides into social reality, the jurist learned that the central position, which until then firmly belonged to the state, now belonged to society. This called for re-examination of basic issues and conceptions. Liberty and property rights were no longer conceived to be absolute values limited only by the regard for the liberty and property rights of others. Individual rights became subordinated to the necessity of conforming with the social order. Property, while serving the individual, constituted a factor in the general welfare: "Property belongs to an individual on the strength of the fact that he belongs to the human society; it constitutes a part of the patrimony of all." This was the new dogma.[59]

The old position of exclusive reliance on positive law, i.e., law formally introduced by the competent authorities of the state, was no longer adequate. Society was now viewed to be governed by its own rules. In consequence, only a portion of the elements of the

58 Geny, *supra* note 19, vol. 1 at 2–3.
59 Renard, Propriété privée et propriété humaine 2–3 (1926): "Beginnings of the new jurisprudence which rejected formal methods of legal interpretation may be traced to Jhering who insisted on the interpretation according to the social purpose of the law which is determined by social goals and not by the individual will." See also 1 Pound, Jurisprudence 335; 1 Jhering, Der Zweck im Recht 74–75 (4th ed. 1904); Jhering, Der Besitzwille, ix–x (1889).

positive law was formally given. Others had to be found through the process of interpretation. Law was partly science and partly technique. Legal rule was conservative and constituted a drag on social development. One of the functions of modern jurisprudence, then, was to gain an up to date understanding of the needs of society. It was to promote reinterpretation of the rule of law, not only in terms of the ageless tenets of legal method, but also in accord with social realities. Hence, the state, but not the legal rule, was relegated to subsidiary status in social ordering. Law was conceived as a function of social rule, the litigious aspect of law enforcement becoming reduced to a matter of technique. Law enforcement was viewed as one of the numerous reasons for upholding the legal rule:

It is quite obvious that a man lives in innumerable legal relations, and that with few exceptions, he quite voluntarily performs the duties incumbent upon him because of these relations. One performs one's duties as father or son, as husband or wife, does not interfere with one's neighbor's enjoyment of his property, pays one's debts, delivers that which one has sold, and renders to one's employer the performance. ... The jurist of course, is ready with the objection that all men perform their duties only because they know that the courts shall eventually compel them to perform them. If he should take the pains, to which, indeed, he is not accustomed, to observe what men do and leave undone, he would soon be convinced of the fact that, as a rule, the thought of compulsion by the courts does not even enter the minds of men.[60]

A different school of thought claimed that: "fundamental changes in society are possible without accompanying alterations of the legal system." [61] Karl Renner, one of the most distinguished representatives of this trend, has suggested the existence of a basic dichotomy between the normative functions of the legal order and the creative functions of social laws. Each of these two social orders, in his view, governed separate realms. The law was addressed to individuals, but was unable to command the economic development of society:

The relations between the individual and the natural object, the technical power of the man, the productive capacity of the individual, all those

---

60 Ehrlich, Fundamental Principles of the Sociology of Law 21 (1936).
61 Renner, The Institutions of Private Law and Their Social Functions 251, 255 (1949); *cf*. Weber, On Law in Economy and Society 35–36 (1954).

develop under the eye of the law but not by means of the law. . . . Where
it aims at the control of groups the law cannot do more than to address
itself to the individual . . . the law must resolve all collective relations
among men into rights and duties of individuals. Wherever men enter
into a definite but extralegal relationship, as for instance in the form
of cooperation for manufacture, or a body of factory workers, in actual-
ity they constitute groups whose collective actions are beyond the reach
of law. Even a casual gathering of the individuals, such as a crowd, develops potentialities for social action outside the direct control of the
law.[62]

Consequently, for Renner, legal rule was not a relevant social
rule. It could not influence the development and transformation of
social forms of action. Economic developments, however, did affect
the legal rule, and deprived of legal force those formally binding
legal rules which no longer applied to changed economic and social
conditions.

The function of the jurist, in Renner's analysis, was to provide
the bridge between these two phenomena, i.e., to link the legal order
with the state and the social forces. Social facts thus were correlated
with the legal order by providing a foundation for its operation. The
legal and social orders acknowledged their allegiance to the central
principle of social organization, described variously as "a complex of
social facts involved in the manifold associations and relations which
make up human society" (Ehrlich), "social interdependence in the
economic order" (Duguit), or "social solidarity" which constitutes
the principle of law (Bourgeois). [63]

The institutions which translate social action into the forms
current in legal commerce have been variously conceived. Jellinek,
still standing astride the two systems of rights and the mechanism of
social functions, resorted to the device of fiction. Thus, true contracts involving individual will were arranged in the same category
with the quasi contracts which clothe social action.[64] Hauriou developed the theory of the institution, which he conceived to be an
"association of human activities" endowed with significance and con-

---

62 Renner, *supra* note 61, at 255.
63 1 Pound, Jurisprudence 335 ff.; Leroy, *supra* note 37, at 38, 277–78.
64 Jellinek, L'état moderne et son droit 74 ff. (1904); *cf.* 1 Pound, Juris-
    prudence 341; Pound, *supra* note 18, at 84.

tinuity in a social milieu. The state was one of these institutions. Along with other institutions, it provided anchorage for the legal system.

Renard developed Hauriou's concept still further. Institutions represented, to Renard, not only the elements of stability and continuity, but contained as well an element of progress. While the contractual forms of relations were sporadic, and represented little or no continuity, institutions represented the dynamism of social life.

Renard's new jurisprudence was addressed to the problem of liberty in the sense that it tended toward subordination of the individual will to the rule of reason. Individual will left to itself was an anarchistic element. Social order grounded on the principle of social discipline provided the element of balance in the conflict of antagonistic forces. The element which unified all people was reason. Therefore, the legal system should be redirected from the principle of individual will and contract to the principle of order based on institutions and reason.

In other words, reason was identified with the scientific approach to the problem of lawmaking. Isolated from politics, the latter was to be directed only by the scientific findings of the supporting sciences which analyzed and established the needs of society. The age of politics, with its struggle for freedom, had passed. Freedom had been won. The need now was for a better rule of law more adapted to social needs.[65]

Various authors of the modern sociological school differ in their understanding of the role of the state and of the legal order. Socialist theories of social change reserve to the state its traditional role as guardian of public order. Contrariwise, the main trend of sociological jurisprudence calls for a more active role for the state and legal order. However, in the system of social organizations the state is only one of several constituents, though perhaps the most important. In order to be creative, the law would then be required to seek harmony with the social rule.

---

65 "[L]e virement de l'institutionnel au contractuel dénote habituellement une malaise, le virement du contractuel vers l'institutionnel un progrès." Renard, La théorie de l'institution 30 (1930); also *id.* at 445–46. *Cf.* Rommen, *supra* note 47, at 40–41, 55, on the relationships *lex-ratio* and *lex-voluntas*.

According to Duguit, formal standards of legality are not adequate criteria by which to test the validity of the rule of law. The
latter was that rule which promoted social solidarity. The force of
law rested in the fact that the people's individual consciences were
persuaded that this norm could be enforced. Law existed and was
valid independently of the technique of enforcement by the state.
But fundamentally, it was not the creation of the state, although
formally it appeared to be.

These two concepts, the purposive character of the legal rule
and the state of individual conscience, determined in Duguit's analysis
the content and binding force of the law; and on this basis, legal rules
were integrated with social laws. On this basis also, individual rights
and interests were identified with the interests of society at large.[66]

The sociological school argued against the division of the legal
system into public and private law, and against the concept of state
sovereignty. Duguit considered both to be contrary to the principle
of solidarity. Renner, on the other hand, rejected private law altogether, as in his opinion it was a system of rules which delegated
the exercise of public power to private entrepreneurs. The homogeneity
of the legal system warranted full judicial control of all aspects of
social activity, whether within the jurisdiction of public authorities,
social organizations, or private entrepreneurs.

No less important among the contributions of the sociological
school were the reforms which increased judicial control of proceedings in civil causes. Thus, with a view to arriving at the material
truth, the court was permitted to control the flow of evidence and to
decide for itself what evidence it needed in order to discharge its
responsibilities. Furthermore, the court was given great powers to
expedite proceedings in the cases before it. After the reform of German
civil procedure in 1924, which may be taken as typical of the reforms
introduced in the period between the wars in the European countries,
the parties, by joint agreement, could no longer suspend proceedings
in the case until further motion. The court, on the other hand, could
order the parties to continue the pleading unless good cause was

66 1 Duguit, Traité de droit constitutionnel 80–81, 93, 174 (1927); *cf.*
Willoughby, The Ethical Bases of Political Authority (1930).

shown. Also, as social harmony was the primary value of which laws were required to take account, European courts were instructed to favor in each stage of proceedings amicable settlement of litigations, and to render necessary assistance to the parties to that effect.

In the field of the criminal law, the sociological school made the courts chief instruments of modern penal policy. Criminal courts were accorded great powers of punishment, of judicial pardon, and the application of preventive, correctional, and therapeutical measures. Their aim in the disposal of criminal cases was to assist those who promised a return to normal life.

Of similar import were the powers accorded to the civil courts in regard to enforcing private contracts and adjusting relations between individual parties according to broader social interests. In particular, courts were accorded great powers in the distribution of risks resulting from the hazards of modern life. An interesting indication of the trend of thought initiated by the sociological school was the proposal contained in the draft of the German Civil Code which was prepared at the beginning of the present century. According to this proposal the court could, in adjudicating a case, adapt the stipulations of a private contract to the requirements of public utility and in accordance with the commands of morals.[67]

At the turn of the century, the work of the sociological school was beginning to produce practical results in the form of legislative reform.[68] Its main achievement was the recognition by the legal profession and the legislators of the need to utilize the new techniques for the purpose of realizing the eternal goals of the rule of law within the context of new social conditions.

The sociologists have demonstrated that, in order to provide a balance between individual rights and the general welfare and security of all, the rule of law must abandon its abstract and general form and become a more flexible tool of social ordering. Sociologists have

---

67 For the listing of the most important works of the early period of the sociological school see 1 Geny, *supra* note 19, v ff.; *cf.* Leroy, *supra* note 37, at 84.

68 Pound, "The Need of a Sociological Jurisprudence," 19 The Green Bag 607 (1907).

also taught that it is necessary to take account of social and economic disparities rather than to insist on the equality of all members of the community under law.

This shift in the ideas concerning the function of the rule of law was occasioned by the realization of social environment as the milieu which shapes the forces of progress responsible for the conditions of life. In addition, it has been recognized that the role of the state has had to be correspondingly enlarged in order to maintain social peace. The state, although no longer enjoying the pre-eminence accorded to it by the positivists, has remained the most important and most general social institution affording protection to individual rights. In the final analysis, then, sociologists have added a new dimension to the concept of legal order, though still inspired by the idea that the rule of law represents a balance between the general welfare and individual liberty.

Chapter II

LAW, STATE, AND SOCIETY

GROWTH OF THE SOCIALIST *RECHTSSTAAT*

A collective work of Soviet jurists to celebrate forty years of Soviet legal order has stressed that the Soviet system has resulted from the achievement of the masses:

The Soviet state emerged not on the basis of some written statutes, but as a result of the direct initiative of the masses, which had destroyed in the course of the revolution of the old order, the old legality, the old system of authorities, which have created in its stead its own system of power, its own governmental agencies.[1]

While this description is undoubtedly true regarding that part of the process which consisted of overthrowing the old regime, the Soviet regime itself was rather the result of political and military action conducted from the center. The victory of the Bolshevik Party was followed by the gradual integration of the revolutionary authorities into a single system of controls. Before its accomplishment, however, large parts of Russia lived without any system of government and without a legal order.

Decrees and instructions which flowed from the center of the revolutionary government might give the impression that from the very beginning the new regime was firmly entrenched and was able to afford new freedoms and a new social structure to the working masses of Russia. The Soviet professors, in continuing their description of the initial years of the Soviet order, have painted a grandiose picture of the various programs of social reform which occupied the minds of the new leaders:

1 Sorok let sovetskogo prava 16 (1957).

It is enough to become acquainted with the first decrees of the Soviet power to realize how energetically the law making of the masses developed.... History shows that building the new social and governmental order in our country is indissolubly linked with the historic decrees of Soviet government on peace, on land, on establishment of the Council of People's Commissars, on the workers inspection, on the nationalization of banks and basic means of production, on the eight-hour working day, on the judiciary, etc.

In the same breath they admit, however, that the legislative activity of those days was far from being conceived as a measure of government. Rather, it was regarded as an act of propaganda and of class warfare. Lenin, speaking to the Eighth Party Congress, indicated that not all of these decrees could be enforced at once and fully. They were only a form of an appeal for bringing the masses into the political struggle on the side of the Bolshevik Party:

[S]hould we have refrained from pointing the way in the new decrees, we would have been traitors to socialism.... Our decrees were an appeal, but not an appeal in the formal meaning such as "workers arise, overthrow the bourgeoisie." No, it was an appeal to the masses, to undertake a concrete task. Decrees were instructions, calling for a mass participation in practical work.[2]

Thus, the first decrees of the Soviet government were not designed to possess absolute binding force, even in the eyes of their authors. They were, according to the definition of Trotsky, "the program of the Party uttered in the language of power" and, as such, "rather a means of propaganda than of administration."[3] In 1917 Lenin wrote:

It does not matter that many points in our decrees will never be carried out; their task is to teach the masses how to take practical steps.... We shall not look at them as at absolute rules to be carried out under all circumstances.[4]

2 *Id.* at 47–48.
3 Trotsky, Moia zhizn 65 (1930).
4 16 Lenin, Sochinenia 149 (1924). As to the temper of the times, see Hazard, Settling Disputes in Soviet Society 2–3 (1960). The author wishes to acknowledge his debt to this capital work on the formative years of Soviet legal institutions. *Cf.* also Reisner, "Law, Our Law, Foreign Law, General Law," in Soviet Legal Philosophy 93 (Babb transl., 1951).

Similarly, the beginnings of the Soviet courts had little in common with the regular administration of justice. There was no order or plan in the activity of the various self-styled courts and tribunals, such as are now included in the genealogy of the Soviet judicial system. Rather, the revolutionary administration of justice was characterized by the activity of several self-organized courts, which took their authority from the general spirit of revolt, and not from the central authorization.[5]

According to the description of a Soviet historian of the early days of the Soviet order, the revolutionary administration of justice began with the activity of several self-organized courts and revolutionary tribunals, avowedly created by the decrees of the Central Executive Committee of the Soviets. The first was the "Petrograd War-Revolutionary Committee" whose "penalizing activity became one of the sources of the new law and the new socialist legality." Several other courts followed, such as "Provisional People's Courts," "Courts of Social Conscience," "Inquiry Commissions," etc.[6]

These courts made their own rules and established their own powers, in such terms as, for example:

Courts of authority, enjoying full confidence among the people; Courts of conscience, not bound by any existing laws. . . . (Rules of the People's Provision Court of the Government of Kuznetz).

The Rules of the Provisional Revolutionary Court of the Government of Novgorod provided:

The Court decides on the issues by conscience, on the basis of its own conviction. (sec. 15.) In imposing punishment upon the guilty person, the court is not bound by any existing laws, but is authorized to use the existing criminal laws for non-obligatory reference. (sec. 18.) [7]

Developments in the first years of Soviet lawmaking and the administration of justice in Russia were dramatically but neatly summarized in the Guilding Principles of the Criminal Law of the RSFSR of December 12, 1919, which stated:

5 *Cf.* Stuchka, "Otchet Narodnago Komissara Iustitsii," 1 Proletarskaia Revolutsia i Pravo 33 (No. 1, 1918).
6 Gertsenson *et al.,* Istoria Sovetskogo ugolovnogo prava 81, 101 (1948).
7 Materialy Narkomyusta 42–48 (1918).

The proletariat, having won power in the October Revolution, smashed the bourgeois apparatus, which served to oppress the working masses. ... It is self-evident that all the codes of the bourgeois law, all bourgeois law as a system of legal rules, had the same part to play, namely to maintain by organized force the balance of interests of the various classes of society to the advantage of the ruling classes. ... Since the proletariat could not adapt to its purposes the bourgeois codes of the outlived epochs, which ought to have been placed in historical archives. Without special rules, without codes of law, the armed masses have been and still are coping with their oppressors. In the course of the struggle with their class enemies the proletariat is applying various measures of force, but it has applied these during the early period without any special system as each case required and without organization. The experience of the struggle has accustomed the proletariat to uniform measures, has led to systematization, has given birth to the new law. Almost two years of this struggle have already provided the opportunity to present the results as a concrete manifestation of proletarian law; to draw conclusions and the necessary generalizations.[8]

While the political aspects of legalistic anarchy were gratifying to the new aspirants to the control of government in Russia, the absence of legal order was not an unmixed blessing. The official optimism of the leaders found the situation on the legal front inspiring and promising of new solutions to problems of law and justice within the framework of the new socialist civilization. This was paralleled, however, by the more sober tone of practical measures, by which it was sought to channel revolutionary sentiment into some common pattern of action. While accepting the repeal of the old laws, the new regime suggested adoption of orderly procedures in the process of repeal. The Decree of December 7, 1917, on the Judiciary instructed the new People's Courts, which were to supplant the courts of the Tsarist regime, to apply the laws of the previous government insofar as they were not abrogated by the Revolution and did not contradict the "revolutionary conscience and revolutionary concept of law." The second decree on the Judiciary, enacted in February 1918, created District People's Courts. These were to dispose of the cases pending in the old courts, and were instructed to follow judicial statutes of 1864 regarding their procedure. Further, the new judges

8 Sob. uzak. sec. 590 (no. 66, 1919).

were required to state the reasons why the court in each case "abrogated one law or another as obsolete or capitalist." Finally, the Statute on the People's Courts of the RSFSR of November 30, 1918, definitely prohibited any citation of prerevolutionary law in court decisions. The courts were instructed to "render their decisions on the basis of the enactments of the Workers and Peasants Government and of the revolutionary consciousness of the judges." [9]

The text of the enactments would suggest that the Soviet government moved step by step in order to replace an orderly administration of justice with a regime of anarchy and terror. In fact, anarchy and lawlessness were present; and while the regime depended on anarchy for the success of the revolution, it attempted to put some order into the operation of its own courts by the correlation of this activity to such laws as were available. The Decree of November 1918 seems to indicate that the regime recognized for the time being the futility of its attempts in this direction. Consequently, one may question whether successive steps toward freeing people's courts from the bondage of the laws of the old regime were the result of the growing revolutionary temper of the Soviet leadership, or rather that the regime was forced to accept the existing situation.[10]

In spite of the official optimism of the leaders, the initial practice of the Soviet courts held little promise that their activities per se could lead to a system of socialist law. A Soviet historian of the early days of the administration of justice indeed demonstrated that without central action no systematic and orderly application of common standards of justice would be possible. Lynch trials were quite common. On many occasions criminals were shot without trial. Sentences of death were imposed frequently by popular vote and sometimes were carried out by burning. In a village near Orlov, a man was put to death by 59 votes against 40. Sometimes whole groups of people suspected of robbery, and on one occasion a pregnant woman, were burned at the stake while the whole community watched. Some death sentences were executed by cutting the convicted man to pieces, or by

9 Grzybowski, "Continuity of Law in Eastern Europe," 6 Am. J. Comp. L. 48–49 (1957).
10 1 Gsovski, Soviet Civil Law 280 (1948).

throwing him onto hay forks. When a Red Army soldier was put on trial for killing a thief, his fellow soldiers nearly revolted because they were unable to grasp what the offender's crime was.[11]

The action of Soviet authority took two courses. In the first place, as their control over the country increased, the central authorities replaced local courts with their own institutions. These possessed standardized organization and standardized jurisdiction and operated on the basis of uniform procedural legislation. Secondly, the regime sought to replace vague ideas about revolutionary justice with statutory enactments which finally grew into a system of codes.

Not in all these fields were Soviet policies clear and well reasoned from their inception. The initial concern was with the mechanism rather than with the substantive law. While a uniform system of courts was established with considerable dispatch, their operation and manner of rendering justice belied their uniformity of organization.[12] Not only was the regime little concerned with legal refinements in the enforcement of the legal order, but it experienced great doubts as to some of the fundamental questions of the legal order in a revolutionary country. In particular, the regime was troubled by the question of what kind of law a socialist country should have.

The original ideas as to the kind of law a socialist country might need were related to the modern trends in Western European thought. This latter tradition tended to favor free judicial interpretation of statutes rather than the formal analysis of text. One might have serious doubts whether extremist views on the subject entertained by some of the Soviet jurists in leading positions were widely shared by their colleagues. Nevertheless, the Commissar of Justice considered the situation in which courts were called upon to administer justice without any substantive law whatsoever as a great achievement of the revolution. Viewing the situation in the Russian Courts at the beginning of 1919, he stated:

Neither Roman law nor bourgeois law gave such authority to a judge. Perhaps we can find some analogy in more ancient primitive law. But one has only to consider the whole complexity of contemporary social relationships and to contrast these with the primitive use which was de-

11 Isayev, Obshchaia chast ugolovnogo prava 63 ff., 86 (1925).
12 Hazard, *supra* note 4, at 477.

veloped into a norm by the elders by custom, and by other sources of primitive law to grasp the immeasurable difference between the sources of primitive law and the new law created by the proletarian revolution.[13]

He emphasized that:

The bourgeois judge can only complete the statute by interpretation. The scope of the proletarian People's Court is much wider. In its basic function—criminal prosecution—the People's Court is absolutely free and is guided above all by its consciousness of law.[14]

He was certain that "the proletariat was not disappointed when it gave the courts such a strong weapon as the freedom of law making."[15]

The idea that the socialist order of economy might dispense with an elaborate legal system was not a Soviet invention, but was born in Western Europe.[16] In the initial years of the revolutionary state, the new legal order was identified directly with a set of principles born out of the revolution. The Decree of November 23, 1917, described them as "revolutionary consciousness of law." The Decree of March 7, 1918, had a similar provision which prescribed that since the courts were not restricted in their functions by any formal law, they should be guided by their "concept of justice." The third Decree on Courts of July 20, 1918, mentioned again "socialist conscience" as a source of law, along with the decrees of the revolutionary government. The same provision also appeared in the Decree of November 30, 1918, which provided that "in deciding all issues, the People's Court shall apply the decrees of the government of the Workers and Peasants, and, in case of the absence of a decree or its incompleteness shall be guided by the socialist consciousness of law."

Thus, the Soviet judge was to be free from any familiarity with the legal rule except for a few applicable governmental decrees. This position was eventually confirmed by the Party program adopted at the Eighth Party Congress of the All Russian Communist Party

13 Kurskii, "Novoe ugolovnoe prave," 2 Proletarskaia Revolutsia i Pravo 24 (No. 2–4, 1919); *cf.* Timasheff, "The Impact of the Penal Law of Imperial Russia on Soviet Penal Law," 12 American Slavic and East European Rev. 445 (1953).

14 Kurskii, *supra* note 13, at 47.

15 *Id.,* at 55.

16 *Cf. supra* Chapter I.

(March 1919). Then the judges, elected by the Soviets, were instructed to realize the will of the proletariat by applying their decrees. In the event of absence or incompleteness of the latter, they were to follow their socialist consciousness of law.[17]

However, there is evidence that even at that early stage there were doubts in high governmental circles as to the wisdom of unguided judicial lawmaking, particularly as the number of decrees enacted by the new regime grew considerably. In this connection, the Sixth All Russian Extraordinary Session of the Soviets passed at the end of 1918 a resolution "on strict observance of laws." The resolution stated that "the working class of Russia has during one year of revolutionary struggle laid foundations for the laws of the RSFSR," the strict observance of which was declared to be indispensable for the further development and the strengthening of the Government of Workers and Peasants in Russia. The resolution further called upon all citizens, official persons and authorities to obey strictly the laws of the RSFSR.[18]

The first step toward providing some order in the administration of justice by the new courts was the promulgation of the so-called "Guiding Principles," adopted on December 2, 1919.[19] By this means was initiated a specifically Soviet legislative technique of providing central government directives for the creative improvisation of the legal order by the lower echelons of authority. After the federal structure was adopted, the Guiding Principles were to provide those basic guide lines to be followed by the legislation of the federal republics. The purpose, of course, was to maintain the uniformity of those legal aspects which constituted the basic principles of policy. Contrary to later practice, however, the Guiding Principles of 1919 were to be directly enforced by the courts, which were, nevertheless, to enjoy a large measure of freedom in devising rules of law applicable to individual cases.

The Guiding Principles did not constitute a complete code of criminal law. Rather, their purpose was to "make a balance sheet of achievements, and, for the sake of economy of effort, to establish rules and methods of defeating the class enemies for the transition

17 *Cf.* Hazard, *supra* note 4, at 62.
18 Sob. uzak., sec. 908 (No. 90, 1918).
19 *Id.,* sec. 590 (No. 66, 1919).

period of the proletarian dictatorship." Their function may be compared, therefore, to that of the General Part in the criminal codes of Europe. The latter provide guidance for the courts in terms of penal policies; whereas, a special part provides penalties for individual crimes.

The second step was the enactment of a series of codes for the Soviet state.

In the system of codes, which represented a response to the new situation under the NEP (New Economic Policy, 1921–1927) when the Russian economy was to return temporarily to capitalist forms of production, only the criminal law was to retain the unadulterated character of a class measure. The new labor code was to establish a regime in which the Soviet worker would again be employed in a private enterprise. The civil codes, the first in Russian history to provide a uniform private law for the entire country, were also to protect the interests of the national economy by promoting conditions which would favor industrial enterprise. Only the criminal law was to protect the interests of the socialist order of things, and only in the field of criminal legislation could the experience of the revolutionary period be used.

The first move for a full-fledged criminal code preceded by some time the advent of the NEP. Such proposals were formulated by the Third All Russian Convention of the Workers of Soviet Justice (June 1920). The code itself was the result of a number of drafts. In the course of the discussion, it was also proposed that Soviet courts should return to the criminal code of 1903, which was a progressive piece of legislation and an outstanding example of modern legislative technique. Commissar of Justice Kurskii came out with a proposal which he believed would salvage as much as possible from the experience of the socialist administration of justice. He proposed that the Code should refrain from providing a full list of definitions covering all possible offenses. In addition to a general part stating the general purpose of the penal policy and general principles of criminal law, the Code should contain, he believed, only a few general characteristics of crimes which the courts would apply to individual situations by the method of analogy.[20]

20 Materialy Narkomyusta, vol. 11–12 (1921).

The Code as it was finally adopted employed a number of the proposals advanced by Kurskii. Such was thought to be essential in a Code without a full list of crimes.

In the first place, the Code of 1922 gave a material definition of a crime as an act dangerous to the social order (Article 6):

Crime is every socially dangerous act of omission endangering the foundations of the Soviet system and legal order established by the Government of Workers and Peasants for the period during the transition to the communist system.

Furthermore, the new Code defined the dangerous character of the offender in terms of activity harmful to society or seriously imperiling social order. It also formulated the principle of analogy which was to remain the feature of Soviet law until its removal in 1958. Article 10 of the Code of 1922 stated:

In case of absence of a direct provision for a particular kind of crime in the Criminal Code, the punishment by means of social defense shall apply, . . . according to those articles of the Criminal Code, which provide for crimes most similar as to importance and kind.

FROM POPULAR TO THE SCIENTIFIC LAW

One of the architects of the Soviet legal system described the situation in the early days of the revolutionary regime as follows:

. . . our Marxists were utterly devoid of interest in problems of law and legal ideology, notwithstanding the fact that even the revolution itself and the period of war communism following thereafter posed problems of the utmost importance . . . as to the relations of the proletariat to law.

He continued:

This accounts for the astonishing sobriety and reality of principles and the plans established exclusively on the basis of expediency rather than upon the basis of justice or of formal principles of abstract authority.[21]

Absence of theoretical formulations in the official doctrines on legislative policies did not leave the early Soviet lawmakers without guidance. Indeed, Soviet legislators fell back on the well established doctrines and teachings of modern legal science. So, for instance, the

21 Reisner, *supra* note 4, at 92.

Section on the Judiciary in the 1919 Communist Party Program indicated that the Soviet courts were applying such advanced institutions as suspended sentence, public censure instead of punishment, and labor instead of confinement. Further, the formula to be employed by the courts in supplying the law in the event of statutory silence sounds very familiar to the ear of one conversant with Article 1 of the Swiss Civil Code or Article 12 of the Italian Civil Code of 1942.[22] Professor Hazard has called attention to the resolution passed by the general assembly of Moscow judges, which protested against setting aside a court sentence by an administrative authority. It is significant that the resolution, introduced by Pashukanis, gained acceptance in spite of the doctrine of the unity of the People's power—a rule of Soviet constitutionalism.[23] The resolution of the Third All Russian Convention of Workers of Soviet Justice, referred to above, in recommending codification of the Soviet criminal law, expressed the conviction that a codified statute was a better method of assuring the proper administration of justice than by appealing to the revolutionary or proletarian consciousness or conscience.

The jurists who sat in the councils of Soviet government were concerned with the improvement of the quality of Soviet Codes once they had been enacted and with the assurance of higher standards of the administration of justice. Their purpose was to avoid favoritism and partiality, and to assure the intervention of the class principle only in cases where the interests of society as a whole, in terms of the communist doctrine, were involved.[24]

The process which took place in the post-revolutionary years in the Soviet Union cannot be interpreted by the conflict between the two prevalent orientations of the day. The first of these had called for the organization of national life and governmental action according to that understanding of Marxism which was inclined to see in legal institutions something which was characteristic of the capitalist society. The other had followed the so-called legal line which posited the usefulness of the legal rule in the period of transition to higher forms of social organization. In the final analysis, the political conflict purged

22 Hazard, *supra* note 4, at 62.
23 *Id.,* at 17.
24 *Id.,* at 433.

both doctrines in favor of Stalin, who could neither be accused of being legalistically minded nor sympathetic to the doctrines of Kurskii, Stuchka, and Pashukanis. The conflict between the two groups, in essence, centered upon the point of whether a modern legal system could be devised for Russia without employing techniques belonging to the European tradition. There was no conflict as to political or social aims of the legal order. Russian jurists, who supported the legal line, wanted socialist law to correspond to certain standards of codification and to certain formal standards of operation. In a sense, Russian jurists, though revolutionaries, could not escape their own background. As Max Weber said:

[A] body of law can be "rationalized" in various ways and by no means necessarily in the direction of the development of its "juristic" qualities. The direction in which these formal qualities develop is, however, conditioned directly by "intrajuristic" conditions; the particular character of the individuals who are in a position to influence "professionally" the ways in which the law is shaped. Only indirectly is this development influenced, however, by general economic and social conditions. The prevailing type of legal education, i.e., the mode of training practitioners of the law, has been more important than any other factor.[25]

Thus, the conflict between the two tendencies was resolved by the introduction of legal doctrines inspired without exception by the patterns and models borrowed from the West.

The problems of simplicity in court structure, of the involvement of the lay element, and of the informality of judicial procedure were major issues of legal reform in the West. European jurisprudence had, in fact, devoted great attention to these questions since the second half of the nineteenth century. The crop of civil and criminal procedures produced in the interwar years was inspired by the same ideas.[26] Soviet criminal legislation represented an effort to formulate the penal policies of the Soviet state in the terminology of the Italian *Scuola Positiva*.[27] Institutions of the Soviet Civil Code of 1922 were framed upon the patterns borrowed from the two modern codes of Switzerland and Germany. And, many of its provisions were incorporated from the draft of the Russian Civil Code prepared before the War.[28]

25 Weber, On Law in Economy and Society 97 (1954).
26 *Cf. supra* at 15, 38–39.
27 *Cf. infra* at 184, 190, 200.
28 1 Gsovski, *supra* note 10, at 24–25; *cf.* Timasheff, *supra* note 13.

In spite of the official theory that Soviet law was the product of popular ideas of law, the initial years witnessed a great concern with the modern techniques of criminology of Western Europe. Indeed, extensive researches were conducted in the best traditions of the sociological school of Liszt.[29]

Long after that period and well into the post-Stalinist period, the Full Civil Chamber of the Polish Supreme Court had adopted a directive which stated the simple convictions animating the work of Russian jurists of the initial years, before Stalin's ascendance to power:

> In every state, irrespective of its type, civil procedure in its broadest form ... serves to protect civil rights, property rights, and claims based on those rights. The qualitative difference of the socialist state and law from the state and law of the exploiters, different class nature of the administration of justice in the socialist state, are unable to affect this function of the civil procedure, as long as the state and law shall continue to exist—which is and will be, to afford protection to private rights in the form of state coercion.[30]

These borrowings did not prevent the products of socialist lawmaking from being inferior. The Criminal Code was a mixture of ideas and concessions made to extraneous influences. The Civil Code was a hasty and inexpert work which again fell short of the great models which it endeavored to imitate. Even so, Soviet legislation, with all its imperfections, was not responsible for the questionable conditions of the administration of justice and the level of juristic thinking in the Soviet Union. The regime in Russia which followed the ascendance to Stalin's power was not a *Rechtsstaat,* but a police state.

THE PATTERN OF STALIN'S STATE

Leon Duguit had made his principle of social interdependence the starting point for an attack on the concept of sovereignty. The state was not an institution with a distinct personality, and public power was not separate from social facts. The state had to enact laws, but these laws were to correspond to the fact of social interdependence. The state had to conform to the laws which it made; and judges, ad-

29 *Cf. infra* at 206.
30 Decision of the Full Civil Chamber of the Polish Supreme Court of Feb. 12, 1955, PiP 290 (No. 7–8, 1955).

ministrators, and legislators were to act within the powers which it created until it was changed or abrogated.

For Duguit, the existence of social groups and the principle of social interdependence dictated the content of laws and determined mutual relations between the mechanism of government, the social structure, and the rule of law. As the content of the legal rule was the result of social solidarity, the governing apparatus could not be sovereign. As society did not perform public services itself (Duguit rejected the concept of public power), society was not sovereign. In other words, the identification of the content of the legal rule with the content of social solidarity and the integration of the mechanism of government into the social structure resolved the problem of the state and social relations. In addition, it eliminated the need for the concept of sovereignty as an attribute of the state, as something separate from the social milieu. Society was simply the environment in which was produced the phenomenon of the state, which, in turn, was the division between the governing group and the governed.[31]

The first Soviet theoretical answer as to the place of each of three components, the state, the law, and the society, in the process of change was dictated by the conviction that social action (class struggle) was the motor of progress. According to Stuchka, Pashukanis, and their followers, law had a function in the society, but once the institution of property disappeared, the state and law would disappear as well.[32] Action by the state could produce little change in social structures. Even the act of nationalization (particularly nationalization of the land) and expropriation of the exploiting class did not by themselves constitute a transition from the lower level of social existence to higher forms of cooperation. This would take time and would be achieved by the establishment of new economic institutions.

31 *Cf. supra* at 38 ff.

In contrast with Duguit, Karl Renner denied the state and law a creative role in social processes. For Eugen Ehrlich law enforcement was a social process, and individual response in terms of obedience to the rule of law was predicated on facts independent of the state power. Nordics, on the other hand, reduced the problem of the correlation of the social structures, the state, and the legal rule to the issue of exercise of power in order to realize the interests of the state.

32 Pashukanis, Allgemeine Rechtslehre und Marxismus (1929); Stuchka, Introduction à la théorie du droit civil (1926).

In fact, the theories of Pashukanis described quite correctly the situation in Russia as it existed after the Revolution, and particularly under the NEP. However, once the state undertook to manage and plan for the economic development of Russia, a new theory had to be worked out.

The new theory was the result of a clash between two Marxist orientations. The deterministic interpretation of history, stressing the spontaneity of social processes, was superseded by the theory which insisted that Marxist determinism and concern with the economic forms of social activity were compatible with intervention in order to hasten the march of history. The policy of the five-year plan brought about a flood of regulations, directives, instructions, and other enactments to marshal national resources and organize industrial enterprises, to regulate consumption and production, and to bring about a conscious and planned realization of socialist society. Direct ties between the legal rule and economic life were not broken, but strengthened. If, as according to Pashukanis, law was bourgeois and the economy was socialist, then under Stalin's theoretical assumption, both law and economy could be socialist in content and function. The nature of the legal rule was determined not so much by its institutions and forms, as by its social purpose.

The Soviet mechanism of change thus represented a marshaling of all three elements—law, social structures, and the state—combined with the principle of a deterministic concept for the purpose of social action. As a Soviet scholar wrote at the time when the Soviet Union was facing mortal danger of German aggression:

Every society, irrespective of its form, follows laws based on objective necessity. In the socialist society this necessity acts as the economic law conditioned by the external situation of the society, by all historical antecedents of its development; this objective necessity perceived by men, infiltrated into the conscience and the will of the people—in the persons of the builders of the socialist society, as the leading and organizing force of the society, the Soviet state and the Communist party, directing the activity of the masses.[33]

This objective necessity was translated into direct and concrete commands of Soviet laws. Thus, Vyshinskii, attacking legal "nihilism"

33 *Pod Znamenem Marksizma* 45 (No. 7–8, 1943).

and sociological tendencies in law, wrote: "Stuchka and his adherents liquidated law as a separate, specific social category, they drowned law in economics, deprived it of its active creative role." [34]

As an important Soviet jurist wrote at the time when five-year plans became a permanent factor in Soviet life:

[I]t would be a mistake to consider economy as the only factor determining the understanding of the historical processes. One must take into consideration Marxian teachings on the mutual relations between the basis and the superstructure and of the bearing which the superstructure may exercise in turn upon its economic basis, so as to cause its further development and change. Politics are not a mere impression moulded from economy, as the vulgar materialists try to represent them, but the conclusion drawn from a generalization of the economy.

Politics are fully expressive of the economic level which conditions the class content of the state activity, in shaping by legal regulation the relations between the classes, the influence of the state on the development of the sciences, of arts, and vice versa the influence of the superstructure on the economic basis.

Politics, state and law—represent the three sides of a single process; politics (a full expression of the economic system) constitutes a transmission belt which sets law and state in motion and correlates their cooperation and relationship. [35]

If for the principle of social interdependence the principle of inexorable progress is substituted, the theoretical construction of the Duguit type resembles Soviet formulations of the correlation of the society, state, and law. The real difference, which on first sight does not seem to be of key importance, is in the concept of the role of the elite. The governing group had to render public services and was bound by its own laws. According to Trainin, the policy of the Soviet government and of the Communist Party was determined by actual economic conditions, not by the content of the law. This was because the governing group had a better understanding of the tasks which faced society than the rest of the social structure.

34 Vyshinskii, Teoria gosudarstva i prava 78 (1945).
35 Trainin, "Gosudarstvo stroiushchegosia kommunizma," Izvestia Akademii Nauk SSSR, Otdelenie Ekonomiki i Prava 7–8 (No. 5, 1945); *cf.* Guins, Soviet Law and Soviet Society 4 (1954).

THE INTEGRATED SOCIETY

The Soviet Constitution of 1936 affords to citizens the right to form associations as well as the unlimited capacity to join already existing ones (Article 126). The best among them may join the Communist Party, which holds a central place in the entire spectrum of social and governmental organizations by providing a nucleus in the state and social organization. Thus, what had begun as a concept of right, has ended as the principle of order, in much the same manner that democracy is predicated upon the citizen's willingness to participate in the government of the community.

Georges Gurvich in his systematization of legal sociology distinguished between kinds of law, frameworks of law, and systems of law. A system of law, in his view, consisted of a number of frameworks of law within which various kinds of law competed. Translated into less technical terminology, any legal system of a polity consisted of a number of legal orders such as state law, cooperative law, family law, and trade union law. Within their framework, these legal orders accommodated different kinds of law such as feudal law, bourgeois law, American law, etc. Without going into further analysis of this formulation, it is enough to state that the present chapter is devoted to an examination of the various frameworks of law and their correlation within the legal Soviet order. This approach will permit the tracing of the interconnections between various social organizations and the system of Soviet authorities. It will further permit the distinction between those parts of the framework of law of each social group which constitute a genuine part of the framework from others which represent an intrusion originating outside and, in the final analysis, representing a distortion of the group's social function.[36]

The theories of Gurvich are, as is already obvious, the result of the observation that a legal system of a polity is never the product of a single lawmaking agent. Rather, it is viewed as owing its existence to the interaction of many sources. Law consists of frameworks born of the needs and functions of what Gurvich calls real collective units. Through these frameworks are introduced elements of a legal system

36 Gurvich, Sociology of Law 198–203 (1942).

which either reflect specific rules for various social groups or for various alien kinds of law.[37]

Article 126 of the Soviet Constitution, which contains the principle of the penetration of the Communist Party into the viscera of each social organization, represents the basic plan for the correlation of social forces and the integration of social and governmental organizations. These latter include local administrative authority, professional organizations, and economic institutions. The characteristic feature of the social and political order of the Soviet society is that none of these organizations exclusively belongs to any of the two categories—society or state—and each of them owes its existence to the fact that it constitutes a channel for the coordination of human masses.

The Soviet administrative system, which finally emerged as a single system of elective authorities throughout the federal Union, has its roots in the dual tradition of public administration in Europe. According to this pattern, national affairs are handled by the central government with field offices, while local affairs are administered by local elective institutions. These latter are sometimes limited only to the communal level and sometimes are organized on the territorial basis; nevertheless, in principle they remain independent on each level, and are not subject to the control from the national center. In pre-revolutionary Russia (1870), territorial and municipal government had been a center of important governmental reforms, and quite early some of the revolutionary parties saw in the institutions of local government a beginning of the future socialist regime for Russia. The Bolsheviks, however, came out against such notions and favored a single system of elective authorities handling all aspects of administrative activities, both national and local. World War I greatly weakened local government in Russia, and after the revolution, earlier territorial and municipal government played practically no part in the establishment of the new order. Functions of local government, if there were any left, were taken over by the revolutionary soviets—workers, peasants, or soldiers—which provided foundations for the future system of Soviet administration. Quite soon, it was resolved

37 Gurvich, L'éxperience juridique et la philosophie pluraliste du droit 138 ff. (1935).

that all distinction between local and national affairs should disappear from the jurisdiction and powers of the administrative authorities of the revolutionary state. This approach to the management of public affairs was combined with the repudiation of the system of the separation of powers.[38] Local revolutionary Soviets wielded, whenever and wherever they could, dictatorial powers without distinction of functions, and frequently clashed with more specialized agencies of the new political order, i.e., judicial agencies. Following the adoption of the Soviet Constitution of 1936, the Soviets were reorganized into Soviets of deputies of the workers and peasants, elected for each level of public administration.

The chief method of integration of various agencies belonging to the various levels of government, whether federal or local, is the power of the purse which under the Constitution of 1936 (Article 14 (k)) belongs to the Union.

In the West of Europe, the original theory of the independent commune, exercising its quasi-natural right to self-government, greatly lost its appeal. It was replaced by the theory that the essence of public administration consisted in the exercise of public power irrespective of the type of administrative authority, and later by the view that public services were the responsibility of both local government and centralized administration. The result has been the integration of administrative systems through the method of delegated powers and a general increase of local responsibilities. This has occurred, however, without prejudice to the original powers of local government, which still retained exclusive jurisdiction, subject to none other but judicial control.[39]

In the Soviet Union, however, the end result has been a unitary system of administrative authorities, with no real means for the formulation of policies regarding local interests.[40]

38 *Cf*. Siezdy sovetov v postanovleniakh i resolutsiakh 121 (1939).
39 Gneist, Self-government; Kommunalverfassung und Verwaltungsgerichte in England (1871).
40 Gsovski & Grzybowski, Government Law and Courts in the Soviet Union and Eastern Europe 71 ff. (1959).
    In Eastern Europe only Yugoslavia and Albania followed the Soviet example. In Poland, Hungary, Czechoslovakia, Bulgaria, and Rumania, councils of all types continued in the tradition of local elective govern-

The principle which aligns the Soviets with the social structure is visible already in the election procedures. The Soviets are principally representatives of social organizations. In the initial period, social organizations of the proletariat and of the poorer peasantry nominated their representatives without any intermediate process of voting. After 1936, members of the Soviets were elected by general vote, but from a single list of candidates nominated by social organizations, which amounts to very much the same thing.[41]

The local Soviet is not the only basis on which the identification of the official authorities with social organizations takes place. Terms of reference which determine social functions and responsibilities of the governmental authorities, and at the same time public functions of the social organizations and their place in the social structure, indicate a great shift in the nature and character of their functions.

Any generalization aiming to distinguish between social and gov-

---

ment parallel with the agencies of centralized administration. Only at a later date were their functions coordinated with those of the centralized administration, and an integrated system of administrative authorities established. *Cf.* Grzybowski, "La continuité légale dans les démocraties populaires," 54 Revue Politique et Parlementaire 57 (July 1952). *Cf.* also Grzybowski, "Continuity of Law in Eastern Europe," 6 Am. J. Comp. L. 58 (1957).

41 Organization of the executive apparatus of the Soviets in the Soviet Union reflects a recent trend toward deep involvement of the masses in the activities of the official mechanism of Soviet polity and identification of the state with social action. Social activists perform official functions either as auxiliaries of the Soviet state or as social organizers. According to statistics published in 1959, in the territory of the Soviet Union there were 121,000 commissions of the Soviets, each in charge of various aspects of local administration. In discharging their responsibilities these commissions, consisting of deputies to the Soviets, mobilized the cooperation of a great number of the so-called social activists affiliated with various social organizations representing associations of the citizens either on the professional or territorial basis. This permitted the commissions to tackle various administrative problems which called for a concentrated effort and a departure from routine procedure with the assistance of those organizations including street committees, commissions for cooperation in the maintenance of housing units, village assemblies, comradely courts, parents' associations, committees for the protection of social order, people's militia, etc. Vlasov, Studenikin, Sovetskoe administrativnoe pravo 37 (1959).

ernmental functions is open to criticism. It seems, however, that economic activity, as a matter of principle, must be considered a social function rather than one typically within the scope of the governmental responsibility. Marxist theories, as well as practical solutions in open societies, have tended toward assigning the management of economic institutions to the field of social responsibility. In the modern state, public enterprises, engaged as a matter of public policy in economic activities, follow the organizational pattern and the techniques of management of private economic institutions. Finally, according to the ultimate pattern of society under communism, responsibility for the processes of production is to be with the associations of producers.[42]

In the Soviet polity, however, the process of the distribution of responsibilities for various aspects of governmental and social services led to a pattern of jurisdiction which contradicts these assumptions.

Initially, Lenin was inclined to stress the need for preserving a degree of independence of social organizations, particularly trade unions, from interference by the state. The soviet state, Lenin argued, was not the state of the workers. It was still the state of workers and peasants. In addition, it had been "bureaucratically deformed." Although the trade unions should not indulge in systematic opposition, they were still bound to defend themselves from interference by the state because: (a) its policy might at times be the result of conflicting interests of workers and peasants and (b) elements of arbitrary bureaucratic rule might lead to defense of their rights on the part of the workers.[43]

When Lenin tendered this advice to the workers' organizations, the revolutionary state had had some experience with the workers' ability to handle nationalized industries. At the outset of the revolution, the Bolshevik Party called for workers' participation in the control of private factories. As the revolution and the nationalization of Russian industries made progress, this gave the workers full control of the economic institutions of the country. Workers' management at the factory level was combined with a most rigorous regimen introduced in the field of industrial relations under the Labor Code of 1918, and with a rigid system of administrative control from above. Conse-

42 Friedmann ed., The Public Corporation, A Comparative Symposium (1954).
43 Deutscher, Soviet Trade Unions 56 (1950).

quently, Lenin's remarks, made on the eve of the NEP, could be understood as anticipatory of changes which removed trade union control of the factories and of a return to a more conservative understanding of their responsibilities. Under the 1922 Labor Code, work contracts were again emphasized, collective bargaining was reintroduced, and the trade unions again became social organizations not fundamentally involved in the administration of economic resources.[44]

Once ousted from management, the trade unions never returned to their previous positions. However, the era of the economic plans meant a new manner of involvement by trade unions in administrative responsibilities. The expansion of industrial plants was identified with the realization of the goals of social action by the workers' organizations; and the workers' struggle was identified with the struggle for fulfillment of the plan. At the same time, trade unions were given an auxiliary role in the administration of welfare services.[45]

In their new position, the trade unions were directly involved in sharing the risks of economic ventures undertaken by governmental enterprises. And this was true in spite of the fact that their position vis-à-vis management differed little from that in the capitalist economy. The Sixteenth Congress of the Party (1930) insisted that the trade unions should take into consideration in their collective agreements the financial status of enterprises, and that their responsibility should cover also the financial and production aspects of the enterprises. In 1933, the Central Board of the trade unions assumed the functions of the People's Commissariat of Labor, and trade union bodies in factories replaced the labor inspectorates in enforcement of the protective provisions of labor legislation. The final step which identified trade union interests with that of management was the reform of the wage system by introducing piece rate as the center of the new system of remuneration.[46]

The basic dogma of the system of public authority, in which there is no hard and fast rule separating governmental and social functions

44 Deutscher, *supra* note 43, at 14 ff., 62.
45 Gsovski, *supra* note 10, at 387, 810–11 in vol. 1 and 342 in vol. 2; Gsovski & Grzybowski, *supra* note 40, at 1413.
46 *Id.* at 1413 ff.

and in which responsibilities overlap, is the axiom of the identity of interests with a corresponding tendency by various agencies of government and of social organizations to assume functions which do not belong to their spheres of activity. Since the state and society are identical in class, there is no reason why various functions and responsibilities should not be freely handed over from center to center. This was vividly demonstrated by the Polish and Hungarian revolts in 1956 and by the challenge of the new workers' councils, which took over government enterprise. There was nothing contrary to the basic doctrines of Marxism about the workers if dissatisfied with the activities of their organizations, the socialist government, and the trade union committees, delegating new bodies to remove shortcomings and improve performance. Gomulka observed in the challenge of the workers' councils and the plans to provide interenterprise institutions a threat to the very existence of the workers' state:

Workers' councils extended upward in all branches of national economy would need some supreme authority. Would this authority be the government itself? The government cannot be the supreme authority for social organizations such as workers' councils. The alternative, therefore, would be to create a new body, either through direct or indirect elections. And thus we see that this concept leads us astray. It appears that the government must cease to concern itself with the national economy and then it becomes superfluous as there is another central body . . . which has taken over the management of the national economy of the country. And in order to do this, the second body must take over from the government central planning, management of banks, procurement, distribution, etc. In other words, it must take over all government powers.[47]

The real cause for the political and social amorphism of the social organizations of socialist societies consists in the absence of identification of individual organizations with the social stratum which they claim to represent, rather than in their exercise of public power or control over social services. The fact that collective agreements, in fact, constitute a rule of law, or that the very process of negotiation is of public interest and therefore must conform to certain procedures, by itself is not harmful to the feeling of allegiance of the membership. The process of institutionalization of social functions is not contrary

47 Nowe Drogi 11–12 (No. 6, 1957).

to the identification of social organizations with class or group inter-ests.[48]

In the Soviet system, however, trade unions are organized to conform to their counterparts in public administration. Furthermore, trade unions exercise their functions, such as participation in the administration of the factory, the administration of social services, participation in the institutions handling labor disputes and enforcing labor discipline in the factories, in a manner which offers little oppor-tunity for demonstrating a protective attitude toward their member-ship. This attitude—bureaucratic deviation—is facilitated by the fact that, as elsewhere within the Soviet system, the representative principle of trade unions suffers.

Furthermore, most trade union functions within the economic system of the Soviet state stem from the external authorization of the state or of the Party. This applies particularly to participation of trade unions in planning processes, in supervisory and inspection activities, and in the administration of public welfare services financed by the state. It is the public authority which involves social organizations in the administrative duties, and the trade unions acting on behalf of the state must assume responsibility for shortcomings in the performance of these services. If trade union legislation is examined in terms of the criteria suggested by the Gurvich concept of frameworks and kinds of law, it would appear that the law of Soviet trade unions contains little of its own legislation. Its functions and social role are determined by legislative activity from without, thus constituting an alien element of legal rules within the trade union framework.[49]

The central principle of the integration of all public and social authority is state ownership of the means of production. This makes of the management of economic enterprises, the exercise of public power, and renders industrial relations, employment policies, and business transactions a matter of governmental policy.[50] Article 1 of

48 Bouère, Le droit de grève 142 (1958) and the literature cited at 142.
49 Deutscher, *supra* note 43, at 121; Gsovski, "Elements of Soviet Labor Law," Bull. No. 1026 of the U.S. Dep't of Labor (1951); Aleksandrov, Sovetskoe trudovoe pravo 50, 56, 271 (1954); Kiselev, "O pravovom polozhenii profsoiuznykh organizatsii v SSSR," SGP (No. 4, 1956).
50 "The country which has gone furthest in applying the Marxist theory of the socialization of means of production, Soviet Russia, had politically

the draft of the General Principles of the Civil Law Legislation of the USSR and the Union Republics states that:

Soviet civil legislation regulates property relations and related non-property relations for the purpose of strengthening and developing the socialist system of economy and social ownership, creating the material and technical base of communism and satisfying the material and spiritual needs of citizens more and more fully.

Public policy stated in these terms is safeguarded, in addition to the monopolistic ownership of the means of production, by the monopoly of forming juristic persons to organize industrial enterprises, distribution, and service industries and to promote production and control consumption.

With few exceptions in the agricultural sector of the national economy, juristic persons are designed to assume charge of the national economic assets which constitute the property of the state. In their corporate character, they are representative of the legal capacity which is centralized in the institution of the socialist state. According to Article 26 of the Hungarian Civil Code of 1959: "The state has legal capacity. Its legal capacity comprises all rights and obligations which by their character do not attach only to man."

Consequently, socialist rules regarding the establishment of corporations could dispense with all those elaborate provisions which have aimed at protecting the safety of commerce and safeguarding the public interest. A juristic person is created by an administrative act, which assigns to the former its respective duties and means of performance according to the economic plan.[51] The fiction that a corporate body exercises its proprietary rights in the same manner as a physical person is replaced by the reality that a corporate body is a government organization. As a socialist jurist formulated it:

The power aspect of the new legal entities (government enterprises) in the midst of all other legal entities within the framework of the national

and legally not only retained the trappings of sovereignty, but reached new heights of concentrated state power." Friedmann, Law in a Changing Society 299 (1959).

51 *Cf.* art. 20 of the Draft of the Civil Law Principles of the USSR and the Union Republics. *Cf.* also Saleilles, De la personalité juridique (1922); Rumelin, Metodisches über juristische Personen (1891); Michoud, La théorie de la personalité morale (1906–1909).

economy represents a socially correct solution in the development of a country on the road to socialism.

A government enterprise becomes an indispensable participant in the process of production, and an essential channel for the execution of the national economic plan.[52]

In this context, the character of business transactions and contractual engagements assumes a new character, which in the West has hitherto been limited to situations involving agreements settling collective standards and conditions of employment. In the socialist legal order, public law character extends to all transactions of the government corporations. Conceived and executed with reference to the provisions of the economic plan, the business activity of socialist enterprises constitutes a legal framework for the coordination of human activity (labor) and natural resources in order to implement a public policy within the "jurisdiction" of each individual economic institution.[53]

THE LEGISLATIVE TECHNIQUE

Wide distribution of governmental responsibilities between the official agencies of government and the organs of the society also takes place in the field of legislation. While the constitution of the socialist state specifies the authorities holding legislative powers, normal criteria of sources of law in Soviet society mean even less than in traditional constitutional arrangements. Nor are the material criteria infallible. Soviet legal theory, which states that the real source of law is the will of the ruling class and that the force of legal enactment is its true reflection, again is little more than a programmatical phrase.

Although the theory of the sources of socialist law limits the power of lawmaking to those authorities representative of the people's power, i.e., to the Soviets alone, the body of Soviet law includes various

---

52 Vasiliev, Grazhdansko pravo narodnoi Respubliki Bolgarii, obshchaia chast 239–40; *cf.* Bolgár, "The Magic of Property and Public Welfare," 2 Inter-Amer. L. Rev. 288 (1960); Savatier, Métamorphoses économiques et sociales du droit civil d'aujourd'hui 6 ff. (3d ser. 1959); Serick, Rechtsform und Realitet juristischer Personen (1955).

53 Vasiliev, Generalni dogovori (1958); Hazard, Law and Social Change in the USSR 50 ff. (1953); Gsovski & Grzybowski, *supra* note 40, at 1413 ff.

enactments from other sources. These sources, although not in form but certainly in content and significance for the public policy of society, represent a type of legislation which sometimes far outweighs legislation derived from formal sources of lawmaking. Pronouncements of leaders and the directives and instructions issued by social organizations and executive agencies of government constitute an important source of regulations, affecting the life of private citizens very much in the manner that a formal law does.[54]

These various acts are covered by a new term of normative acts which, in the words of a Polish jurist:

[E]ither establish new institutions for the socialized sector of the national economy or introduce important changes in our civil law. Among those of supreme importance are the instructions of the highest authorities of the economic administration of the country. There is no doubt today that these are sources of the civil law and abrogate within the jurisdiction of those authorities the provisions of the civil codes.[55]

The number of these normative acts is extremely large, and their great proliferation adds to the uncertainty as to the legal situation in the socialist countries. Furthermore, there are no satistics, no adequate compendia with a systematic arrangement of various regulations. According to an estimate made public a few years ago in Poland, the number of normative acts which the central authorities made binding upon the courts was in the vicinity of 10,000 enactments.[56]

In addition to the normative acts of the highest category, each local administration has the right to issue regulations. These, too, constitute the law, unless found contrary to some higher regulation. Some indication of the size of the legislative output is the growth of various official and unofficial publications, law gazettes, local official gazettes, reporters for special branches of administration, and technical publications containing standards worked out for use in national industries, which have a bearing on the private rights and calculation of wages and either directly or indirectly affect the operation of government. But in addition, it has appeared from time to time that a key

54 Gsovski & Grzybowski, *supra* note 40, at 41–42.
55 Wolter, Prawo cywilne, część ogólna 49 (1955); 1 Gsovski, *supra* note 10, at 222–24.
56 Gsovski & Grzybowski, *supra* note 40, at 730.

regulation, which on occasion had vitally affected legal commerce, had been issued in the form of a circular letter which was never published. Thus, a circular of the Central Board of the Trade Unions of Poland changed the law on collective agreement; and the sale of real estate was prohibited in a circular addressed by the minister of justice to the notaries public.[57]

It seemed for a while that this practice would be seriously curtailed after the official policy of the socialist countries tended to emphasize a need for restraint in the flow of regulatory activity. However, it is clear now that the practice of normative acts will survive the drive for the reform and reorganization of the legal order in the socialist states. The only practical step in this direction would be to grant binding force only to certain types of enactments. This was the principle of the hierarchy of statutes developed in the nonsocialist countries. Then the courts would be able to reject administrative regulations contrary to, or issued without or beyond statutory authorization. This, however, is a step which would affect vitally the government's ability to implement expeditiously their current line of policy. The need for the continuance of this latter practice was recognized in Article 1 (par. 2) of the Polish draft of the Civil Code (1960), which provided that its force extended to relations between governmental organizations only insofar as these relations were not regulated in a different manner by another statute or regulation issued by the highest governmental authorities. Thus, precedence was afforded to ministerial instructions.

A large bulk of normative acts belongs to the field of economic administration because neither the economic plan nor the system of planned contracts between enterprises and agencies involved in its enforcement are able to provide for all contingencies arising from business activities. Furthermore, factory managers are administrative officers. In consequence, they require authorization to change the techniques or policies which in the West would be dictated by conditions of the market, but which in the socialist economy must be replaced by administrative regulations. In order to keep the economy going, it is necessary that administrative authorities on all levels adjust the premises of the plan and of the standard contractual engagements

---

57 Grzybowski, "Reform and Codification of Polish Laws," 7 Am. J. Comp. L. 395 (1958).

between the socialist business partners, and that they determine more closely business operations either for industrial branches or within each governmental enterprise. Some illustration of the great number of regulations issued in this connection is obtained by examining the legal reform introduced by the General Law of Management of Working Collectives in Public Economic Institutions and Higher Economic Associations of July 2, 1950, in Yugoslavia.[58] In order to bring order into the mass of earlier enactments, a special Executive Order on Bringing into Conformity the Decrees of the Federal Agencies with the new Economic System was necessary.[59] This listed 468 decrees enacted in the period of 1945–1950 as abrogated. In addition, an unspecified number of decrees issued on the basis of those expressly abrogated regulations were declared repealed. At the same time, 176 decrees were still retained on the statute books.

A similar operation was again repeated in Yugoslavia after the enactment of the Constitutional Law of January 13, 1953. Following the reorganization of the Yugoslav Federation, the Federal Executive Council enacted the Executive Order on the decrees of Federal Agencies of September 21, 1953. This terminated the force of 865 decrees.[60]

In both cases, repeals on federal levels were followed by mass repeals of legislation enacted by the individual republics of the Yugoslav Federation. Serbia, for instance, repealed in January and May 1953 some 575 decrees concerning the management of the national economy, still retaining 80 such decrees. In April 1954, Croatia repealed 600 similar decrees, still retaining the imposing number of 194 legal enactments of this type. One can only speculate as to the number of similar regulations on still lower levels of economic administration which all have their own specific spheres of responsibility.

Socialist courts are also engaged in vigorous lawmaking. Although the official theory is that the courts are excluded from the process of lawmaking, the very nature of the legal system in which they operate forces the socialist courts to contribute to the development of socialist

58 Law No. 391, S.L. 22/1952.
59 Law No. 389, S.L. 40/952.
60 Maksimovich, "Experiments in Legislative Technique in Yugoslavia," 2 Highlights 385–86 (1954).

law in a manner very reminiscent of court practice in the common law countries. A fast tempo of change and a great output of legislative material compel the courts to interpret the legislation in force, either in a manner which brings it closer to the current political line of the regime (although contrary to the express wording of the law), or in a manner which amounts to the virtual repeal of outdated but not yet formally abrogated enactments.[61]

In addition to providing a more general guidance for the lower courts, particularly when urgent interests of the regime call for immediate support for its policies from the entire mechanism of the state and of social organizations, an institution of directive rulings by the highest tribunals of the law has been created. Its purpose is to restate, in connection with the enforcement of specific legal provisions, those policies of the regime which are contrary to the express wording of the law or to reverse time-honored interpretations of the legal rule. Directive rulings are issued on the initiative of the Minister of Justice, the Attorney General, or the Chief Justice. According to the Polish Judiciary Act of 1950, which in this respect follows the standard provisions found in the judiciary acts of other socialist countries, the purpose of the directive rulings is to determine "concrete tasks of the administration of justice, and the manner of their performance in accordance with the economic, social, and political conditions of the country within the limits of the laws in force." Directive rulings are binding on lower courts, and violation of their terms constitutes an appealable error. In fact, directive rulings formulate governmental policies not contained in the statute. Among the jurists of socialist countries there is a good deal of controversy on the subject. According to some, rulings are new legislation. Others, quoting the provisions of the constitutions, deny that they have such an effect.[62]

Soviet techniques of lawmaking cannot be interpreted as having no principle by which to determine the legitimacy of legal rules and thereby to bring the *disiecta membra* of the legal order in a socialist

---

61 Grzybowski, *supra* note 9.
62 Gsovski & Grzybowski, *supra* note 40, at 534,641; Sipkov, "The Bulgarian Supreme Court and Its Directive Rulings," 6 Highlights 139 ff. (1958); Grzybowski, "Directive Rulings of the Supreme Court in Criminal Matters," 6 Highlights 149 ff. (1958).

state into a single system. The techniques of lawmaking reflect the peculiarities of the social organism and the relationship of its various parts to the problems of public policy by which it lives. Social change and the emergence of modern societies have made obsolete all theories that laws come from a single source. In the France of the early civil code, this theory was based on the idea of the superiority of the statute, which provided a firm guidance to the courts. In the Anglo-American tradition, the courts were the source of the law, and statutes had to be tested in the courts in order to become part of the legal system. Modern life destroyed the fiction of the internal symmetry of the legal order. It was discovered that modern societies live by law from many sources, and that legal systems supplemented by rules from various social centers obtain their cohesive character from the interplay of social forces, which all have an interest in maintaining the social and legal order.

A socialist legal order of the Soviet type is the product of the fast rate of social change, of the great flow of legislative enactments from numerous sources, and of the experimental character of governmental policies. Thus, Soviet law represents not a system, but rather an armory which stores various instruments of policy to be used according to the needs of the day. The content of the legal rule is no longer important. Rather, the question is how it is used. The old law may always be infused with new meaning to achieve the social aim according to the current line. Uniformity of the legal system, normally guaranteed by the formal hierarchy of various statutory enactments, was replaced by the singleness of inspiration which is assured by the place of the Communist Party in both the social structure and the mechanics of government.[63]

RESPECT FOR LAW IN THE SOCIALIST SOCIETY

The appearance of public authority in any other role than that of a law enforcing agency represents a disturbing factor in legal commerce. Disguised as *fiscus,* and assimilated almost totally to the private holder of rights, the state enjoys privileges and is free from execution. As an administrative authority, charged with duties and given the power to manage social interests and render services, it is judged in-

---

63 Cardozo, The Nature of Judicial Process 112–13 (1921).

competent in the fulfillment of its obligations or negligent in the performance of its duties, according to standards falling far short of those which apply to private persons or corporations in a similar situation. The state cannot go into bankruptcy; and for moral weaknesses, a polity is not answerable in law.

The difference in standards is due to a number of causes. A partial explanation is afforded, however, by the more rigid procedures which a public authority must follow, by the stricter accounting standards which prevail as to financial policy, and by a greater limitation of action owing to the public interests involved.[64]

As the state and public authority became more involved in social and economic activity, their impact upon the respect for rule, and generally upon law enforcement, has increased. In open societies, this influence is tempered by the fact that the public management of national economic interests is still an exception, and that public corporations tend to assume the coloring of private economic institutions in order to avoid political control of their economic activities.[65] In the socialist world, this aspect appears in altogether different proportions. This is due to the fact that, as a rule, socialist countries manifest planned economies, the government owning the industrial plant and all the means of production. Standards and methods of law enforcement

64 Gsovski & Grzybowski, *supra* note 40, at 507; Orlovskii, "Zadatchi pravovoi nauki v svete reshenii XX siezda KPSS," 26 Vestnik Akademii Nauk 5 (No. 8, 1956).

In regard to this problem in the legal practice of the Western societies, abundant illustration is to be found in the splendid study by W. Friedmann, Law in a Changing Society. *Cf.* Ransom and Luck v. Surbiton B.C. [1949] 1 Ch. 180 and William Cory & Son, Ltd., v. City of London Corpn. [1951] 2 K.B. 476, cited by Friedmann at 364, and East Suffolk Catchment Board v. Kent [1941] A.C. 74, also cited by the same author at 365.

The problem of methods to assure respect for the legal rule on the part of public authority or public corporation represents an important issue in the legal practice and theory today. There is a tendency to follow a course normally effective in relations with private persons or corporations. However, it has also been pointed out that the fact that fines must come from the public budget limits their effectiveness. In this connection see the discussion in Dennings, The Changing Law (1953) at p. 28 of the case of the Yorkshire Electricity Board which was fined for erecting a building without proper license.

65 Friedmann, *supra* note 42.

and the formal respect for law in socialist countries are primarily influenced by the nature of government operations. In addition, there is the influence of the character of the governmental machinery itself. Its design is to effectuate government purposes according to the standards set up not so much in legal rule as in the directives and inspiration emanating from the party.

In the course of 1958 and 1959, the Polish Fishermen's Association, which has a fishing monopoly in all inland waters in Poland, sued some thirty government enterprises for polluting streams and rivers. The pollution had caused damage to the fishing industry and to the national resources of primary raw material and had violated antipollution legislation. According to statistics submitted to the courts, there were at that time some 700 major industrial establishments (all of them government-owned) which were guilty of such practices. The Association won its cases and proceeded to file some more, but the end result was not the enforcement of the rule of law. The Association was adjudged damages, which were promptly paid, and the enterprises continued in their disregard of the laws in force.[66] Obviously, the regime could enforce its own laws in terms of the physical means of enforcement, but was prevented from doing so by higher policy. It was cheaper to pay damages, and even fines, from the budgets of the enterprises and to provide appropriate sums for these and similar contingencies than to engage in large reconstruction and rehabilitation projects. Indeed, this latter could change the plans of individual enterprises and affect the calculation of the cost of industrial construction in Poland on a national scale. In the final analysis, then, the fishing rights of the Association were transformed into the right to sue for damages. Full enforcement was simply not feasible politically.

The cost of industrial construction, however, is not the only reason for these and other manifestations of disregard by governmental authorities of administrative regulations providing for orderly procedures in industrial activity. Industrial expansion is conceived in terms of revolutionary enterprise. As such there is neither time nor room for restriction in the name of vested rights, even though these vested rights are none other than those of the community at large. The Soviet polity, striving to cover in one leap the progress of the

66 Pietek, "W imieniu ryb," PiZ, Jan. 11, 1959.

decades, has found it easier to make up for the neglect of the past by re-creating the atmosphere of the industrial revolution in the West, when profit and cheap expansion were the only law.

This is especially apparent regarding the legal force of all those administrative regulations issued by the local authorities. After the 1956 upheaval in Poland, during which a marked tendency toward decentralization of governmental authority had developed, public opinion began to press for greater respect by central authority for local conditions, sanitation, urban development regulations, and building and zoning restrictions. Socialist industrial and urban planners now claim that they have mastered the anarchistic tendencies marking the capitalistic forms of industrial organization, and that the socialist state has found a formula for balancing the various interests which claim precedence in any development program. Under socialism, they claim, it will be possible to avoid the monstrosities created in the period of early capitalist development. In fact, however, as the Polish press has disclosed, industrial ministers demonstrate an attitude quite similar to that of capitalist industrial pioneers in seeking the best locations without regard to local urban development plans.

This attitude of the higher authorities toward the responsibilities and plans of the lower echelons of administration is further complicated by the absence of proper administrative procedures tending to coordinate official actions from various centers. This difficulty, in turn, is compounded by the absence of a strict delimitation of powers between the central and local government regarding the residual prerogatives of the local government. In 1959, considerable uproar was caused by the fact that after the municipal government of a Polish city had reserved a certain area for suburban development, one of the industrial ministries then declared its intention to use the same area for the construction of apartment blocks according to plans kept secret from eyes of the local authority. In the meantime families had built their houses, paved the streets, paid the cost of sewage and other services, planted their lawns and gardens. In spite of this, however, the ministry, using its powers of a supervisory authority, proceeded with the annulment of the deeds issued by the city fathers, evicted individual owners, and proceeded with the construction of its apartment blocks.[67]

67 Młynczyk, "Rzecz o grzechach administracji," PiZ, Dec. 13, 1959.

A Polish analyst of the administrative mechanism of the Polish state has traced its shortcomings to two causes. In the first place, administrative authorities have no respect for their own decisions and those of other government departments. In the second, the administrative machinery of the popular state is staffed by two categories of civil servants, each with a different role within the same governmental setup. Those in office on the strength of an electoral mandate enforce the policy, but not the law. Those constituting the professional establishment of governmental agencies, on the other hand, are saddled with the responsibility of finding the law to substantiate the decisions of political leaders. Matters are complicated by the fact that basic policy decisions come to the executive departments from the party centers, which are involved in the planning and supervision of government operations through its members in key positions.[68]

Thus, respect for legal rule is affected by Party control of the governmental apparatus in two directions. In the first place, the concept of the socialist state and the legitimacy of governmental operations imply an institutional reliance upon Party motivation:

No institution, organization, or person could or should stand above the Central Committee, above the Politbureau. No decision of importance should be made without the Central Committee's consent and approval. This should become an iron law to all. . . .[69]

Secondly, construction of the legal rule must follow the inner meaning of the socialist law. This, in turn, is always the actual will of the people. As the Polish Supreme Court stated:

Interpretation of the law should not be concerned with its literal meaning but should aim at the realization of its social purpose and take into consideration that it is an expression of the will of the broad social masses.[70]

While conformity to the policy line is assured, the authority of the law as clear guidance for private parties, courts, and government departments must suffer. This reflects not only on the official life of the state and of social organizations, but, in the final analysis, on the

68 *Ibid.*
69 Rabotnichesko Delo, Feb. 4, 1950.
70 PiP 146–50 (No. 7, 1950).

relations between individuals in respect of their private rights, as well.

Insufficient law enforcement regarding private relations in socialist societies is the direct result of a system which sanctifies outside intervention in the performance of government business. The Party exercises influence through public propaganda campaigns, through the personal intervention of Party members with the governmental apparatus, or through Party spokesmen. As a result, the process of government follows channels which cannot be contained within regular procedures defined by the law or within the official edifice of the state. Socialist public order sanctions private deals and the exercise of personal influence by persons in high party positions. Further, this is true not only regarding the shaping of governmental policies, but also regarding their implementation by the government agencies. This result is observed in the role of Party committees at all levels of government operations, in economic administration, and in the factories. The 1957 reform of the economic administration of the Soviet Union was specifically designed to bring the Council of National Economy, which had taken over the functions of the economic ministries, under closer supervision of the provincial Party secretaries.

While this system of operation has obvious advantages with relation to the high degree of response of the governmental setup to Party demands, there are compensating disadvantages; inasmuch as the Party may influence the governmental machinery all along the line, there results great possibility for the abuse of personal power. This disadvantage is compounded by the difficulty of distinguishing between legitimate uses and abuses of influence. While no regime may boast a foolproof system for excluding abuses of power and of official authority, the Soviet order is particularly susceptible to such shortcomings owing to the manner of governmental operations.

Examples of a quite unfortunate state of affairs, in regard to the protection of individual rights in socialist countries, are to be found in all provinces of official activity. There are cases of systematic prevention of criminal prosecution of embezzlers of government property, of refusal to execute sentences passed by criminal courts, of lack of respect for decisions of courts made in civil causes, and of eviction of lawful owners from their apartments. In practically all these cases, the press had traced failures in law enforcement to the personal influence of important Party members.[71]

One of the students of Soviet life has thus summed up the reasons for this state of affairs:

Two basic causes seem responsible for the disrespect for laws, courts, and government attorneys as law enforcement agents. One cause is the attitude of party organizations and their leaders that they are above the law. Party members constitute a higher class of citizens, and the Party has its own code of behavior. Its censure and discipline take precedence over court action, and its members are under special protection. This protection extends not only to Party members directly, but also to their families and to nonrelated persons involved in illegal activities which the Party condones. . . . It seems that Soviet bureaucrats have not been trained to perform duties and functions with a view toward conformity to provision of the law. The reason for this seems obvious. In the past, whenever the law in force and the rights of the individual conflicted with the policy of a government agency, laws and rights gave way to policy. One might even say that whenever a major policy change occurred, it almost invariably involved violation of the laws in force and of the vested rights of the individuals.[72]

A vast majority of the cases which affect adversely private rights and general law enforcement result from the exercise of Party influence to force the authorities to depart from normal procedures and to disregard express provisions of the laws in force. There are, however, broad areas in which rights and law enforcement suffer owing to their direct connection with the production processes and their dependence on performance. Particularly is this true with regard to industrial relations and the provisions of the labor law.

In Soviet practice, the provisions of laws governing the field of labor relations are translated into reality by means of collective agreements. As everywhere else, conditions of labor are not subject to contractual stipulations, and departures from the standards established in the contractual transaction are permitted under specific conditions and in accordance with the legal rule administered by the public authority.

71 Kryvickas, Illustration of the Rule of Law in Lithuania, 6 Highlights 193–204 (1958); Rusis, Law Enforcement in Soviet Latvia, 6 Highlights 273–87 (1958).

72 Rusis, *supra* note 71, at 286–87.

At the same time, rights contractually established and formulated in labor law as general standards are made relative by a system of devices. These include the piece rate system, the provision of the wage fund in terms of a share in the general plan of costs and profits of the economic venture, and the cession of the administration of the labor law and of the collective agreements to the trade unions themselves. Thus, trade unions are turned into public agencies which have the authority to depart from the stipulated standards of labor conditions. At the same time, they remain financially interested in the success of the economic venture. In this system, the risk of economic operation is borne by factory crews in the form of the extension of working hours, the violation of provisions concerning overtime pay by means of voluntary production campaigns, and the lowering standards of work safety and hygiene conditions. The relaxation of the administrative regime in Polish factories after the October 1956 upheaval revealed a complicated situation in the national industries of the country whereby factory managers were forced to resort to the systematic violation of the labor law as the only method of efficient administration.[73] Thus, standards of performance realistically determine the conditions of labor and are to be found in the calculations of the economic plan.

The over-all effect of the deep involvement of the entire governmental and social mechanism in economic management is that the attention of the entire society and of law enforcement agencies is directed toward collective achievements rather than in the direction of realizing the individual's status. The very ethos of the legal rule is to emphasize the significance of collective action. By this means, the general welfare is guaranteed in terms of positive gains. This is the function of law enforcement; its role in determining individual rights is de-emphasized. The center of legal order is not the bill of rights contained in the socialist constitutions. It is, rather, the economic plan administered by the Party. In consequence, the litigious aspect of law enforcement is no longer a social technique for bringing about social harmony, but is, instead, adjustment and conciliation with a view toward assuring the realization of social aims.

73 Grzybowski, "Trade Unions in Communist Poland," Problems of Communism 16 ff. (No. 5, 1956).

Chapter III

FORMS OF ADJUDICATION IN SOCIALIST ECONOMY

FORMAL AND SUBSTANTIVE JUSTICE [1]

In the course of the debates at the Third Congress of Workers of the Administration of Justice (1920), a proposal was made for the abolition of lay judges on the bench of the People's Court. The representative of the Commissariat of Justice, however, came out strongly in defense of the lay element. Lay judges, he maintained, were necessary "so that the court would always be the most living, the most authentic echo of that concept of law which had currency among the population, so that in the decision and sentence of a court there would be made apparent that concept of the people, and that the court, and so-called 'public opinion' would not present two points of view having nothing in common as has been the case in the former court." [2]

The attitudes of those members of the Congress who were critical of the lay element stemmed from the increasing momentum of a tendency toward greater stability and expertise in the administration of justice. The question was raised of the codification of the procedural and substantive laws of the Soviet Republic. In addition, it was insisted that greater stability and uniformity of judicial practice were desirable. Consequently, lay judges, whose role on the bench had been useful in the revolutionary period, were now thought to be an obstacle in the orderly pursuit of justice. Thus, professionalism constituted the preeminent goal of the critics.

However, in the eyes of the Soviet leadership, other values were

1 For the full discussion of these two terms see Weber, On Law in Economy and Society, ch. 8, at 224–55 (1954).
2 Hazard, Settling Disputes in Soviet Society 104 (1960).

of greater importance. In the Soviet society, courts were to reflect popular convictions as to what was right and wrong. It was also obvious that judicial effectiveness would suffer if its action demonstrated differences of views on problems of law and order. The solutions adopted showed a clear preference for the idea that, in the administration of justice, political orientation should predominate. The people's courts, although guided by recognized rules of procedure, were still to be bound by revolutionary concepts rather than by formal rules of law.[3]

In contrast with the past, the presence of the lay judges on the bench indicated that Soviet courts had broken away from the tradition of formal justice administered by the imperial courts of Russia.

The debates at the Third Congress cast a good deal of light on the intentions of the architects of the Soviet court system. Integration of lay and professional judges on one bench, according to the pattern of the German *Schoeffengerichte,* was intended to assure that Soviet courts would always act in public as a source of one official attitude.[4]

In a sense, the Soviet judicial reforms undid the transmission to Russia of the achievements of the French Revolution, which had reformed the courts of France. French reformers had been dissatisfied with the courts of the ancient regime, which had been staffed mostly by lay judges and governed by antiquated laws. Drafters of the French Civil and Criminal Codes saw the cause of the unsatisfactory performance of the old court system in the bad laws and the absence of professional legal education on the bench. They were convinced that

3 *Cf. supra* at 44.
4 Debates at the Third Congress of Workers of the Administration of Justice explain why Soviet leaders preferred the German court pattern to the French for the organization of the judiciary in the revolutionary state. In the German Schoeffengerichte lay judges are organized with their professional colleagues in one bench, which renders its decisions by the majority vote in all stages of the proceedings. The French jury system (at that time) accorded distinct roles to the professional and lay judges in the court. This permitted distinguishing between their respective pronouncements and, generally, their functions. The jury was thought to represent a concept of justice more closely reflecting the current public opinion than professional judges. For obvious reasons Soviet leaders aiming at the great ideological cohesion of the society thought this was to be avoided. *Cf.* Kucherov, Court, Lawyers and Trials Under the Last Three Tsars 214 ff. (1953).

injustice could be avoided if laws were good and just, and were interpreted in a scholarly manner. Portalis, who fought for greater respect for the courts of the new order, claimed that their role would be beneficial if the level of judicial interpretation were raised:

Jurisprudential construction (*par voie de la doctrine*) means to grasp the proper meaning of the laws, to apply them with discernment, to supplement them in cases where there is no specific rule. Without this kind of interpretation, how can one imagine the fulfillment of the office of the judge? [5]

The chief object of Portalis' argumentation was to demonstrate that the administration of justice might be conceived as a separate department of government. He was opposed to the ideas that French courts were unable to fill the gaps in the law and that cases where no rule applied should be referred to the legislature for proper legislative action. Formality in the administration of justice in conjunction with scholarly legal method would, he believed, assure independence of the courts and thus expand the field of their activity. At that time, the defender of judicial independence could not foresee that formal justice meant also a serious restriction of judicial activity. It guaranteed to the parties maximum control over the proceedings and the greatest opportunity to present their interests. But it was also conservative; and a formal interpretation of the law made it difficult for the courts, as was later discovered, to adjust the rule of law to the process of social change.

Because of its characteristics, formal justice, although able to provide a main channel for the administration of justice in the modern state, has been subject to attack from many quarters. It was consistently supported only by those who wielded economic power and were interested in freedom from public control. Formal justice was opposed by authoritarian and totalitarian tendencies because it less-

5 Portalis, Discours préliminaire, Projet de Code Civil présenté par la Commission nommée par le Gouvernement, le 24 Thermidor an 8, at xi; "Les parties qui traitent entre elles sur une matière que la loi positive n'a pas définie, se soumettent aux usages reçus, ou à l'équité universelle, à défaut de tout usage. ... Les lois intervenues sur des affaires privées, seroient donc souvent suspectes de partialité, et toujours elles seroient rétroactives & injustes pour ceux dont le litige auroit précédé l'intervention de ces lois." *Id*. at xi–xii.

ened individual dependence on the state and public authority, thus limiting the power of the state. It was attacked by conservative tendencies because of its rationalistic, antiemotional attitude to social processes. At the same time, it was opposed by radical and democratic movements which sought to promote social change in the interest of higher standards of social and political justice.[6] Finally, formal justice was subject to attack on the purely practical ground that, in some situations, reference to legal standards alone was not able to provide an efficient basis for the solution of minor criminal cases and private law conflicts.

The usual policy in modern states has been to reserve room for both types of administration of justice and to accommodate within the system of courts dispensing formal justice a method permitting a more flexible approach to settling disputes and even to administering criminal justice. A historical perusal of the jury trial in criminal cases in Europe discloses that its *ratio existendi* consisted in its ability to provide an opening for substantive justice.[7] Another reason for departing,

6 Weber, *supra* note 1, at 228–29. "[T]he development of the trial into a peaceful contest of conflicting interests can contribute to the further concentration of economic and social power. In all these cases formal justice, due to the necessarily abstract character, infringes upon the ideals of substantive justice. It is precisely this abstract character which constitutes the decisive merit of formal justice to those who wield the economic power at any given time and who are therefore interested in its unhampered operation, and also to those who on ideological grounds attempt to break down authoritarian control or to restrain irrational mass emotions for the purpose of opening individual opportunities and liberating capacities. To all these groups nonformal justice simply represents the likelihood of absolute arbitrariness and subjectivistic instability. Among those groups who favor formal justice we must include all those political and economic interest groups to whom the stability and predictability of legal procedure are of very great importance, i.e., particularly rational, economic, and political organizations intended to have a permanent character. Above all, those in possession of economic power look upon a formal national administration of justice as a guarantee of 'freedom,' a value which is repudiated not only by theocratic or patriarchial authoritarian groups but, under certain conditions, also by democratic groups."

7 "When, for example, French jurors, contrary to formal law, regularly acquit a husband who has killed his wife's paramour caught in the act, they are doing exactly what Frederick the Great did when he dispensed 'royal justice' for the benefit of Arnold, the miller." Weber, *supra* note 1, at 229.

in the settlement of civil and criminal cases, from strict law enforcement was that sometimes the interest of the parties and of the society was better served by the process of composition and official conciliation. Thus, justices of the peace in the French and Anglo-Saxon traditions have played a useful role. Those judicial administrations which provide a level at which simple justice is handled by laymen take account of the fact that strict observance of the legal rule would be of little importance in the settlement of disputes where minor infringements of the law or those of small value are involved. The function of justices of the peace is primarily, and particularly in regard to civil law litigation, to arrive at the composition of cases to the satisfaction of everybody concerned, or to a decision which follows rules which tend to reflect substantive rather than formal justice.[8]

In spite of serious doubts as to the usefulness of the institution of the jury in the American court system, it is admitted that in the conflict of formal and substantive justice an important step forward in the evolution of legal ideas has been achieved in many cases.[9]

Social change, by producing a new attitude in the courts and among the professional lawyers to the problem of law enforcement, delivered the most serious blow to the idea of formal justice. It was

---

In monarchial regimes of the nineteenth century, jury trial of political crimes, or offenses committed by the means of press, served to protect political tendencies and movements which though contrary to those protected by the legal order and political regime found support in the popular sentiment.

8 Mendelssohn-Bartholdy, Das Imperium des Richters 167 ff. (1908).

9 Tort law was one of the important fields of litigation which was strongly influenced by the common sense of justice or prejudice evinced by juries. Dean Green's description of the method by which juries influenced the progress of law provides a classic example of a conflict between formal and substantive justice and the contribution of the lay judges to the formulation of the new legal standards: "Seemingly juries saw only parties before them, and placed the risk where they thought it could be best borne. The judges had been interested in principles; juries were interested in doing justice between the parties. The judges evolved a nice scheme for determining responsibility, the juries gave verdicts which wrecked the scheme. Juries held their ground here until legal theory could catch up with the new order of things which had emerged under the very eyes of the judges without most of them noticing it." Green, Judge and Jury 122–23 (1930). *Cf.* also 2 Harper & James, The Law of Torts 890–92 (1956); Holmes, Common Law 110–11 (1881).

claimed that in the new conditions, the judicial function could not be confined to the formal construction of statutes and to strict adherence to the "stare decisis" where the courts had reigned in the past.[10] Furthermore, the very concept of the judiciary as a symmetrical system of courts was shattered. In order to meet new situations in the areas of new legal regulation, special courts and tribunals were established with an organization indicating that their role was something more than the administration of formal justice. They had to take into consideration community interests, ethical and political interests, and the demands of social justice. Other semijudicial bodies were charged with functions which combined adjudication with conciliation and mediation.[11]

In the general movement of modern societies from the principle of formal toward substantive justice, the concept of the judicial interpretation of statutes was greatly modified. In the wave of reform, civil procedures in a number of countries were amended to give the courts greater powers to act as arbitrator and mediator. In this way, it was sought to promote the amicable composition of differences between the parties. In addition, the courts were awarded greater powers in the discovery of material truth, thereby facilitating the discovery of the essence of litigations.

Further, the courts reinterpreted old laws and were given new directives in order to redistribute the hazards of modern life according

10 *Cf. supra* at 39; also Pound, "The Need of a Sociological Jurisprudence," 19 The Green Bag 607 (1907).

11 E.g., French provisions for arbitration and conciliation of labor industrial conflicts under the law of Feb. 11, 1950, as amended by the law of July 26, 1957 (J.O. of July 28, 1957, 7459); *cf.* West German Law of Sept. 3, 1953, on Labor Courts.

Tsarist Russia had only the beginnings of the modern social legislation. In the period between the wars in all countries of Eastern Europe, which at present belong in the Soviet sphere of influence, various forms of adjudication of disputes in the field of industrial relations, whether individual or collective, were adopted. As a rule labor courts were concerned with conflicts regarding individual contracts of work, while various arbitration and conciliation boards dealt with collective aspects of industrial relations. *Cf.* Grzybowski, "Evolution of the Polish Labor Law 1945–1955," in Legal Problems Under Soviet Domination 90 (1956); Gruenbaum-Ballin & Petit, "Les conflicts collectifs du travail et leur réglement dans le monde contemporain (grêves, procédures de conciliation et d'arbitrage)," Travaux et récherches de L'Institute de droit comparé de L'Université de Paris, ix (1954).

to a new pattern. The old liability doctrine was abandoned as the courts were enjoined to take account of the economic inequalities of the parties. Finally, the role of the court as social arbitrator within the limits of the legal order was recognized.[12]

While this new orientation toward problems of modern life was taking place within the framework of the traditional mechanism of the administration of justice, new courts, tribunals, and conciliation boards came into existence. Responsible for maintaining social peace and balance within new areas of social action, they reflected in their organization the fact that their function was not the scholarly interpretation of the statutes but was rather the combination of judicial with administrative action. In organization they resemble the Soviet people's courts, with the representatives of conflicting industrial and social interest seated together with the professional judge as umpire. Thus, formal justice received a function within a structure serving primarily as an instrument of substantive justice.

This complicated mechanism of social adjustment stands in a singular relation to social and economic reality. In a sense, its function is to preserve the conditions which make possible the existence and the function of the public organization and of the state itself. On the other hand, its role is to serve social and economic interests. It is no longer feasible for the courts and the judiciary to live in another age.[13]

CONTRACTS IN PLANNED ECONOMY

The system of judicial and quasi-judicial institutions in charge of adjudicating and adjusting disputes in the Socialist polities of the Soviet type is highly reminiscent of judicial institutions in the free world of the civil law tradition. A special quasi-judicial branch, roughly corresponding to the commercial courts of Europe, handles

---

12 *Cf.* Frank, Law and Modern Mind 126–27, 157 (1936).

13 With reference to the judge-made law in the course of the nineteenth century Dicey was convinced that: "However this may be, we may, at any rate as regards the nineteenth century, lay down that as a rule judge-made law has, owing to the training and age of our judges, tended at any given moment to represent the convictions of an earlier era than the ideas represented by the parliamentary legislation." Dicey, Relation Between Law and Public Opinion in England During the Nineteenth Century 390 (1952).

litigation arising out of business transactions. Litigation between individuals is assigned to courts of general jurisdiction, while labor disputes take special channels.

The jurisdictional competence of judicial institutions in the Soviet polity is determined by the relationship of the cause at issue to the central piece of economic legislation—in a socialist state, the economic plan. In the broadest sense, the plan sets out all those conditions which in an open society are left to the free interplay of economic forces. While in the free societies a transaction translates the conditions of the market into business relations, in the socialist economic order it translates into similar relations the provisions of the plan.

Litigation, which is the responsibility of the Government Arbitration Boards, stands in the most proximate relationship to the economic plan. Labor disputes are also intrinsically related to the provisions of the plan. In this latter instance, however, the provisions of the plan are translated into more concrete terms by the intervening method of collective agreements concluded between the trade unions and industrial branches. However, not all the issues arising in the course of labor-management disputes may be decided exclusively with reference to the terms of the plan. Private litigation before the people's courts is of such nature that it can be decided in a manner which only sporadically will require intervention of the agent representing the over-all interests of the community.

This gradation is also reflected in the procedural characteristics of each of these three types of causes alluded to above. Conflicts of interest arising from business transactions within the socialist sector of the economy are handled according to the rules of nonadversary procedure. Another field where nonlitigious methods have wide application is the field of industrial relations. The prevalence of non-adversary techniques and the resort to arbitration and conciliation are influenced by the fact that the nationalization of the means of production has made the state and its various organizations the principal business partners, as well as the only industrial and commercial employer.

A Soviet textbook on civil law, a collective work of a group of leading jurists, characterized the function of contractual engagements between the enterprises which belong to that circle of business institutions which correspond in most general terms to the business work in the free societies as follows: "The question of concluding a contract is not a private business of the two managers of the socialist enterprises; concluding such a contract is the function of government." [14]

Business transactions in the socialist system are, in consequence, official acts which implement in detail the directives of governmental policy as formulated in the plan which occupies a central place in the entire system of rules regulating this activity. The Czechoslovak Civil Code of 1954 thus determines the place of various pieces of legislation within a special order of precedence regarding their force for the determination of mutual rights and duties between the parties (sec. 212):

(1) The uniform economic plan shall be enforced through contracts specifically adapted to the needs of economic planning (economic contracts). Competent organs shall create specific obligations according to the requirements of economic planning.

(2) To the thus created legal relationships, the provisions of this law shall have application, in the absence of provisions to the contrary.[15]

14 1 Genkin, Bratus, Lunts, & Novitskii, Sovetskoe grazhdanskoe pravo 397 (1956).

15 E.g., Article 2 of the Draft of the Principles of Civil Legislation of the USSR and of the Union Republics. Hungarian Civil Code of 1959 (Law No. IV) Sec. 199: "In order to realize the obligations arising from the people's economic plan, contracts shall be made, unless statute expressly provides otherwise. The basis for such contracts shall be the approved Plan." Sec. 297: "Socialist organizations—if statute does not provide otherwise, shall enter into contracts with each other for the detailed determination and performance of all of their mutually existing obligations regarding product delivery, construction and other performances coming within the scope of their enterprises, for the realization of the people's economic plan (plan contracts)." East German Gesetz über die Vetragssystem in der sozialistischen Wirtschaft (Vertragsgesetz) of Dec. 11, 1957, provided as follows, Sec. 23 (1): "The purchaser is obliged to submit to purveyor an offer for a contract or, if such is impossible for him, to request the purveyor to make a contract or, if such is impossible for him, to request the purveyor to make an offer for a contract. This shall be done ... within a month from the day on which the temporary or final government assignment was delivered." Sec. 1: "Socialist enterprises are under obligation to make contracts regarding those of their mutual relations which, on grounds of and in concurrence with the goals of the people's economic plan, concern the purveyance and sale of products or production and sale of work or other performance."

The special position of contractual engagements between the units of the economic order of the socialist state is further strengthened by the general provisions of the civil codes of the socialist countries. These emphasize the fact that the over-all purpose of planned economic activity applies to all aspects of legal commerce under the rules of the civil law. Article I of the Draft of the Priniciples of the Soviet Civil Legislation (1960) defines the purpose of its provisions as follows:

Soviet civil legislation regulates property and related non-property relations for the purpose of strengthening and developing the socialist system of economy and socialist ownership, creating the material and technical base of communism and satisfying the material and spiritual needs of citizens more and more fully.

The Hungarian Civil Code of 1959 states that:

(1) This Act regulates the property relations involving material value and certain personal relations of the citizens, as well as of the state, economic and social organizations, with the object of meeting systematically and to an ever increasing extent the material and cultural demands of society and of building socialism.
(2) The provisions of this Act shall be construed in full conformity with the economic and social order of the Hungarian People's Republic.

Article 343 of the Polish draft of the Civil Code (1960) states in its provisions on the law of contracts:

[S]ocialist organizations are obligated to cooperate both in concluding contracts as well as in their execution, taking into account the influence of their action on the execution of the contract by the other party, on the meeting the needs of economic life, efficiency of production processes and commerce, and on safeguarding the national economy from losses.

Thus, while maintaining the fiction that the general provisions of the civil law apply also to the contractual relations between the socialist economic units, economic contracts, in fact, constitute a separate category of legal transactions. This is due not only to the application of special legal provisions not included in the civil codes, but, in addition, to the fact that civil codes themselves provide separately for the interpretation and enforcement of such contracts. These special regimes, either within or without the civil codes of socialist countries, follow from the fact that public authorities, responsible for performance of public duties, are partners in socialist economic and legal commerce. This is reflected in three institutions which constitute the heart of the law of contracts of the socialist economic sector: (1) the duty to contract, (2) the effect of administrative action on the terms of the contract, and (3) the consequences of nonperformance and default of the parties.

The institution of the duty to enter into the contractual relations, which is imposed upon the socialist enterprises, endeavors to combine two opposite principles of action. These are: a contract which is an expression of individual calculation, and the central direction of the national economy according to the plan. "Planned contracts" between socialist enterprises, states a Soviet civil law treatise, "represent a formulation of planned assignments received by the parties of the contract."

Soviet Contract is a form of liaison between the individual socialist enterprises directed towards the best accomplishment of the general socialist plan. This task is equally in the interests of both parties. The fact that both parties have this task in common results in the equality of socialist organizations as parties to contracts. The equality of parties is secured by the national economic plan itself and is reflected in all normative acts (laws and decrees) relating to contracts between the government agencies engaged in commerce and industry. . . .[16]

Originally, the assignments of the plan were distributed by two types of contracts. General contracts were entered into between the central government agencies in charge of the industrial branches which determined the distribution of the national product according to the plan of the distribution: consumption, production, investment, reserves, etc. Within this basic breakdown of production and distribution assignments, enterprises, factories, and distribution chains determined concrete obligations, fixing dates of delivery within the general terms of the accounting and financing system. In order to assure an orderly conduct of business according to the plan, these types of contracts were to be entered into promptly, and a special system of pre-contract disputes was devised.[17]

In this system of strict military-like discipline, direct dealings

16 1 Sovetskoe grazhdanskoe pravo 369 (1950–51).
17 Gsovski & Grzybowski, Government, Law, and Courts in the Soviet Union and Eastern Europe 1150 ff. (1959).

between individual units of the Soviet economy were frowned upon and were permitted only when expressly provided for by the regulations issued by the higher administrative authorities. By the end of 1935, the policy was changed and the government began to favor direct dealings between the individual enterprises.[18] On January 15, 1936, this practice was sanctioned as a regular form of business relations.[19]

In 1949, however, the Council of Ministers reversed this practice and ordered that the method of contracts general and local be tried again.[20]

The resolution of the Council of Ministers of May 22, 1959, again changed the method of business transactions between the units of socialist economy. The practice seems to demonstrate that the system of contracts general and local was a failure. Since 1952, the prevailing tendency has been to rely on direct contracts for business transactions between government enterprises. Critics of the previous system have pointed out that contracts general, although conceived as an institution of civil law, have in fact acquired the character and the function of an administrative act. This, of course, was inconsistent with its form of a contract. Fine points of law notwithstanding, what was more important, the system of two-staged contracts was cumbersome and took a long time to take shape. In addition, the necessity of waiting for the yearly elaboration of an intricate system of contractual obligations between the parties, so as to provide a basis for economic cooperation between Soviet enterprises, contributed to a yearly lag in business transactions. Contracts general were concluded late, and without them all transactions were fundamentally illegal. Enterprises which proceeded with their usual deliveries without adequate contractual engagements were exposed to the danger of financial loss. The practice of legalized *ex post* deliveries made prior to concluding contracts general undermined the sense of the system and reduced it to a purely superfluous formality. The final blow to the system of two-

18 Resolution of the Council of People's Commissars of Dec. 14, 1934, Concerning the Making of Contracts for 1935, Sob. zak. SSSR sec. 45 (1934).
19 Sob. zak. SSSR sec. 27 (1936).
20 Resolution of the Council of Ministers of April 21, 1949, Sob. zak. SSSR sec. 68 (1949).

staged contracts was delivered by the administrative reform of 1957. This reform abolished the centralized economic management of the country from the federal and republican level, and replaced it by economic districts under councils of national economy. Thus, the idea of contracts general, as based upon the idea of the central management of national economy, was rendered completely out of tune with the real situation.[21]

The 1959 Resolution of the Council of Ministers on Deliveries simplified the system. It provided for one type of contract to be concluded in the execution of instructions concerning the distribution and supply of technical equipment and materials for production purposes directly between the interested enterprises. In regard to articles of general consumption, direct business relations were to be established between the producing enterprises and distribution centers, which then were to enter into contractual arrangements with their units of the distribution network.[22]

While undoubtedly simplification of the system of contractual relations might contribute to a more efficient handling of the distribution of goods, the essential nature of contractual relations between the units of the socialist economy was not affected. The validity and tenor of their mutual obligations are primarily determined by the dispositions of the economic plan, and their authority is based on the instruction of the administrative act.

In Poland, where a system of planned contracts, similar to that introduced in the Soviet Union by the Resolution of 1949, has been in existence since 1950, a decree of May 16, 1956, on Contracts of Delivery [23] introduced a method of direct contractual engagements between the enterprises. Although it simplified the method of business transactions, it failed to convert them into the civil law institutions. This is apparent from the provisions of the decree that in case the directly interested parties should fail to reach an agreement, the mutual obligations of the parties are to be determined by a joint

---

21 Bratus, "O nekotorykh chertakh istorii sovetskogo grazhdanskogo prava," SGP 97 (No. 11, 1957).
22 Lys, Lesnik, & Borzova, "Struktura dogovornikh sviazei i nekotorye voprosy ulutshenia organizatsii materialno-tekhnicheskogo snabzhenia," SGP 85–92 (No. 2, 1960).
23 DU 16/87.

decision of higher economic agencies to whom the interested enterprises are subordinated.[24]

Thus, the core of the system is in the intimate relationship between the contractual agreements, the plan, and the decisions of the
higher government authorities.[25] The logical consequence of this fact
is that should a change occur in the policy decisions as they are
formulated in the plan, the contracts between trading partners are
directly affected. A typical provision, in this respect, is the Bulgarian
Statute on Obligations and Contracts of November 2, 1950, which runs
as follows:

Sec. 6. . . . If a contract is concluded in connection with the fulfillment
of the planned task, the repeal, lapse or change in this task has retroactive
effect on the provisions of the contract, its repeal, its validity in the
future, or the change in its provisions.[26]

The Hungarian Civil Code, which contains a full treatment of all
aspects of contractual relations under the economic plan, provides in
Section 403 that in case the plan or some specific task included in it be
cancelled, all contracts concluded with reference to the assignment are
accordingly modified or cancelled. Similarly, the arbitration board
might "within the limits of the plan and their statutory authority
modify, terminate or dissolve any planned contract."

Administrative control extends also in other directions. In countries which, as in Poland, still allow some degree of private enterprise,
administrative directives limit the choice of partners for socialist trading in order to restrict private economic initiative.[27] According to the

---

24 Gsovski & Grzybowski, *supra* note 17, at 1335.
25 Sec. 400 (1) of the Hungarian Civil Code of 1959 states: "The enterprise approved plan and instruction issued by mutual consent of the
   directing organs shall determine the content of the plan contract. In
   case of construction contracts, the state may provide that technical plans
   and budgets shall be basis of the contract." The Code further provides
   that (sec. 409 (3)) a statute may provide that the rules on plan contracts shall apply to contracts between socialist enterprises even if such
   are not intended for product delivery, construction, or other undertaking.
26 D.V. No. 275/1950.
27 Polish Decree on Delivery Contracts of Dec. 28, 1957 (DU 3/7/1958)
   provided that: "Delivery contracts, construction contracts and general
   service contracts over certain value may not be given to private entre-

Draft of the Polish Civil Code, "Separate provisions determine in what cases state organizations may not make contracts with other persons, or may take them only under specific conditions." Thus, contractual activity is another channel for the implementation of government policy. It may require that needs of economic enterprises be satisfied according to a scheme of distribution worked out centrally in order to promote newly opened sources of supply of raw materials and semifinished products. Quite frequently, new sources offer products inferior in quality or on a noncompetitive basis. However, the support for the new production is a matter of policy.

The direct relationship among business deals, the economic plans, and the instructions of governmental agencies is further illustrated by various regulations concerning substitute methods for creating quasicontractual obligations. These tend to emphasize the fact that the complex system of agreements between socialist business partners represents the mechanism of the socialist economic system. Consequently, remedial and corrective provisions for meeting the default of one of the parties has had to be designed in a manner differing fundamentally from similar institutions of the civil law. Under the traditional legal system, the purpose of such provision was to indemnify the innocent party. Under the socialist legal system, on the other hand, it is to assure greater discipline in the legal commerce between the business partners.

According to the Soviet draft of the Principles of civil legislation of the USSR and the Union Republics (1950), Article 35:

In the case of obligations between state organizations, collective farms and other cooperative and public organizations, the payment of a forfeit (fine, penalty) for non-fulfillment or improper fulfillment of an obligation and the recovery of damages do not constitute a release from fulfillment of an obligation in kind except in cases where a plan assignment on which the obligation is based has lost its force. In the case of obligations between the above-mentioned organizations, agreement of the parties concerning limitation of their responsibility, as established by

---

preneurs on the basis of public bidding." The purpose of this provision is on one hand to restrict the economic significance and, in general, the expansion of private enterprise and on the other to aim at the elimination of competition between the government and private economic initiative.

USSR and Union-Republic legislation is not permitted. The release may be effected only by the decision of the higher authority.

Consequently, in addition to the system of planned contracts, the higher authority may, in the process of adjustment of the plan to the realities of the economic conditions of the moment, act to establish mutual obligations in organizing economic or commercial activity. The Polish Draft of the Civil Code (1960), provides (Article 364) that an administrative instruction may obligate a socialist organization in favor of another party in the same manner as a contract. Further, the Code provides (Article 365):

Provisions of the foregoing article apply accordingly if a socialist organization was instructed to modify or dissolve a contract, or refrain from performance of a contract.[28]

Another aspect in which the economic conditions of the country, influenced by the governmental policies, determine the nature of the contractual obligation is that of the contract of work. In a planned economy, the terms of employment constitute one of the basic conditions determining the cost of production and the share of the national product which remains to implement governmental policies of industrial expansion. Viewed from the central position of the economic plan, labor conditions are not a matter of individual accommodation, but of basic decisions concerning the size of the workers' share in the gross national product. Looked at from the center, wages and marginal benefits, representing an individual entitlement under a contract of work and the terms of the labor law, represent planned participation of an individual worker in the general framework of labor conditions in the productive processes managed by the state. As the interest of the state is determined by the terms of the plan, fluctuations in the fulfillment of its tasks occurring in the course of the period of its operation are adjusted by proper management of the wage fund. From this

---

28 Polish Decree of Dec. 28, 1957, *supra* note 27, stated (art. 7): "In exceptional cases...the Council of Ministers may authorize supreme governmental agencies to issue decisions instructing subordinate units of the socialized economy to make deliveries to other units of the socialized economy without entering into contracts. These instructions create rights and obligations for the recipient and purveyor in lieu of contracts."

vantage point, it is also difficult to see the conflict of interests between the two sides in industrial relations. Indeed, the interests of the state and of the workers are considered identical. A Soviet scholar describing changes which have occurred in labor legislation in the people's democracies, stated that:

In countries of people's democracy, labor organization and wages are put on a scientific basis after the example of the Soviet Union.... (A scientific basis is provided by the fact that social-labor relations are in fact) material relations independent on human will.... People cannot exist without producing the means of their existence ... the material character of social-labor relations consists in their dependence on the level of development of the productive forces; qualitative changes in the level of their development unavoidably result in changes in social-labor conditions.[29]

Thus, the contract of work as a method of a personal coming to terms is only a formula for the statement that a set of predetermined conditions applies with regard to a concrete individual, provided that some terms of the contract are related to the calculations of the plan.

In this doctrine of the function of the contract of work in the general setup determining industrial relations, the axiom that economic management is a public function of the worker's state is of central importance:

In the popular state the function and the tasks of state administration are basically different. Its basic function is a creative and planned influence on the formation of the economic foundations for the construction of a new social order. In this perspective restriction of administrative activity to the forms typical for the bourgeois state of the liberal period ... would serve no purpose ... administrative acts in the fields of relations between the state and the individual in the new type of economy have acquired a different nature; now their purpose is not only the protection of individual rights, but primarily, through the regulation of rights and duties of the individual, his integration in the planned socialist construction.[30]

Thus, the function of the collective agreement is to translate the provisions of the plan into concrete conditions of individual enterprises

29 Aleksandrov, Sovetskoe trudovoe pravo 7 (1954).
30 Jaroszynski, Zimmerman, & Brzezinski, Polskie prawo administracyjne, część ogólna 324 (1956).

and work establishments. Wages and working conditions are thus worked out as a result of the successful accomplishment of planned assignments. The very procedure for fixing various elements of the working conditions by government decree and in consultation with the central trade union authorities reflects the change in industrial relations from the contest of human wills into the creative influence of the socialist worker on the industrial environment.[31]

Thus, in final analysis, the nature of the legal transactions out of which litigious causes arise have little in common with transactions under the rules of the civil law. In open societies, the intervention of the administrative authority into economic and social life, when it assumes the forms of private law activity, has caused a good deal of doubt as to the nature of such action.[32] In the socialist society, economic management is always a matter of public policy.[33] The process of expanding the activities of the socialist state means gradual restriction of the provinces of life subject to the rule of civil law in its tradi-

---

31 *Cf.* Gsovski & Grzybowski, *supra* note 17, at 1446–47, 1465–66, 1542–43; Aleksandrov, *supra* note 29, at 198–200.

32 *Cf. supra* at 17–19. "The distinction between 'administration' and 'private law' becomes fluid where the official actions of the organs of official bodies assume the same form as agreements between individuals. This is the case when officials in the course of their official duties make contractual arrangements for exchange of goods or services either with members of the organization or with other individuals. Frequently such relationships are withdrawn from the norms of private law, are arranged in some way different from the general legal norms as to substance or as to the mode of enforcement, and are thus declared to belong to the sphere of 'administration.' As long as claims treated in this way are guaranteed by some possibility of enforcement, they do not cease to be 'rights,' and the distinction is no more than a technical one. However, even as such, the distinction may be of considerable practical significance." Weber, *supra* note 1, at 48.

33 "In People's Poland one of the functions of the state is to direct national economy." Decision of the Polish Supreme Court of May 5, 1949, ZOIC 13 (1950). Art. 18 of the General Principles of the Civil Law of the Soviet Union and of the Union Republics stated: "The state is the sole owner of all state property, regardless of what it is or who manages or uses it." *Cf.* Venediktov, Gosudarstvnennaia sotsialisticheskaia sobstvennost 4 (1948): "All government property, whoever controls it, forms a single fund of state socialist property; the right of property of that fund is vested in the Soviet people as represented by the socialist state."

tional sense. Recent socialist codes leave little doubt that truly private law transactions, particularly those between individuals, are reduced to insignificant proportions, and although in all probability they will continue to be present until the final millennium, their social function is quite unimportant.

ADJUSTMENT AND CONCILIATION

When the Soviet government embarked upon the experiment of providing a separate channel for the adjustment of conflicts arising within the socialist sector of economy, there was little awareness of the impact which the method of planned contract would have upon the techniques of adjudication and upon civil law institutions in the future. In 1932, Commissar of Justice Krylenko wrote:

I believe that in our society there can be no difference between the nature of cases coming up for arbitration and those coming before courts of justice, no difference in the methods of passing of them and no difference in the principles of substantive or procedural law applied.[34]

Writing in 1943, Ginsburg, a Soviet scholar of note, stated:

The state arbitration system is the economic tribunal for the period when the foundations of the socialist economy and of the second five-year plan are laid. It is a tribunal, since its method consists of the use of state compulsion for the enforcement of economic and contract discipline. It uses compulsion to accustom economic agencies to discipline. However, methods of its work, its organization, and the principle on which its rulings are based contain a number of new elements; these elements reflect a new climate of economic development and the full victory of socialism and transform the state arbitration system into one of the agencies of economic administration which use the methods of struggle for economic accounting and contract discipline.[35]

The state arbitration system was established in the Soviet Union in 1931. And after World War II, with proper modification, it was

34 Krylenko, "Sudebnaia sistema i Gosarbitrazh," SGP 39 (No. 7–8, 1932).
35 Ginsburg, "Voprosy sovetskogo khoziaistvennogo prava na dannom etape," in Voprosy sovetskogo khoziaistvennogo prava, Part I, p. 14 (1943); *cf.* Shkundin, "Gosudarstvennyi arbitrazh i arbitrazhnyi protsess," in Arbitrazh v sovetskom khoziaistve 20 (1938); Berman, "Commercial Contracts in Soviet Law," 35 Cal. L. Rev. 205 (1947).

adopted in the socialist countries in Eastern Europe as an indispensable appendage of economic planning.[36]

The 1960 regulation defining the duties of the State Arbitration Board under the USSR Council of Ministers [37] leaves little doubt as to the nature of the Board's functions. In addition to protecting property rights of disputing parties, it also enforces a policy which aims at promoting the efficiency of the economic mechanism of the state. Its decision must foster the cooperation of governmental enterprises, facilitate the fulfillment of economic plans and prevent a narrow and self-centered approach to business transactions. The Board is called upon to "assist in the fulfillment of plans and assignments for deliveries of products and other obligations and also in the elimination of shortcomings in the economic activity of enterprises, organizations and institutions which came to light . . . in the course of hearings. . . ."

The most important function, however, follows from the arbitral activity itself. The Board is enjoined to cooperate with the federal government of the Soviet state in determining the terms of trade in individual types of goods. It is also authorized to issue instructions concerning the procedure for "receiving products and goods in terms of quantity and quality."

The State Arbitration Board representing the apex in the hierarchy of such institutions in the Soviet Union, has special duties in the area of foreign trade. It is authorized to adjust or annul the terms of contracts between the parties for the purpose of achieving conformance to the regulations and governmental directives in force. In addition, it negotiates proper changes in contract terms, and codifies and arranges systematically the laws and regulations governing Soviet foreign trade.

According to Article 5 (point d):

In order to assure the necessary uniformity in the settlement of disputes, (the Board) studies and generalizes the experience of state arbitration boards, or economic councils, ministries and agencies, instructs them on question of the application of the regulations on deliveries of products

36 Gsovski & Grzybowski, *supra* note 17, at 585–87, 719–29, 820–21, 893, 1147–51, 1199, 1220–23, 1259–61, 1288–93, 1376–80, 1449–51; Hazard, Law and Social Change in the USSR 50 ff. (1953); Berman, *supra* note 35.

37 Sov. iust. 30–32 (No. 12, 1960).

and all other All-Union normative acts regulating economic regulations, and instructs state arbitration boards on questions of statistical accounting.

It also reports to the government on the most flagrant violations of "state discipline and of legislation regarding the quality and completeness of products, as well as on manifestation of local tendencies and on other violations of socialist legality in the economic work of enterprises, organizations and institutions."

The importance of these functions to the operation of the planned economy was enhanced by the 1957 reform of economic management in the Soviet Union. The reform's main achievement was in removing the bulk of administrative functions from the level of the federal government. In fact, it substituted for the economic ministries at the center a system of territorial councils of national economy. At the same time, however, the over-all direction of the planned economy in terms of national goals and targets remained in Moscow. In this situation, the federal echelon of the arbitration mechanism serves primarily as an analyst of the progress of business operations in the entire Soviet empire. In this manner it permitted intervention from the center for the purpose of maintaining the unity of the national economy and the assurance of the soundness of its business activity.

In this vast array of responsibilities, arbitral functions serve only as a means of achieving other more important results. The Board acts as an economic and social organizer, advisor as to sound business practices with reference to Soviet legal regulations, legislator in the field of the actual conduct of business activities, and as a source of information for the federal government in the proper enforcement of the economic policies of the state, leading eventually to the modification of tasks and assignments.

The characteristic feature of the Board's activities, particularly regarding the function of adjusting conflicting interests, is that it pays no attention to the principle of the sanctity of contracts, which elsewhere constitutes the core of judicial functions. The issues in each case before the board are defined not so much in terms of contractual performance as by conformance to the economic plan, which provides the rationale and content of the contractual activity in the first place. Obviously, the role of the plan is basically different from the role of the Civil Code with regard to contracts between private parties. Contracts in the former instance are truly only a form of "liaison" which could as well be established by the decision of a higher economic authority. Thus, decisions of the economic arbitrator can be made exclusively in terms of economic policy and without reference to abstract rules of law.[38]

This type of judicial action has but limited application in labor disputes, which constitute another category of litigious issues arising out of economic planning in the socialist polities of the Soviet type. Labor disputes involve personal interest. In the final analysis these are expressed in concrete claims based variously on the provisions of governmental decrees, on the collective agreements, or on the labor code. And the decrees, agreements, and code are couched in the form of abstract commands addressed to a multitude of legal relationships in the area of industrial relations.

Thus, the presence of personal interests influenced the techniques devised in the Soviet Union for the settlement of labor disputes. In so doing, conciliation was combined with an opportunity for a judicial review of the disputed issues.

Litigations arising in the area of industrial relations fall into three broad categories. (1) Some disputes arise from the struggle of labor organizations for improvement in labor conditions and a larger share in industrial profits. These are hardly disputes in the legal sense of the word, representing rather a form of social struggle. Nevertheless, the modern state seeks to regulate the process of adjustment of conflicting interests in order to assure the welfare of the entire society. (2) Some disputes arise from the enforcement of the provisions of the law governing labor conditions and are handled by public agencies exercising supervisory and punitive powers to maintain certain standards. These include the hygiene and safety of work, employment of certain categories of workers, hours of work, conditions of work, etc. (3) Other disputes result from individual contracts of work and concern individual claims for minimum pay, leave, terms of contracts, etc., which are handled by the regular courts of justice. Such courts are normally specially organized for that type of dispute, and proceed according to the normal rules of judicial procedure.[39]

38 See note 16 *supra.*
39 See *supra* at 84.

Originally, all types of disputes under the Labor Code of 1922 and the Law of August 1928 were handled by the piece rate and conflict boards, which applied conciliation and arbitration to cases within their jurisdiction. Gradually, however, many of their functions, e.g., determination of the standards of output and piece rating, were taken over by the administrative agencies of the Central Boards of the Trade Unions, which assumed the functions of the Commissariat of Labor. The only jurisdiction left to the boards was, in consequence, the settlement of individual disputes, preliminary to transferring the case to the court.[40]

The edict of January 31, 1957,[41] abolished the old boards. In their stead, labor dispute boards were established, whose only functions have been to deal exclusively with labor disputes concerning claims arising out of the contract of work and to enforce the labor regulations in force. In no case have labor dispute boards the right to intervene in order to improve either labor conditions or to raise the rates of pay. The board consists of an equal number of representatives of management and of the factory committee, and its decisions are taken unanimously. If either party is dissatisfied with the ruling of the board, it may file a suit in the competent court.[42]

According to the draft of the Basic Principles of Labor Legislation of the USSR and of the Union Republics, which was published in 1959, the 1957 regime is to continue without change.[43]

From the decisions of labor boards, appeal lies to the local trade union committees. These also have jurisdiction to deal with controversies not settled in proceedings before labor dispute boards, i.e., where the necessary unanimity was not reached. Courts have exclusive jurisdiction only in cases involving dismissals, or where either of the parties is dissatisfied with the decision of the trade union committee.

Labor dispute boards have been introduced into all Eastern European countries of popular democracy,[44] thus replacing methods of settling labor disputes which were modeled after patterns evolved

40 1 Gsovski, Soviet Civil Law 803–4 (1948).
41 Vedomosti, item 58 (1957).
42 Gsovski & Grzybowski, *supra* note 17, at 1449–51.
43 Sots. zak. I–XIV (No. 10, 1959).
44 Gsovski & Grzybowski, *supra* note 17, at 1470–72, 1494–95, 1520–22, 1546–47, 1565–67.

in the industrial societies of the West. Polish developments in this connection are highly instructive.

In pre-World War II Poland, labor disputes were handled by labor courts in which lay judges represented the interests of both worker and employer.[45] Conciliation was used in order to settle collective grievances and to establish future conditions of work, and was obligatory only in disputes which "could endanger national economic interests." In making their decisions, conciliation boards had to take into consideration the "interests of employers, and those of labor, and also the economic and social welfare of the nation." [46]

After the war, labor courts were reconstituted in their old form, and shop committees were given jurisdiction to conciliate disputes between the workers and management of individual factories. All cases which could not be settled amicably within the factory were sent to the District Inspectors of Labor, a government agency which enforced the laws concerning general labor conditions. In 1950, pursuant to the reorganization of the Polish judiciary along Soviet lines, labor courts were abolished and labor cases were transferred to ordinary courts. In 1951, labor arbitration boards were introduced in all Polish industries, and in 1954, in all government enterprises and institutions as well.[47]

Labor arbitration boards have jurisdiction in all labor disputes except those involving the use of dwellings allotted to employees. These disputes concerning financial responsibility for damage attributable to the employees and those disputes involving personnel in higher managerial positions in the excepted areas are the responsibility of the administrative authorities.

An arbitration board is a replica of the Soviet model, and its decision requires unanimous agreement of labor and management representatives. In contrast with Soviet legislation, however, the Polish decree contains a directive regarding the nature of awards made by the arbitration boards. Thus, a board makes its decisions "having the interests of the working masses and the welfare of the

45 Decree of March 22, 1928, DU 37/350, and 95/354 of 1934.
46 Decree of Oct. 27, 1933, DU 37/313.
47 Decree of Feb. 24, 1954, DU 10/35.

national economy in view, and taking into consideration the law in force, provisions of the work contract, and shop rules."

In other words, its function is not limited to discovering the rights of the parties involved in the litigation. Rather, it is directed to seek the achievement of a compromise which would safeguard the interests of production, and of the larger interests of the society as a whole, although the issue is the alleged violation of a contractual stipulation or of the legal provision in force.[48] In the final analysis, it contains elements of administrative action aimed at the correlation and integration of individual claims into the general pattern of economic policy.

In the period which followed the 1956 upheaval in Poland against the harshness of Stalinist rule, doubts were expressed as to the possibility of achieving a greater respect for the individual rights of workers without a basic reorganization of the economic management of the country and the replacement of the administrative rule by forms of economic initiative shaped by the institutions of the civil law. Insisting that respect for individual rights was incompatible with a high degree of centralization, one of the partisans of economic self-government in the factories exercised by elective organs known as workers' councils, suggested that:

[T]he scope of the decision making of the administrative authorities should be seriously restricted. Relations between enterprises and central authorities should assume the form of a system of contracts in which central authorities would act as representatives of the national interests, while workers' councils would act in the interests of the enterprises and of the crews. This arrangement would make possible a full participation of the crews in the factory management, . . . leading to the separation of responsibility for the state of the national economy.

In this pattern of economic management, administrative regulation would no longer be the only source of mutual rights and obligations. Indeed, the revival of civil law to govern relations between the various units of the national economy either representing local or national interests would appear to be a logical consequence.[49]

48 Grzybowski, *supra* note 11, at 90–91.
49 Grzybowski, "Polish Workers' Councils," 17 J. Central European Affairs 284–85 (1957).

CIVIL CAUSES AND PUBLIC INTEREST

The forms of judicial procedure followed by Soviet courts of general jurisdiction result from the fact that only occasionally will the public interest of the socialist society claim recognition. Article 2 of the Draft of Principles of Civil Procedure of the USSR and of the Union Republics limited the jurisdiction of Soviet courts to cases involving disputes arising from civil, family, labor, and collective farm legal relations. These, as a rule, cannot be expected to affect the economic and social policies of the state.

In such circumstances, the forms of civil procedure appear to the lawyer's eye to be an external form not directly related to the social or economic order of the polity:

Civil procedure in each state, irrespective of its type ... serves to uphold civil law relations and claims arising therefrom. The qualitative difference of the social state and legal order as compared with the state and law of the exploiters, different class nature of the administration of justice in the states of a socialist type have not affected the nature of this function of the civil procedure, which, as long as the state and law shall continue—is and will be to afford to individual claims protection through state power.[50]

At the same time, the protection of private rights cannot but be affected by the fact that the legal protection of private rights is extended by the public authority. Such is inspired by the policy aiming primarily at the realization of general welfare. The Soviet draft of the Principles of Civil Procedure makes it clear that collective interests take precedence over individual claims (Article 1):

The aim of Soviet civil procedure is to ensure correct administration of justice in civil cases in order to safeguard the socialist system of economy and socialist property and the defense of political, labor, housing and other personal and property rights and interests of citizens protected by the law, and also the rights and interests protected by the law of state institutions, enterprises, collective farms and other cooperative and public organizations.

Civil procedure should help to strengthen socialist legality and ensure precise and undeviating execution of laws by all institutions, enterprises,

50 Decision of the Polish Supreme Court, Full Civil Bench, of Feb. 12, 1955, PiP 120 (No. 7–8, 1955).

organizations, officials and citizens, and also educate citizens in a spirit of solicitous attitude towards socialist property, observance of labor discipline and respect for the rules of socialist society.

From the most general point of view, these reservations as to the degree of legal protection afforded by the socialist courts to private rights and claims resemble similar reservations in the civil codes of the Western World which limit the enforcement of rights by the commands of public order and good morals.[51] However, it is easily discernible that the reservations set out by the socialist codes refer to situations which represent concrete obligations of the socialist society vis-à-vis its individual members. The socialist judicial process seeks to meet higher and more concrete standards of individual behavior by more precise and powerful methods of intervention by public authority in individual litigations in order to protect those collective demands.

In this respect, socialist judicial procedure represents only an aspect of similar solutions in the judicial procedures of open societies. Modern codes have given effect to the principle that on some occasions the court, in response to broader interests, has the power to go beyond the wishes of the parties to the case and proceed ex officio. This is particularly true of proof adduced by either of the parties, which the court may consider as insufficient. It may then demand the submission of additional evidence if it appears to be in the public interest to probe deeper into the real nature of the issues at stake. However, this power of the court may be limited by agreement of the litigants, and settlement between them always constitutes a barrier to its action.

In the socialist legal order, the criterion of interest which authorizes the demand for legal protection exceeds the persons of the litigants or those who are under legal duty to represent them. Article 6 of the Draft of the Principles of Civil Procedure provides that:

A court begins examination of a case upon the application of the interested person, or upon the application of a prosecutor, and also upon the application of a governmental, trade union, or other public organization or individual citizen if under the law the case may be instituted independently of the demand of the interested person.

51 E.g., art. 6 of the French Civil Code.

In other words, a claimant may find himself involved in legal proceedings without making a move himself, a situation which is highly reminiscent of proceedings before the *volost* courts in Imperial Russia, where the interested party was merged in a collective action of the village community of which he was a member. Elsewhere, where more traditional criteria of legal interest prevail, thus giving the right to resort to judicial protection, this possibility has been almost exclusively limited to matrimonial causes.[52]

Of the third parties entitled to take part in the civil suit, the most important is the public prosecutor. His participation in the trial is mandatory whenever the law so provides, and where the court calls for it. Otherwise, he may always institute civil proceedings, practically without restriction or limitation. Article 23 of the Draft of Principles of Civil Procedure states the limitation: "if the safeguarding of state or public interest or of the rights and legally protected interests of citizens demand this." In contrast, other agencies of government and public organizations may enter a case or be called upon to participate only in cases where the law expressly provides for it (Article 24 of the Draft).

The Soviet court has full control of proceedings and is not restricted to the evidence offered by the parties. In Soviet civil procedure, the inquisitorial principle has found its full expression; the usual reservation that court action would be barred by the joint opposition of the parties to the litigation is not the law in the Soviet judicial procedure. Furthermore, amicable settlement, the withdrawal of the claimant from the case, and the agreement to submit disputed issues to settlement by arbitration require approval by the court.

Finally, appellate proceedings favor public interest. Here also Soviet procedure followed the well-beaten path of similar institutions in the civil procedures of Western Europe. The appeal by the public authority in the defense of the law, known to some European civil procedures, is based on the fact that only at that final stage of the proceedings may the importance of the judicial decision for the public order be properly appraised. Thus, the representative of the state is permitted to step in and intervene to uphold the principle of legal order. This right is reserved exclusively to the attorney general

52 See *supra* at 105.

(*procureur général*), and proceedings in the case have no effect on the case itself.[53]

In the Soviet Union, the institution of the Supreme Court has been devised to serve exclusively that type of action, and private parties have no access to it. In addition to various other methods of Supreme Court supervision of lower courts, public prosecutors, presidents of the courts (therefore courts higher than people's courts), and their assistants have the right to move for the reopening of finally decided cases. Under the draft of the principles of civil procedure, it proposed that this right be exercised only within a period of three years from the moment of the final determination of the case.[54]

The Polish Supreme Court, in a decision of the full civil bench, explained the meaning of the reform of Polish civil procedure introduced after the Soviet pattern as follows:

The quest for the determination of material truth is one of the principles of the socialist order, and is expressed in a number of positive rules of the Code of Civil Procedure. . . . These provisions were enacted still by the bourgeois legislator, but only now they are fully enforced. . . . In particular, article 218 section 1 of the Code of Civil Procedure should be construed . . . that it instructs the court . . . to adopt an active attitude in the course of the proceedings and to bring to light true circumstances of the case.[55]

At the same time, Polish courts have distinguished between various categories of cases, depending upon the nature of the interests involved:

The inquisitorial principle . . . is not equally applicable to all cases. . . . It should have full application, when the interest of the People's state is at stake.

The Court supported this position by pointing out that similar practice is followed by the Soviet courts.[56]

The difference in the degree of legal protection offered to the public interests, as compared to the private causes, extends also to

53 Morel, Traité élémentaire de procédure civile 515 (1949); *cf.* Dalloz, 1 Nouveau répertoire de droit 436 (1957).
54 Gsovski & Grzybowski, *supra* note 17, at 531–34.
55 Civil Bench CPrez 195/52, PiP 536 (No. 10, 1953).
56 Decision of July 5, 1952, C. 1285/52 ZOIC 81/53; *cf.* also the Decision of the Polish Supreme Court of Oct. 3, 1951, C. 223/50, ZOIC 72/51.

other fields of legal regulation. In a case involving shortages, the Polish Supreme Court stated that the one-year statute of limitation under Article 473 of the Polish Code of Obligations for the recovery of the shortages did not apply to the socialist employer. The court reasoned that:

The statute of limitation provided in the Code concerns claims arising exclusively from the contract of work. However, the present claim arose not from a contract of work, but from the fundamental principles of the popular legal order (which calls for a special care for the socialist property).[57]

Another example of this type of reasoning was evidenced in a case in which the Polish Supreme Court stated that the mere breach of a contractual obligation constituted a criminal offense only when it affected the interests of the state. Otherwise, it gave grounds to a claim for damages under the general rules of civil law. When a private party was involved, the breach resulted in liability *ex delicto*.[58]

The presence of dual standards within the same order of legal procedure is due to the basic change which occurred with the transition of the national economy from private enterprise to socialist planning. The concept of the state as the subject of proprietary rights, and therefore as assimilated in their exercise to all other subjects of the private legal relationships, has disappeared.[59]

In all its forms—acting through the medium of government enterprises, socialist organizations, governmental agencies, and elective institutions—the state exercises public power and enforces public policy. The Polish draft of the Civil Code of 1955 stated, in the attached report of the codification commission, that it objected to the concept of the treasury as a party to legal transactions or as a subject of rights and duties in its own capacity as apart from the state conceived as a public power:

This recalls the bourgeois theory which makes a distinction between two fields of state activity: one in the province of public law and the other

57 Decision of Dec. 4, 1951, C. 1539/51, PiP 372–73 (No. 8–9, 1952); *cf.* Shargorodskii, "Tolkovanie ugolovnogo zakona," Uchonye zapiski Leningradskogo Gosudarstvennogo Universiteta 306 (No. 1, 1948).
58 Decision of Jan. 1, 1955, ZOIK 29/55, PiP 510 (No. 3, 1955).
59 *Cf. supra* at 16, 86 ff.

in the province of private law.... The state as the owner of national property unifies indivisibly the quality of authority with that of ownership.[60]

This development reflects, in an interesting manner, on the meaning and function of procedural institutions. In its traditional form, the state, in its autonomous function as guide for the conduct of all members of the society, had a concrete interest in upholding the legal rule. Socialist legal order is identified with the policy of the socialist state.[61] And, therefore, the institution of appeal in the interest of the law has assumed a new meaning. The intervention of public authority in civil trials in the form of a motion for the ex officio reopening of the case simply cannot be limited to the reconsideration of the legal issues involved without materially affecting the substantive interests involved.

60 Nagorski, "Draft of the New Civil Code for Poland," in Studies of the Polish Lawyers in Exile in the U.S. 69 (1956). In the case of the Soviet telegraphic agency *Tass,* sued for libel in Britain, the defendant claimed diplomatic immunity and submitted a certificate from the Soviet Ambassador to the United Kingdom which stated that *Tass* "constitutes a department of the Soviet state ... exercising the rights of a legal entity." 77 Journal du droit international 892 (1950).

61 Jaroszynski, Zimmerman, & Brzezinski, Polskie prawo administracyjne, część ogólna, 343 (1956): "In the absolute state bureaucracy was not bounded by its own acts ... in the capitalist legal order ... individual rights were a limit to the revocability of the administrative acts. In the socialist state all these moments are no longer valid, as public administration is a part of the social order.... Those aspects of life which demand some stability will call for a degree of stability of the administrative act.... Acts of the administration of creative nature ..., the legislator permits to change as the conditions change...."

Chapter IV

HOMO SOVIETICUS

THE MODEL

Standards of human behavior in relation to the exercise of individual rights are necessary in any legal system. Their function is to correlate legal provisions with individual activities and to provide uniform criteria for their evaluation. In legal systems closer to our world, these standards are personified under such concepts as "average prudent man" or "bonus pater familias" (Articles 450 and 1374 of the Civil Code of France). In addition to providing a yardstick for the evaluation of human actions, these concepts serve also in the elaboration of legal rules to assure desired social goals. In other words, the legislative technique in our mass society is that the legal rule addresses itself not to a number of real individualities but to a standard model, i.e., to a hypothetical member of human society.[1]

The more realistic this model is and the closer its approximation to what people and individual members of a polity actually are, the greater will be the chances that the legal rule will command "natural" obedience. Contrariwise, the more removed from reality or the less average the model to whom the law appeals, the fewer are the chances of success of the legal order.

As with everything else which pertains to social order, the proper correlation of a legal command to the model human being to which it is addressed is only one of the reasons for the success of the rule of law. A highly reformist legal order which operates with an idealistic model type may still be successful, if social regimentation, either by force or in combination with ideological doctrines, is adequate. On

---

1 Savatier, Métamorphoses économiques et sociales du droit civil d'aujourd'hui, 6–7 (ser. 3, 1959).

the other hand, a legal order conservatively conceived will be outdated and its institutions will have to be adapted to new conditions, if owing to social change a new type emerges, widely differing from the model envisaged by the legal order.

It seems, therefore, that a prescription for a legal order, which will fulfill its role of providing standards for human behavior with economy of force, must depend upon a keen understanding of actual social conditions and a feeling for the future. The model type of the member of a society to whom the legal rule is addressed is one of those characteristic features of the social order which determines its character.

Examples of unrealistic concepts of the model type are quite numerous. Among the most significant of such legislative errors were the provisions of the French Civil Code which took no account of the Frenchman's inclination to form associations. This mistake was corrected by later legislation, including the *Code de Commerce*. Of even greater significance was the general attitude of the legislators of the nineteenth century toward workers' associations. A most characteristic statement of the hostility toward workers and professional associations in the name of individual liberty was the French decree of March 2–17, 1791, which instituted a prohibition of workers' and employers' associations for the purpose of exposing fully industrial relations to the impact of the forces of the market. These laws were followed by a long list of prohibitions against forming associations and were reinforced by penal provisions for violations of their rules. They were gradually reversed by a series of laws beginning with the decree of February 25–29, 1848, and ending with the law of July 24, 1867. The latter re-established the freedom of professional associations.

Other countries of Europe have undergone similar experiences. Thus, Great Britain authorized workers' association in 1824; whereas, in Germany, the recognition of workers' rights to form associations had to await the passage of the law of June 21, 1861.[2]

While the French Civil Code was predicated upon a single concept, i.e., of a hypothetical Frenchman, and purported to implement the postulates of equality and liberty by determining the rights of

2 Bouère, Le droit de grève 20–40 (1958).

all members of the French society in a single act, no modern legal system may operate on the basis of a single standard of behavior and a single model type. One may say that the progress of modern societies is characterized by the emergence of an ever-growing number of social types to whom various legal rules address their commands, without prejudice to their universality. These rules take into account special obligations, as well as professional functions and qualifications. Doctors, lawyers, soldiers, businessmen, journalists, members of the trade unions, etc. are called upon to adhere to higher standards of behavior than other members of the social order. Their privileged position, a position of trust, is thought to be counterbalanced by higher obligations. Enforcement of these standards is often guaranteed by special provisions of the criminal law, prescribing responsibility for negligence or failure to act when another person would escape responsibility. Or enforcement may be occasioned by special charters of professional associations, which thus become universal laws to the same extent as provisions of the criminal law providing for qualified penal sanctions.[3]

In the forty years of Soviet legal order, it is possible to distinguish at least three model types, i.e., the average Soviet man, to whom Soviet law has addressed it commands.

In the legal theory of Pashukanis, the citizen of the revolutionary state was an economic man who differed little from a member of capitalist society. This was because the capitalist institutions of law and barter, as means of regulating human relations, continued to function in the Soviet economic order. The emergence of the new man was predicated upon the fulfillment of the new economic order in which economic relations would no longer be regulated by law, but by administrative arrangements and planning. Then *homo sovieticus* would cease to be a legal concept. It would become rather a social category, as the law was to disappear together with the laws of value and the market.

This concept of Soviet citizen was replaced by that of an integrated man whose duty and instinct was discipline. The new man

3 *Cf.* Grzybowski, "Soviet Reform of Criminal Law of 1958," 6 Osteuropa Recht 114 (1960); *cf.* Soviet Criminal Code of the RSFSR regarding the responsibility for economic crimes, or for disregarding of authority.

was the product of a re-evaluation of the political and social situation in Russia. It was accepted as axiomatic that the victory of socialism was a concrete fact and not relegated to an unknown future, and that a classless society had been created as a result of the reforms initiated by the regime. By the same token, the law governing the Soviet Union was promoted to the rank of the socialist law.[4]

Socialist law was thought to be inspired by the postulate of subordination of individual rights to the collective interests of society:

Not Roman law based on private property . . . but the public law principle provides a foundation of . . . Soviet socialist civil law. This principle found its expression in our code of civil procedure (of 1923) which in Article 2 stated the right of the procurator, both to initiate proceedings or to enter the case, irrespective of the wishes or motions of the parties, in any phase of the proceedings, if . . . this is required by the interests of the state or of the working masses.[5]

The Stalinist concept of the Soviet man was the result of an evolution of ideas in Soviet psychology, connected with the decision to reshape through a series of economic plans the economic potential of the Soviet Union, and later, of the satellite countries. The concept of the individual in a socialist society (or rather in a society which builds socialism) has been formulated in terms emphasizing its ideological importance. It is thought to have a political and social meaning. Its appearance was the result of the victory of that tendency in the Communist Party of the Soviet Union which favored active implementation of the rules of history. These rules were said to lead toward the communist society. A plan was preferred to spontaneity. Determinism was played down, and emphasis was placed on the consciousness of the members of the socialist society. The individual was considered capable of response to social incentives, able to train and reform himself. The influence of the individual on his environment was stressed. While social institutions were tightly integrated into the mechanism of the state's undertaking of the task of social economic reconstruction, demands and opportunities for the individual increased.[6]

4 Vyshinskii, Osnovnye zadatchi nauki sovetskogo sotsialisticheskogo prava 38 (1938).
5 Vyshinskii, *supra* note 4, at 54.
6 Bauer, The New Man in Soviet Psychology 2–24, 128–50 (1952).

As a Soviet author explained, the chief characteristic of the Soviet citizen is his ability to identify his interests with those of his nation and with its ideology:

The harmony of the national and individual interests in the socialist community finds expression in the identity of two great forces, the people and communism.[7]

Employment in governmental enterprises and institutions represents the most important form of individual participation in the social and economic activity of the socialist order. In consequence, work determines individual status irrespective of all other criteria of social status. A Soviet jurist who wrote on the development of Soviet labor law (1949) thus described the legal position of the Soviet worker under Stalin's regime:

In the socialist society there is no difference in principle and quality between draftee labor and labor performed by voluntarily entering into labor relations by taking employment. When we say that in the socialist society the principle of voluntary labor is recognized, we are not speaking of some kind of abstract principle of free labor and trade in a liberal and bourgeois sense, a principle which would be treated as a value per se.

Under the conditions of socialist society . . . it is impossible to secure the principle "from each according to his ability" without pressure by the state and law regarding the universal duty of work.[8]

The collapse of Stalin's regime initiated a new attitude toward labor. For quite some time changes in production methods, refinements of modern industrial equipment, the need for higher skills in the labor force, and individualization of human contribution in the processes of production militated against the militaristic approach to the discipline of labor. It thus became necessary to adopt new methods of control and to base the participation of the Soviet citizen on a higher degree of voluntary support for the regime and its policy. The Draft of Basic Principles of Labor Legislation of the USSR and of the Union Republics defined the new policy as follows:

Soviet social order established all conditions for stimulating and developing among the working people a new socialist attitude to labor. In

7 Aleksandrov, O moralnom oblike sovetskogo cheloveka 30 (1948).
8 Dogadov, "Istoria razvitia sovetskogo trudovogo prava," Uchonye Zapiski, Leningradskogo Universiteta 163, 168 (No. 2, 1949).

socialist society an increasing role belongs to moral incentives to labor for the good of the society. One of the manifestations of the new attitude to labor is demonstrated by the active participation of the working people in industrial management and general all-national socialist competition which aims at raising the productivity of labor, and continued raising of social welfare.

Communist forms of labor are on the increase. Simultaneously with the gradual disappearance of the fundamental difference between intellectual and physical forms of labor ... are created conditions for the transformation of work into a primary necessity of life for all members of society.

A major role in the education of workers in the communist attitude to labor and the realization of the workers' participation in industrial management, increasing their material welfare and level of culture belongs to the trade unions.[9]

Thus, the discipline of regimentation has been replaced by the discipline of voluntary involvement in the affairs of the state and social organizations. Soviet society and *homo sovieticus* have arrived, according to this view, at that point in the general progress of the techniques of social ordering where it is possible to realize the highest ideal of social discipline. At the same time the highest degree of freedom is possible, since the ultimate attainment of social discipline will be followed by the disappearance of all forms of state coercion. This moment will arrive, Lenin predicted:

[W]hen all will learn to govern, and will really manage social production themselves, they will themselves be in charge of accounting and control ... then avoiding this, all-national accounting and control shall become so extremely difficult and exceptional, and will be followed indeed by such quick and serious penal repression ... that the necessity to abide by simple, fundamental rules of social life shall become a habit.[9a]

A draft of the law regarding the increased role of society in the struggle with violations of Soviet legality and rules of socialist coexistence provided in Article 1:

Each Soviet citizen has a duty not only to obey the laws, conform to the discipline of labor, protect and strengthen the state and social property, follow the rules of socialist coexistence, but also to insist on the same from other citizens and actively to struggle with all anti-social doings.[10]

9 SGP 3–4 (No. 10, 1959).
9ª Lenin, The State and Revolution, 33 Soch. 155.
10 Izvestia, Oct. 23, 1959.

The law thus proposes to establish a new relationship between the governmental mechanism of law enforcement and the functioning of social structures. They share the same role with the state, and the individual citizen is drawn directly into the processes of government and enforcement of the rules of social behavior, which consist of formal commands of the law and rules of socialist coexistence.

Thus, the state aims at encompassing in the domain of public control that area of life which hitherto has been beyond the reach of legal rule. A higher stage of social development, in the opinion of the Soviet leaders, calls for the control of personal relations between the citizens of the soviet polity. While the province of *laissez faire* was shrinking in the realm of contract and property, the province of personal relations remained the last bastion of freedom.[11]

A high degree of regimentation of individual life in Soviet society is a necessity. This follows from the need for new types and methods of social action in the achievement of social goals unrealizable through normal methods of ordering and coercion. Some of the difficulties in this connection may be gauged from the decisions of the Polish Supreme Court, which has proved hesitant to enforce full control of private affairs. In one case, an employee, dismissed from service for refusal to participate in "social action," sued for damages. The Court stated:

The duty of social work is one of the principles of socialist coexistence in the People's State. It is independent of the fact whether a citizen is employed by a socialist enterprise . . . and violation of a duty of social

11 In the words of Scrutton L.J. in the Court of Appeal: "[It] is quite possible for the parties to come to an agreement by accepting a proposal with the result that the agreement concluded does not give rise to legal relations. The reason of this is that the parties do not intend that their agreement shall give rise to legal relations. This intention may be implied from the subject matter of the agreement, but it may also be expressed by the parties. In social and family relations such an intention is readily implied. . . ." [1923] 2 K.B. 261 at 288.

In the case of Balfour v. Balfour, Lord Atkin observed: "[I]t is necessary to remember that there are agreements between parties which do not result in contracts within the meaning of that term in the law. The ordinary example is where two parties agree to take a walk together or where there is an offer and acceptance of hospitality. Nobody would suggest in ordinary circumstances that those agreements result in what we know as contract. . . ." [1919] 2 K.B. 571 at 578.

work cannot be considered per se a violation of duties resulting from the contract of employment, and as such may not be used as a reason for the dissolution of the contract of work. On the other hand it cannot be ruled out that, in some circumstances a drastic non-compliance with the duty of social work may justify a loss of confidence in the employee so that continued employment even for a short period of time is no longer possible. This may, however, apply to exceptional circumstances, which would indicate such a hostility toward the institution in which the employee works, that leaving him there would jeopardize the work of the institution.[12]

The high standards of conformity by the Soviet masses has been achieved by propaganda and by the monopoly of all forms of political and social advancement. The new tasks, however, call for a much broader and deeper degree of conformity and for the rise of labor productivity. In particular, the improved situation in the supply of durable consumer goods has opened new channels for effecting further the total conformity of *homo sovieticus,* not only in political and social ideals, but also in the style of "socialist coexistence." As an editorial in the leading Soviet legal periodical pointed out:

Until recent times, the problem of meeting the property interests of the citizens was linked in the civilistic literature with the question of the transfer of objects of material value into personal ownership. In the present conditions of the developed communist construction, as never before, arises the necessity to develop legal provisions concerning such relations of the citizens with the socialist organizations, which would make available the use of various objects of material value without making them personal property.[13]

This new development represents the single most important step in the reconstruction of the attitude of the Soviet citizen toward his social duties. The fact that social organizations shall control the means of adding meaningfully to individual existence, either through the control of recreation or travel opportunities, or ownership of car pools, or other means of recreation, while sharing with the state an interest in individual performance at the place of work and in various forms of social actions, will strengthen general discipline at work, in the streets, in public meetings, and even at home.

12 Nowe Prawo (No. 4, 1955).
13 "XXI sjezd KPSS i zadatchi pravovoi nauki," SGP 7 (No. 2, 1959).

RE-EDUCATION

In spite of the abolition of capitalist forms of economy, ideologies and habits rooted in capitalist forms of production have survived into the new social and economic order. Crimes, common weaknesses, and various shortcomings of human nature, which according to Marxist doctrines were a reflection of the old order of the society, have also failed to disappear, and human nature continues to be out of tune with the new shape of things. As late as 1936, which was the year of the Stalin Constitution and its announcement of the liquidation of the classes, *Pravda* reported with a good deal of exasperation: "Egotism, indifference, laziness and cowardice, will survive the abolition of the subdivision of the society into classes by which they were produced." [14]

Direct concern with the moral and ethical convictions of the socialist citizen was also caused by another phenomenon. As Soviet leadership and society have discovered, this called for an educational campaign since laws and regulations were unable to provide an efficient remedy. As stated in a Polish periodical:

A dissatisfied guest in a tourist hotel, a passenger whose bus is late, a client poorly served by the water department, etc., have no legal powers against the institutions which are obliged to serve their needs. The only remedy, writing complaints to the authorities, brings no results. This state of affairs is accepted as a necessary evil which will disappear in some indefinite future. . . . We remain powerless before the ill will and lack of courtesy shown by various people in various state-run enterprises. We still have the legal code of the capitalist system which simply did not envisage situations which occur today. In the capitalist system, incompetence was restricted by free competition. Today we are ready to accept the principle of priority of national interests, and the resulting hierarchy of public needs, but this does not mean that we can tolerate the lack of legal equality in cases when we can afford certain services. . . . If for national reasons we cannot afford all types of public services as yet, we must nevertheless be assured that in the services we do have, we are equal partners and the law defends both sides.[15]

Quite early, therefore, the general education of the public into the ways of the new social reality had to accomplish two goals. One

14 Pravda, editorial, April 7, 1936.
15 Przegląd kulturalny, March 31, 1960.

consisted of eradicating the remnants of capitalism in the minds of the people. The second was to make the Soviet citizen conform to the new reality under socialism, and later communism. For the time being, the Soviet citizen, although not hostile to the regime, was found unable to participate spontaneously in the great task of socialist reconstruction without proper direction and control and a simultaneous process of re-education in the course of law enforcement. Many of the communist leaders were convinced, upon observing the state of the collective and individual mind in Soviet society, that the achievement of the final goal would depend upon the total reconstruction of the Soviet man.[16]

From the very beginning, the courts were considered the most important instrument for the inculcation of the new attitudes. Vyshinskii, the standard bearer of the idea of the legal offensive in the struggle for more perfect forms of social life, was convinced that:

The Soviet court participates directly in the historic venture of the construction of the Communist society. Punishing pitilessly plunderers of the socialist property, thieves, swindlers, speculators, hooligans, do-nothings, and absentees from work, our courts burn out the familiar stigma of capitalism which have still survived in Soviet life. Our Courts struggle against these survivals in the human conscience, . . . educating the bearers of such survivals.[17]

The Soviet Supreme Court, in its directives issued by its Plenary Session, required the judges

. . . to bear in mind when rendering judgments their most important role as acts of socialist justice which demand from the judge a particular consciousness of his responsibility for their correct political content. . . .[18]

The 1926 Judiciary Act, which first formulated the educational role of the Soviet courts, defined their tasks to include, among others (Article 1c): "To strengthen social and labor discipline and the solidarity of the toilers and to educate them in law." The 1933 Act used a somewhat broader formula:

By all its activities, the court shall educate the citizens of the USSR in the spirit of devotion to the country and the cause of socialism, in

16 Komarov, "K voprosu ob unichtozhenii klassov," SGP 11 (No. 3, 1936).
17 Vyshinskii, Teoria sudebnykh dokazatelstv v sovetskom prave 25 (1950).
18 Karev, Sovetskoe sudoustroistvo 23 (1951).

the Spirit of precise and unswerving execution of the Soviet laws, of watchful attitude toward socialist property, of labor discipline, of an honest attitude toward governmental and public duties, and of respect for the rules of socialist community life.

The educational role of the Soviet courts was restated in the various legislative acts which followed the end of the Stalinist regime and initiated the reform of the legal system in Russia.[19]

In Eastern Europe, which became a part of the Soviet bloc, the educational functions of the socialist courts and of the socialist law were fully recognized. So, for instance, Article 40 of the Hungarian Constitution of 1949, stated that "courts of the Hungarian People's Republic shall . . . educate the workers to respect the rules of socialist communal life." A Czech textbook, commenting on Section 4 of the Czechoslovak law on the judiciary (1952) which contains a provision similar to that of the Hungarian Constitution, stated that it is a duty of the Czechoslovak court to educate backward citizens who have violated the laws of the country "under the influence of the survivals of capitalism in their minds." [20]

19 Article 20 of the General Principles of Criminal Legislation of the Soviet Union and of the Union Republics stated: "A penalty . . . aims at reforming and re-educating the convicted person in the spirit of an honest attitude toward labor, of strict execution of laws, of respect for the rules of a socialist community. . . ."

A similar formula insisting on the education of citizens in the spirit of strict observance of Soviet laws and of respect for the rules of everyday life in a socialist community is contained in the general principles of criminal procedure (art. 2) and in the general principles of legislation on judiciary which defines the duties of the Soviet courts as follows:

"By all its activities the court shall educate the citizens of the USSR in the spirit of devotion to their country and the cause of communism, the spirit of precise and unswerving execution of Soviet laws, a solicitous attitude towards socialist property; observance of labor discipline; an honest attitude toward governmental and public duties; and respect for the rights, honor and dignity of the citizens and for the rules of socialist community life."

The Draft of the General Principles of Civil Procedure was less specific and mentioned that the educational goal of the Soviet civil law courts was to instill into the minds of Soviet citizens a "solicitous attitude toward socialist property, observance of labor discipline and respect for the rules of life in a socialist society."

20 Trestni Pravo (general part) 13 (1955); *cf.* also Hungarian Judiciary Act, Law II, 1954 TV.; *cf.* Albanian Law No. 1284 of June 9, 1951,

In the process of re-education, remnants of the capitalist order were to be eradicated and replaced by obedience to socialist laws and adherence to the "rules of life in the socialist community." In this connection, the term "rules of life" seems to indicate a certain style of life under socialism. But this concept is also used with reference to more concrete tasks within the legal system. Thus, "rules of life in the socialist community" are held to constitute an additional source of rules for guiding judicial action when more specific rules are lacking.[21] They also provide a general guide for the validity of individual legal transactions.[22] The "rules of life in a socialist com-

---

on the Judiciary (G.Z., Law No. 1284, No. 20, 1951). According to the Albanian Law on Government Attorneys (G.Z., Law No. 274, No. 86, 1946) the duty of the government attorneys is to educate private citizens in the understanding of the law of communist order. The Polish judiciary act of 1950 (art. 3) calls upon the courts "to exert all their efforts to educate citizens in a spirit of loyalty to the People's Poland, so that they will observe principles of the People's legality, the discipline of labor, and will have a solicitous attitude to socialist property."

21 *Cf. supra* at 24–26.
22 *Cf. supra* at 104–5.
Sec. 9 of the Bulgarian Law on Contracts stated: "Parties have the right to determine freely the content of the contract as long as it is not contrary to law, to the national economic plan and to the rules of life in a socialist community."

Article 58 of the Civil Code of the RSFSR permits the use of one's property within the limits determined by the law. Polish law on the General Principles of the Civil Legislation (art. 3) stated:

"Law shall be applied and construed in accordance with the principles of the order and the aims of the people's state. Nobody shall use his rights in a manner contrary to the principles of social life in the people's state. Any legal transaction contrary to the law or rules of social life shall be invalid. Any declaration of will shall be interpreted in accordance with the principles of social life in the people's state" (DU 34/1950).

The Czechoslovak Civil Code of 1950 expressed the same principle in somewhat different terms: "The Social order of the People's Republic and its socialist construction guaranteed by the constitution are the foundation of private rights" (sec. 1). "Nobody shall abuse his private rights to the prejudice of the society" (sec. 3).

The Hungarian Civil Code of 1959 contains the most developed system of provisions dealing with the effect of social and political conditions in a socialist state on the private rights: (sec. 4) (1) "In exercising civil rights and performing civil obligations the parties shall show such conduct as to ensure that the enforcement of their interests be in conformity with the interests of society."

munity" thus appear in a double role. In the first place, they provide
a general ethical and moral code of behavior for a member of socialist society to guide him in areas of life which are not easily regulated by the formal provisions of the law. In the second place, they
provide a central concept in the legislative techniques peculiar to
Soviet lawmaking, which must resort to vague and broad formulas
in order to meet constant fluctuations of policy. As conditions of life
change, it becomes possible to force upon the Soviet citizen new,
stricter, and more exacting standards of behavior. Thus, "rules of
life" acquire new meaning tending toward ever higher individual
involvement in the affairs of the socialist community.

Soviet laws are deeply concerned with the enforcement of the
new mode of life, which, however, seems to take root with great difficulty. Hence, the resort is made to extralegal concepts which constitute the rationale both of the legal order and of individual behavior.

The common characteristic of the two orders, that established
by the law in force and the other by the rules of life in a socialist
community, is that they both contain identical commands vis-à-vis

---

(2) "In civil law relations everybody shall act by mutual cooperation and in accordance with the demands of socialist coexistence.
Cooperation shall be achieved by strictly performing all obligations and
by exercising all rights in conformity with the function of such rights."
(sec. 5) (1) "Misuse of rights is prohibited by this Act."
(2) "The exercise of a right shall be deemed to be the misuse
thereof if such exercise aims at an object incompatible with the social
function of the rights, particularly where such exercise might result in
damaging national economy, in interfering vexatiously with the citizens, in prejudicing their rights and lawful interests, or in producing
undue advantages."
Polish Supreme Court, in one of the rare cases which involved the
analysis of art. 3 of the General Principles of Civil Legislation, stated
as follows:
"Article 3 of the General Principles . . . determines general principles
of individual rights, stating that the use of individual rights is permitted
inasmuch only as it is not contrary to the principles of life in a people's state. . . . Consequently . . . article 3 constitutes a valid defense
against a claim addressed to the defendant, but it may not serve as a
basis for independent claims to the creditor, in particular a claim for
the reduction of the debt or any other modification of his liabilities or
obligations. Such a claim would have to be based on a concrete legal
provision permitting for the reform of the legal relationship between
the parties." Decision of April 25, 1955, in PiP 529 (1955).

the socialist citizen in the form of two institutions: the economic plan [23] and labor discipline. Both are absolute. Human transactions contrary to the plan are not valid. Commands of the discipline of labor are equally absolute. As a Soviet treatise stated:

Socialist labor relations can by no means be reduced to the rights and obligations of the parties. . . . The social position of the citizen as a member of the socialist enterprise cannot be defined in terms of rights and duties.[24]

With reference to these two institutions of the Soviet social and economic order, commands and prohibitions are formulated in much the same manner as are good morals in civil codes, i.e., as determinative of the proper attitude of the individual to problems of collective life. But their striking feature, directly pertaining to the task of re-making the Sovict man, is the diversity of legal provisions concerned

23 *Cf. supra* at 94–95.

As the Polish Supreme Court stated: "One of the functions of the state is the management of the national economy. Consequently, a violation of socio-economic interests of the state must be considered as the violation of public order. . . ." Decision of May 28, 1949, ZOIC 13 (1950).

This statement must be read with reference to the basic assumptions of the Soviet legal and social order. By itself a statement of this type means nothing novel, as economic life determines the content of human relations and conditions of individual life. According to the traditional view, a legal system operates independently of the economic laws, while socialist planners claim that the economic plan, which is a legal enactment, has subordinated the laws of economy to human will. Economic planning integrated laws of economy into the positive legal system. *Cf. supra.*

"Such a phrase as laws of political economy, laws of history, laws of statistics has no dependence whatever on any conception of a tribunal or a lawgiver, or of doing justice. It signified only the normal results, as collected by observation or deduced by reasoning, of conditions, and (where human action is concerned) habits and motives, assumed to exist and to have effect. Whether we like these results or not, whether and to what extent these conditions are within the control of deliberate human action, and in what direction, if at all, we shall endeavor to modify the conditions or counteract the results,—may be matters deserving to be most carefully weighed; but they belong to a different order of consideration." Pollock, First Book of Jurisprudence for Students of Common Law 20 (1903).

24 Aleksandrov & Pasherstnik, Sovetskoe trudovoe pravo 120 (1952).

with the effect of legal transactions contrary to the economic plan or the consequences of the breach of labor discipline. Sanctions in civil laws applicable to breaches of rules of life in a socialist community are combined with criminal provisions in the penal laws. A proper labor record is not only a matter of the individual's economic position. It is also a matter of social status and is rewarded in many intangible forms, determinative of ethical level and progressive attitudes. The draft of the law on increasing the role of society in the struggle with violations of Soviet legality and the rules of socialist coexistence makes it quite clear that the main problem is the question of proper technique in achieving the basic target, i.e., the reformation of practical human ethics:

Soviet citizens work nobly in all sectors of communist construction, honor strictly their social obligations, follow Soviet laws, and respect the rules of socialist life. However, there are still people who live an ignominious life, commit criminal offenses and other anti-social acts. By their behavior they make it difficult for other Soviet people to live quietly and work, and cause damage to the society. It is necessary to struggle decisively with such violators of Soviet legality and rules of the socialist coexistence. However, not in all circumstances is it necessary to apply to them measures of administrative coercion, or penal repression. In a number of cases such people may be reformed under the influence of the collective.[25]

A ruling for the guidance of Hungarian courts issued by the Supreme Court provides an illustration of the extent of the mental reorientation required from a member of a socialist society. The Supreme Court stated that the so-called stabilization clause provided for in private contracts was invalid because

. . . at the time of the stabilization, it was the court's duty toward our people to regard the value of the forint with realistic optimism, faith and confidence, and this is still our duty. A covenant lacking these characteristics may not be enforced by the courts.[26]

The ruling was issued despite the fact that an express provision of an act issued during the interwar period definitely permitted such

25 *Cf. supra* 115.
26 Biber, "Reevaluation of Money Claims in Hungary," 2 Highlights 228 (1954); Leading Decision of the Hungarian Supreme Court of March 1, 1950, Pkt 5837/1949.

stabilization clauses in private contracts. An act of prudence permissible under the law, an act of foresight calculated to minimize the effect of economic instability, was declared incompatible with the duties of citizens toward society. The new social order required that a contract between private citizens be inspired by confidence toward the new state. Under the new order, the success of the individual depends far more upon the success of the whole than upon his perspicacity and the arrangements which he can personally make. The competitive spirit of the capitalist economic system is replaced by the paramount interests of the whole.

The need for the re-education of the new man is carried down to family relations. Divorce and guardianship cases are a mine of information on the struggle for the reshaping of the legal convictions of the citizenry at large. Thus, the Polish Supreme Court issued a ruling for the guidance of lower courts amounting to a real *privilegium Paulinum:*

Conflicting ideologies on political and social questions, especially if one of the spouses represents a progressive conception of life, and the other, on the contrary, a backward one, justify divorce.[27]

The reshaping of the national economy and the ideological reconstruction of society have given a new meaning to problems of guardianship and arrangements substituting for parental care. Thus, the East German Supreme Court ruled (April 27, 1951) that, in general, antiquated notions such as raising a child in a family home was healthier and better than any other arrangement were no longer valid. It asserted that sometimes it is salubrious for the spiritual and physical welfare of the child to separate him completely from the influence of the parents. The court remarked that

... in the new socialist order the weakened influence of the parents, particularly in divorced families, is fully compensated by the influence of the ideological youth organizations.[28]

27 Dec. 11, 1951; *cf.* Schmied, "Das Familienrecht der Volksdemokratien, 1945–1951," 17 Zeitschrift für ausländisches und internationales Privatrecht 227 ff. (1952); *cf.* canon 1127 of the Codex Iuris Canonicus of 1917; Woywod, A Practical Commentary of the Code of Canon Law 811 ff. (1948).
28 1 OGDDR 136 (1951).

In the same spirit, the District Court of Moravska Ostrava (Czechoslovakia) ruled (January 28, 1953):

When deciding the question whether guardianship of a child should be left to its mother or to a social welfare institution, the probation of the mother during work is to be taken into consideration. If the mother is a shock worker, or a member of the Communist Party, the child can be left to her, as her moral and political qualifications guarantee honorable education.[29]

In another case, the same court removed a son from the care of his parents and placed him under the guardianship of a social welfare institution. The court cited the son's nonaccomplishment of the shift in the mines, the parents obviously having failed "to educate their son in the proper attitude toward his working duties." [30]

29 Socialisticka Zakonnost 20 (No. 1, 1953).
30 *Ibid.*

A Soviet manual for the people's assessors explained that "Soviet law plays an important and progressive role in strengthening and perfecting the productive relations of the socialist society. While fulfilling this function, Soviet law supports the development of productive forces of our society. Technical development, improvement of work habits ... constitute indispensable conditions for a gradual transition to communism." Posobie dla narodnykh zasedatelej 9 (1955).

An important tool in the implementation of the moral reconstruction program in the Soviet Union was created in the form of a network of boarding schools following a recommendation of the Twentieth Congress of the Party. It expanded with great rapidity and has had a marked success. It is said that parents have swamped the new schools with requests for admissions. Schools are credited with important achievements concerning the development among their students of these moral virtues which should characterize good members of the socialist society. An article in *Pravda* by the director of the new school system listed these achievements in the terminology which is familiar to those who are conversant with those aspects of Soviet laws which describe the life in a socialist order: devotion to and love of work; ability to provide for their own needs; and students have become more polite, full of consideration for the collectivity in which they live. In order to improve the performance of the schools the director asked for better cooperation of the Komsomol (Organization of Communist Youth) in selecting leaders for the organization of Pioneers, an organization of Communist children. Kozmin, "Two Years of Boarding Schools," Pravda Oct. 9, 1958. *Cf.* Hazard, "Le droit soviétique et le dépérissement de l'État," in 8 Travaux et conférences, Université Libre de Bruxelles 91 (1960).

The educational quality of the Soviet legal system is due primarily to the fact that rules of law are identical with rules of the moral code:

Communist morals include observance of Soviet socialist laws, with the idea that this is the most important social duty. . . . Socialist law formulates the same principles as do socialist morals. There is not, and cannot be, a division between them. . . . Socialist law is an instrument adapted to the realization of the same goals as socialist morals. Socialist law does not know any other goals than to aid the destruction of the capitalist world and to build a new communist society.

The unity of content of legal and moral command is, as a Soviet jurist has observed, a result of the fact of their common origin, i.e., from the economic conditions in a socialist society:

Morals, as other forms of social consciousness—law, science, and politics —depend on social existence and on the economic conditions of the development of the society.

Soviet morals support all those values, and only those values, which support the march of humanity toward communist forms of life. The most important is the abolition of contradictions between the individual and social interests:

Liquidation of private property as regards means of production, has liquidated the contradictions between the individual and society. Socialist property, the economic basis of the new social ties between humans, is also the basis for new morals.[31]

31 Aleksandrov, O moralnom oblike sovetskogo cheloveka 4–5, 30 (1948); *cf.* also Kareva, Pravo i nrastvennost v sotsialisticheskom obshchestve 11–13 (1952); in a special audition, "Morals of yesterday and today" (May 12, 1961), Polish Radio complained of a discrepancy between public opinion and the courts as to what constitutes a criminal offense: "When criminal offenses in the classical sense are tried," the commentator stated, "public opinion and courts are in agreement. When, however, crimes against the state are prosecuted, not only public opinion sides with the offenders, but their fellow workers defend them, and witnesses are reluctant to incriminate them. . . . All that which is connected with traditional morals is properly understood by the public. However, offenses directed against new forms of life, resulting from socialist transformations, escape social censure." Reported by the FEC News from Poland, May 22, 1961.

Thus, the Soviet man has no need for an *echelle de valeurs* which would motivate his behavior as an independent factor of social life. The identification of morals with legal commands suggests that normal legal techniques are not sufficient to meet the needs for social regulation in the Soviet order. And, indeed, the commands addressed to citizens to improve their work habits, their sense of obligation toward society, and the sense of sacrifice and to see the welfare of their children in terms of their ability to serve the community are beyond the range of legal rule. Identification of the law with morals tends to formalize moral sanction and provide for effective channels for its enforcement in a manner highly resembling and indeed sometimes identical with the enforcement of the law.[32]

The Polish Supreme Court drew the attention of the lower courts to the impact which the new morals have had on the problems of criminal law:

Homicide under the stress of emotion . . . may mean something else in the capitalist state, and something else in our society in view of the basic difference between bourgeois and socialist morals.

A most classic example of the crime committed under the impulse of strong emotion is . . . homicide motivated by jealousy. At the basis . . . of the judicial practice in capitalist states lay morals qualitatively different from socialist morals. In People's Poland, vengeance and jealousy arising from craving for power of man over man are considered as base emotions and contrary to the foundations of her order, and in the process of liquidation through the raising level of culture. An offender guilty of the crime from such motives cannot invoke a state of strong emotion.[33]

A different use of the force of morals is represented by the technique which makes criminal trials in courts also trials by public opinion. This is expressed in the conviction that the interpretation of criminal law is a political interpretation.[34] The administration of

32 I Co 5/55 PiP 847 (1955); *cf.* Decision of the Polish Supreme Court of Sept. 18, 1952, No. C, 1283, ZOIC 84 (1953).
33 PiP 895 (1952).
34 "Any interpretation of criminal law is primarily a political interpretation. This fact is camouflaged by the bourgeois jurists who think that by acknowledging political interpretation of criminal laws they admit thereby the reactionary content of the bourgeois laws. Soviet science of criminal law declares openly that interpretation of criminal laws is essentially a political interpretation. The only correct and truly scholarly

justice in the socialist states emphasizes the need for direct involvement of public condemnation in the process of sentencing by the court. In order to arouse the public, to involve the masses in the eradication of social errors, trials are held on the spot. Contrary to all precepts of orderly judicial procedure, journalistic campaigns are conducted demanding imposition of harsh punishments, making an example of the criminals, etc. A directive of the Soviet minister of justice instructed Soviet judges (1947) to concentrate on the propaganda aspects of the case:

> The judge must know how to conduct court proceedings and how to write the decision . . . to show with the utmost clarity the political significance of the case, so that the defendant and those present in the court could see clearly the policy of government in the court action.[35]

It is not surprising, in view of the growing involvement of social organizations in governmental functions, that the new tendency is to identify punishment with social censure. The new methods not only dispense with the legalistic mechanics of the judicial process but also with the institution of courts. The administration of justice, including the imposition of severe punishments, is partly transferred into the hands of the public. Since the Twenty-first Congress of the Party, which was followed by a series of legislative measures seeking to draw social organizations into the process of enforcing the rules of life in socialist society, there is no longer a hard and fast distinction between the realm of judicial action and that of moral condemnation, between the technique of public censure and judicial process, between the correctional measures provided by the law and administered by courts and those applied without the guidance of the law by social organizations.[36]

CRIMES OF OFFICIALS

A high degree of integration of individual life into the general scope of the activities of the state has blurred the line dividing what

---

interpretation of criminal law is interpretation permeated by communist partisanship." Chkhikvadze, *Sovetskoe ugolovnoe pravo, obshchaia chast* 115–16 (1952).

35 *Sots. zak.* 5 (No. 2, 1947).

36 *Cf. infra* at 249 ff.

is private and accountable only in terms of personal responsibility from what is public and therefore subject to stricter criteria of accountability. The extent of change in the position of the individual in socialist polity is intimately connected with changes which legislation and court practice have introduced regarding the criminal responsibility of public officials for violations of laws while in office.

The principles governing the criminal responsibility of officials, as formulated in modern European criminal laws, are readily evidenced in the Polish Criminal Code of 1932, which may be taken as an expression of modern standards in the field of criminal legislation.[37] The Code, still in force, has a separate chapter dealing with offenses of officials. This covers various specific offenses such as abuse of power (Article 286), disclosure of official secrets (Article 289), receiving material or personal advantage (Article 290), etc. The Code also provides that, in addition to those offenses directly connected with the exercise of public duties, for any offense committed by an official in the performance of his duty or in connection therewith, the court may impose a penalty higher by one-half than the highest penalty fixed for such an offense in the relevant statutes (Article 291). Public officials are defined as not only those in the service of the central or local government but also as persons charged with duties connected with the affairs of the central or local government and employees of any public institution (Article 292).

As soon as the Code went into operation, controversy arose as to the meaning of the concept of "public official" and as to the definition of his offense. Polish courts tended toward a restrictive interpretation of these two concepts. The Supreme Court considered as public officials only those who in some manner were connected with the functions charged to public administration. The mere fact that a person was employed by the government was not enough. He had to be responsible for public functions involving what was known in European jurisprudence as "imperium," which might be rendered as "exercise of sovereign power." Persons employed in government economic enterprises, e.g., members of the administration of national

37 Lemkin & McDermott, The Polish Penal Code and the Law of Minor Offenses (1939).

forests, farms, or state railways, were not held to be public officials unless they exercised governmental functions based upon legislative authorization. For instance, a guard protecting game against poachers was under the protection of the law and was responsible for crimes committed in the exercise of his duties in this connection as a public official.

After 1945, the continued expansion of government control over various fields of the national economy, i.e., the nationalization of trade and industry and the collectivization of trades, agriculture, and the professions, created a new situation. The administration of economic resources and the management of enterprises became functions of the government. This, in fact, was reflected in a great number of laws providing for penal sanctions in connection with the responsibilities and duties of the officials employed in new areas of government activity. These new laws reflected a new attitude toward the two concepts which were restrictively interpreted before the war, namely, who was a government official and what constituted a crime in office. The Small Penal Code of 1946, which contained most of the regulations adapting the criminal law of Poland to new conditions, provided that employees of central or local government enterprises, or enterprises in which the government had financial interest or which were under its administration, as well as employees of organizations in charge of functions delegated to them by the central or local government, should be considered as officials. In addition, managers and employees of cooperatives and audit unions came under the penal legislation applicable to officials.

Similar provisions have been enacted in other countries of Eastern Europe. In this field, as in other realms of socialist law, the purpose of the new legislation was to adapt the function of government to new responsibilities which differed profoundly from what was traditionally considered to be the function of government. The purpose of the new laws was to initiate a new attitude on the part of a public servant toward his duties. It was also a method of re-education. As a Soviet jurist wrote:

The causes for the commission of criminal offenses by government officials in the Soviet state have their root not in the socialist social relations ... but in the survival in the minds of the individual Soviet citizens of the remnants of bourgeois psychology and of morals, and views and convictions inherited from the bourgeois feudal apparatus of Tsarist Russia.[38]

The central problem which the new socialist legislation faced was the necessity of combining governmental functions with business techniques. Soviet legislation endeavored to achieve this by dropping the distinction between those functions involving the exercise of the public power of "imperium" and other duties. Thus, for instance, "abuse of power" involved all departure from the normal operation of government institutions or enterprises which caused financial losses, the violation of the social order or the rights of citizens protected by the law. Departures from the normal operations of the enterprise might include, as a Soviet jurist explained: "nonfulfillment of the plan, improper distribution of manpower or violation of the adopted technical process." [39]

In addition, Soviet legislators considered as crimes and violations of official duties bureaucratic *modus operandi* and attention to formal aspects of official duties as opposed to the business-like management of economic assets. Hence, a group of crimes grew up under the denomination: "careless attitude to official duties" (Article 111 of the RSFSR Criminal Code) and "bureaucratic attitude." Article 99 of the Criminal Code of the Ukraine defines the crime of the bureaucratic attitude as consisting of

... formalistic attitude to official duties, demonstrated in ignoring governmental or social interests or causing delays, or narrow mindedness in solution of problems, ignoring the control of the broad masses, and also careless and insensitive attitude to workers....

Furthermore, criminal liability in such situations was not predicated upon intent. The result was that any type of action or inaction, or simply the inability to make up one's mind, could be considered

38 Kirichenko, Vidy dolzhnostnikh prestuplentii po sovetskomu ugolovnomu pravu 5 (1959).

39 For the detailed analysis and case material *cf.* Grzybowski, "Directive Rulings of the Supreme Court in Criminal Matters," 6 Highlights 149–60 (1958); also Grzybowski, "New Trends in the Administration of Penal Justice in Poland (Offenses of Public Officials)," 2 Highlights, 37–42 (1954).

as a crime, provided that a causal relation between it and the economic failure of an industrial or business enterprise could be established.

The new Soviet legislation focused the courts' attention upon the objective elements of the crime rather than upon the personality of the offender and his criminal intent. The fact that a government official caused damage to the national economy was considered a sufficient ground of criminal responsibility. In Eastern Europe, where modern legislation emphasized the subjective elements of crime, it was necessary to perform a major operation in order to adapt penal policies to the Soviet pattern. This was accomplished for the most part by the means of directive rulings by the Supreme Court, ordering the lower courts to enforce the old and new criminal statutes with regard to the damage aspect of official actions or inactions.

So, for instance, in Poland the Supreme Court issued a directive ruling concerning criminal liability for crimes of officials committed under the influence of alcohol. In the code of 1932 such crimes were considered misdemeanors. Under the new ruling, however, the Court raised the degree of responsibility for offenses so committed to the responsibility for intentional crimes. On another occasion, the same Supreme Court instructed lower courts to measure their punishments according to the extent of the damage suffered by the public interest. The Court, however, admitted in the directive ruling that such was not the position of the Code itself, as the latter was concerned with the personality of the offender rather than with the extent of material damage. On a still different occasion, the Supreme Court identified this public interest with the fulfillment of the economic plan:

The plan is the fundamental law of the state and everything that delays or hampers the execution of the plan constitutes a violation of public interest which is protected by the law.[39a]

Under the Code of 1932, the adverse effect of a criminal act upon the success of the plan could be considered punishable only if the offender had this particular effect of his action or omission in mind. Under the new ruling, the personal attitude of the offender— his intent, negligence, or recklessness—was no longer essential.

Another feature of the impact of the Soviet model on the laws

[39a] *Ibid.*

of the satellite nations is the considerable extension of the function of the public official. Such followed from the new functions of the state. As the Bulgarian Supreme Courts explained:

The People's democratic state fulfills ... the function of organizing the economy and directing the cultural educational activities. This function is unknown to the bourgeois state. The bourgeois theory of the public law differentiates between acts of the state through which it exercises imperium ... from the acts through which it develops its economic activity. ... Such a theory cannot have currency in the people's democratic law, and the people's democratic state in which the functions of organizing the economy and leading the cultural-educational work are as important as the other function. The People's democratic state exercises its functions through the council of ministers ... and the enterprises. ...[40]

When in 1951 Bulgaria adopted the new criminal code, it defined (Section 333) as a public official

... anyone who is charged with the performance of service in a government office, cooperative, or other public organization, or who is entrusted with safeguarding public property—employed for a salary or gratuitously, permanently, or temporarily.

The meaning of this provision is clear when it is realized that all employment in industry and trade is government employment. As mere custody (even temporary) of the government property is enough to qualify the custodian as a public official, there is hardly anybody in government employ who could not be subject to stricter liability as a government official.

In its decision No. 37 of June 19, 1952, the Bulgarian Supreme Court declared the manager of a cooperative to be public official because he held a leading position in a cooperative. Similarly, the Court held responsible any person who exercised an official function in the absence of the regular occupant of the governmental position. The same applied, the Court stated, to those who were given the trust of safeguarding public property, even if there was involved only transportation of such property from one place to another. In one case, the Bulgarian Supreme Court held that a person appointed by

40 Sipkov, "The Concept of Public Official and Offense in Public Office," 2 Highlights 274 (1954).

the village policeman to guard a piece of agricultural machinery was a public official.[41]

A full theoretical explanation of the conceptual revision applied to the term "public official" in the socialist order was given by the Polish Supreme Court in its decision of August 22, 1950:

The concept of the official is linked in the pre-war practice in the capitalist order with the exercise of the sovereign power.... Although the term official was popularly used to designate a white collar worker in general ... the Criminal Code used this term with reference to state and local government officials.... In the capitalist order where economic activity was in the hands of the private owners, and the bureaucracy, both state and local, served to protect the domination of the exploiters, it had as such no economic functions....

The other characteristic of the bourgeois bureaucracy was its ... elite character which was among the others expressed in the different legal position of the government official.... In the new conditions of the People's Poland the administration of justice must be aware of the change in the meaning of the concept "public official" and of the criteria of his activities....

Elite position, caste, privileges of the hireling class, separatistic tendencies of the "class of officials" must be replaced by the equalization of all citizens on the basis of common participation in the management of the socialized property and common responsibility for the development and security of the state of the working people.

In view of the liquidation of the exploiting classes, the vast majority of the society is employed by the state, or industrial and agricultural cooperatives.... This fact has broadened the narrow traditional concept of the "official," as a servant of the oppressive apparatus of the exploiting classes and fills it with an altogether new ... content. "The economic official" in the people's state is a co-manager of the economic assets, which constitute the national property, and which is under the protection of the people's state.[42]

This theoretical position led to some extravagant consequences in practice. "All persons," stated the Polish Supreme Court, "employed in a government or government-controlled enterprises and therefore also workers at the workbench, must be considered as government officials." [43] In another case, the same Court found that

41 Sipkov, *supra* note 40, at 275.
42 Case No. K. 430, PiP 195 (No. 12, 1950).
43 Case No. K. 1290/48, Pip 639 ff. (No. 11, 1952).

a milkmaid on a government farm might be prosecuted under Article 286 of the Criminal Code, since Article 46 of the Small Penal Code of 1946 extended the application of penal provisions applicable to officials to the functionaries of government enterprises.[44]

According to the resolution passed by the bench of seven justices of the Polish Supreme Court (June 16, 1951), even a barmaid in a government restaurant might qualify as a government official.[45] In the Bulgarian practice, managers of cooperatives, storekeepers in cooperatives, cafeteria employees, and cashier-auditors in a co-operative have been declared liable under the Code for crimes of officials.[46] Soviet practice also tended to extend criminal punishment for crimes in office to persons engaged in purely technical functions. However, the Supreme Court of the Soviet Union put a limit to this practice and at the plenary session of November 30, 1956, refused to consider a crane operator, who had dropped sixteen bags of sugar into the sea while unloading a ship, as responsible for an offense in office.[47]

A purely pragmatic attitude defying any restriction of criminal responsibility either by the nature of the criminal act or by the class of persons involved was declared to be the rule in this type of criminal responsibility by the Polish Supreme Court:

All offenses, and in particular those committed by officials, must be considered in connection with the nature, spirit, and direction of the present social and political organization of the State, and the present political reality.

It is impossible therefore to consider offenses by officials from a purely formal or abstract standpoint, in view of the fact that various provisions regulating the scope of their powers, and providing restriction of their interference with the rights of the citizens have lost validity.[48]

A person performing certain services for a government office or enterprise may be considered as a public official and be punished as such even if he is not employed, occupies no position in a govern-

44 Case No. 1344/49, PiP 639 ff. (No. 11, 1952).
45 ZOIC 4 (1952).
46 Sipkov, *supra* note 40, at 272–73.
47 Kirichenko, *supra* note 38, at 276.
48 1 ZOIK 78 (1949).

ment office or enterprise, appears on no payroll, and even when his services are gratuitous and constitute an act of personal courtesy. Thus, a hunter (a private person) who was authorized by the district hunting inspector in Bulgaria to issue hunting licenses to other persons has been declared to be a government official.

It is not essential that rights and authorizations exercised by a person should be officially defined in any manner. A private person, obliged by a contract with a government commercial enterprise in Bulgaria to purchase on its behalf and in its name dried prunes and nuts and to report the amount of money received and the purchases made, was declared by the Bulgarian Supreme Court (decision No. 600 of September 18, 1951) to be a public official:

[A]s the text of Section 333 of the Criminal Code shows, the form of the act, on ground of which the work is assigned to a person or on ground of which he is under duty and obligation to safeguard public property, is of no decisive importance for the solution of the problem whether he is or is not a public official.[49]

Finally, it is not essential that obligations, rights, or powers should be precisely determined in connection with the economic, administrative, and professional tasks which are to be accomplished. Thus, the Supreme Court of Bulgaria stated that (September 18, 1952):

Each person who is given or entrusted with a labor order, a task or service with salary and compensation in any form whatsoever, or without compensation, and who is authorized to exercise administrative, economic or other functions, adherent to a public official or on the grounds of a given mandate, acts as a public official. Every employed person, no matter how unimportant his function in the entire system of government and socialist economy is, should be considered a public official.[50]

It is readily discernible that the practice of qualifying practically everybody who enters into some relationship with the government authority in a socialist state as a "public official" has contributed seriously to the harshness of Soviet penal repression. Its purpose is not only to prevent occurrence of crimes. In addition, the practice

49 Sipkov, *supra* note 40, at 276.
50 *Ibid.*

seeks to alert society to the need for singular effort and devotion to duty, exceeding a civil servant's loyalty to his office or function. As the Polish Supreme Court explained:

In order to arrive at a proper understanding of charges brought against a government official occupying an economic post connected with his managerial activity, and in order to determine his responsibility, it is necessary to review his actions and omissions from the point of view of his duties of a good manager.... An official in such a post ought to take on his own initiative all measures to prevent loss or destruction of government property under his care, irrespective of whether his superior issued proper regulations.... Vigilance of that kind is obligatory in the system of planned economy, in which every public official ought to consider himself as co-manager of public property and to care for it in the same degree as if it were his private property.[51]

Stricter standards of criminal repression are necessitated in socialist societies by the absence of that criterion of efficiency provided by the market which reacts to mistakes or omissions irrespective of the intent or degree of culpability. Although its mechanisms are the judicial process and moral condemnation of society, penal sanction for the lack of success in the socialist society, nevertheless, had to assume the role of an economic sanction. Again, Polish practice is perhaps the best yardstick for appraising the new methods. So, for instance, the Polish Supreme Court found a captain of a harbor tug guilty of a criminal offense committed in office when he caused a collision with another ship. In describing the facts which in its opinion established the captain's guilt, the Court stated:

The accused, overestimating the resistance of ice, ordered higher speed than required, with the result that his order to reverse speed came too late.[52]

Similarly, Soviet courts consistently followed the practice of imposing harsh penalties for shortages caused by the inability to maintain proper accounting procedures. And this was true even though the error was due to illiteracy, or to lack of training and experience. That sentences of this type were still occurring after World War II seems to indicate that competence and qualifications were not

51 ZOIK 19 (1951).
52 PiP 650 (1950).

necessarily the qualities deemed essential for making appointments to official positions.[53]

In Poland, court practice followed strictly the Soviet pattern. So, for instance, the Supreme Court rejected an appeal from a lower court conviction by a manager of a cooperative whose failure to keep proper books resulted in chaos in the affairs of a cooperative. The defendant claimed that he had no training and no idea of book-keeping. The Court stated that this fact alone constituted no defense.[54] In 1951, a manager of a cooperative meat factory was found guilty because two other employees of the factory were processing meats from illicit slaughter, although it was proved that the accused had no knowledge of their practices.[55] In another case, the Supreme Court upheld the conviction of a forester who, owing to drunkenness, neglected his duties. His negligence resulted in several thefts in his section of the forest. The accused was, nevertheless, found guilty of abuse of power, a crime which under the Code of 1932 required intent.[56]

A considerable number of criminal cases involving the criminal responsibility of officials result from the conflicting criteria which decide the promotion of communist officialdom to leading positions in the economic or public life of the country. Some cases make it clear that some of the defendants had gained positions as a result of the "social promotion," which is a by-word for political reliability. As progress from capitalism to socialism means growing integration of various aspects of human activity into various forms of collective effort, the expansion of governmental function is also the process of constant re-education of members of the socialist society in the new forms of cooperation. Thus, a Bulgarian jurist explained the ethos of the reform of criminal law in his country, respecting its provisions concerning the responsibility of officials, as aiming at the application of stricter criteria of "criminal responsibility which will make its educational impact upon a greater circle of persons." [57]

---

53 Kirichenko, *supra* note 38, at 44.
54 Case No. K. 287/51, PiP 654 (1951).
55 Case No. I.K. 1690/51/1, PiP 568 (1953).
56 Case No. I.K. 1946/51, PiP 148 (1953).
57 Busov, Iuridicheska misul 37 (No. 2, 1953); *cf.* Mead, Soviet Attitude Towards Authority, An Interdisciplinary Approach to Problems of Soviet Character, in particular at 44–51 (1951).

A more recent trend in criminal practice of the Soviet Union,[58] started by the pronouncement of the Twenty-first Congress of the CPSU, to the effect that the Soviet Union has passed over to the period of communist construction, blurs even further the dividing line between government officials and private citizens engaged in work or performance of duties of public significance. One of the distinctions between the two categories of citizens had consisted of special protection to those who discharged public functions. The transition to communist forms of economic and social organization, which called for the cooperation of the people in enforcing the rules of life in a socialist community, also brought the demand that special protection be given those who, endowed with a greater sense of responsibility, took upon themselves the enforcement of the more perfect code of social behavior. As a Soviet jurist proposed:

It would be well to institute certain legal guarantees of the safety of citizens who voluntarily participate in the drive on law violations. The Draft Law on Increasing the Role of the Public in Combating Violations of Soviet Laws and the Rules of Socialist Society stresses that the activity of citizens in upholding public order and combating law violations is under the protection of the law. Supreme Soviets of the Union Republics are charged with establishing criminal liability for insulting, committing violence upon, and threatening reprisals against citizens in connection with the performance by them of their duty in the safeguarding of public order. The draft also formulates the principle of encouragement for citizens' taking an active part in the struggle against public disturbances and crime. Article 17 plainly states that these citizens shall be encouraged by state agencies and public organizations.[59]

LIBEL

The insulation of individual honor against libel represents a minor incident in the emergence of the socialist legal system. The problem of affording such protection is directly related, in the new regime, to the political role of the press. The latter has become one of the most important instruments of social control and official action. Its duty is to inform and exhort and to expose the enemies of the

58 *Cf. infra* at 249 ff.

59 Denisov, "O sootnoshenii gosudarstva i obshchestva v perekhodnyi ot kapitalizma do kommunizma period," SGP 29–40 (No. 4, 1960).

new order and the shortcomings of governmental and social organizations. It, indeed, leads the official apparatus of both government and
society in joint actions.

The growing complexity of the mechanism of the state and the
social structure of Soviet society has been accompanied by the increasing importance of the press. In Soviet reality, the criticism and
initiative of the press represent the only efficient means of cutting
through the tangled web of Soviet agencies and of striking directly at
problem spots in the social or economic life of the polity. Consequently, to impede its action in the name of individual interest would
be tantamount to raising an obstacle to a social action in which an
attack on a person would be only an incident.

In this method of social control, the position of the individual is
determined by the principle of self-criticism. It is the duty of the
Soviet man to embrace and emulate the criticism by the press and to
assist in the elimination of mistakes and shortcomings. The nature
of this response is dictated by the fact that press criticism is not solely
a matter of objective truth. In addition, there is involved a question
of party policy, which uses it as a method of progress. Zhdanov, the
Party's expert in matters of philosophy in the days of Stalin, explained the function of criticism and self-criticism as follows:

In the new Soviet society ... the struggle between the old and the new,
and consequently transition from the lower into the higher takes place ...
in the form of criticism and self-criticism, which forms the real force
of our progress, and a mighty weapon in the hands of our party. Undoubtedly this is a new pattern for progress, new type of development,
the new dialectical legality.[60]

Thus, suits for libel and damages in this context have disappeared
from the dockets of the socialist courts.

Inasmuch as the authority of the press as a social censor reflects
the authority of the party, the ideological upheaval in Poland in the
fall of 1956, resulting from the moral crisis in the Party ranks, has
produced a significant change in the attitude of the courts and of
those who have suffered from the methods so employed by the press in
the process of social control. Protection of individual dignity became,
in consequence, an issue of great practical importance, and a number

60 Zhdanov, Voprosy filosofii 270 (No. 1, 1947).

of libel suits against the communist press acquired the significance of political action to restore some of the personal freedom lost in the Stalinist period.

Under Article 255 of the Criminal Code of 1932, the accused was free from liability if the facts were proved to be true. Truth was a good defense. However, if the allegation was made publicly (and through the press), the law required that the accused prove additionally that he acted in defense of a well-founded public or private interest, either of his own or affecting other persons, and libel did not pertain to facts from the private or family life of the injured party.

The revival of the provisions of Article 255 of the Criminal Code has greatly restrained the censorial and educational activities of the press in Poland. As a countermeasure to these undesirable developments, the government has ordered that a draft of a new press law be prepared for enactment by the legislature. The regime hoped, by thus relaxing the strict provisions of the Code regarding criminal responsibility for slander, that some degree of freedom of action might thereby be restored to the government press.

It has been proposed to distinguish between private libel and libel committed by mass communication media. In the first instance, the former provisions of the Code would apply, and private persons would continue to be responsible under the strict rule of responsibility. In the second instance, i.e., libel by mass communication media, good faith would constitute a sufficient defense. Thus, under the proposed regime, defense would be easier in cases in which possible damage to individual honor and dignity was greater, while a private slanderer would have to prove the facts alleged against the injured party.[61]

In the discussion which followed, partisans of the strict legal protection of individual dignity insisted on continuing the old pattern on the ground that there was no compelling reason for departing from it:

Criticism represents an important force of progress under any, not only a socialist order. However, honest criticism and criticism attacking personal honor are two different things.

61 Sawicki, "Dobra wiara a zniesławienie w projekcie prawa prasowego," PiZ, Jan. 25, 1959; Papierkowski, "Niebezpieczne prawo," PiZ, April 19, 1959; Merz, "O dobra wiare," PiZ, June 16, 1959.

They went on to claim that there were no specific reasons why the protection of human dignity should be less important under socialism than under any other social order.[62]

In opposition to the view stressing the need for the strict protection of human dignity, the apologists for the less strict approach claimed that:

In the socialist order criticism is a vital necessity for social development; its function in our society is basically different from that in a society which is based on the system of exploitation of man by man.

The reason for different standards, they continued, lay in the nature of the interests involved. Although an innocent person might suffer harm, socialist criticism was in the interest of all.[63]

The proposed solutions are not a novelty in socialist legislative techniques. Indeed, the duality of approach in the legal protection of individual and socialist interests is typical of the criminal law of the Soviet type. Crimes which are not characteristic of the socialist social and economic order, i.e., those which represent an attack on traditional social and ethical values, are prosecuted according to the normal rules of responsibility. In these instances, the type of guilt (intentional and nonintentional) is decisive to determine criminal liability and severity of punishment. Definitions of crimes against the new regime tend to establish absolute criteria of responsibility. Punishment and its measure are determined exclusively by the objective criteria of social danger.[64]

In all likelihood, the Polish press law will be adopted as proposed by the government; otherwise, its ability for political action would be seriously curtailed. The very fact, however, that public pressure has brought about some limitation on governmental power to initiate political campaigns by means of attacking individual honor is highly significant. It suggests that a degree of the autonomous status of individual existence has survived the process of socialist integration.

In this respect, Poland is not an isolated example. In Hungary, Decree No. 17 of 1959 and the executive order adopted by the

---

62 Papierkowski, "A jednak contra legem," PiZ, Aug. 23, 1959.
63 Merz, "A jednak zgodnie z ustawą," PiZ, Aug. 23, 1953.
64 *Cf. infra* at 185 ff.

Council of Ministers of the same year on the responsibility for press offenses provide a mechanism for the defense of private honor against attack by the press. A journal is under obligation to publish, on the demand of an injured party, a refutation of charges which appeared in its columns. Criminal responsibility has been provided in the following situations: (1) seeking material advantage for publishing or not publishing a press material; (2) press activity without proper license; (3) failure to comply with a duty to publish a refutation; (4) willful publication of false information together with the refutation of earlier charges.[65]

The new press law of Yugoslavia, enacted in the fall of 1960, followed the Hungarian pattern. It gave the citizen the right to demand equal space and display in the newspapers, magazines, and radio and television programs for the purpose of refuting allegations made by public information media.[66]

REGIME OF PROPERTY

The theory of absolute rights inhering in the individual has always been little more than a symbol. Indeed, rights have always been subject to limitation by the interests of the collectivity. It is enough to point to the antiquity of the institution of eminent domain in its various forms and to modern developments reflecting on the institution of property and the freedom of contract to see all individual rights qualitatively restricted: a system of relative rather than absolute concepts. Even in the face of these limitations, however, it would be unrealistic to rule out of the legal system the idea of rights as defining the autonomous position of the private individual vis-à-vis the surrounding reality of persons and things.

One of the fundamental bases of the claim by the Soviet legal and social order to an exceptional place in human history lies in its novel approach to the institution of private rights, which are totally subordinated to the interests of society. Section 1 of the Soviet Code of 1922 declared that: "The law protects private rights except as they are exercised in contradiction to their social and economic purpose."

65 Obzor Wengerskogo Prava (No. 3, 1959).
66 Arts. 7, 34–51, Sl. L., No. 45, 1960.

However, it seems that the heart of the matter is not in the conditional guarantee of private rights, but in the presence of powerful forces of social change which affect the position of the individual in regard to collective existence. Provisions similar to that in the Soviet Code are a common feature of all civil law legislation which endeavors to describe systematically various aspects of human and social relations.[67] Policies of government, either in the form of the nationalization of the means of production or of planned transformation of the economic and social structures, cannot be related to the provisions of the Civil Code in the Soviet order. In this respect there is little difference regarding the function of civil law provisions between the socialist order and the traditional society. The civil law must be regarded as consisting of general statements of principle, the contents of which are shaped by events beyond its scope.

While initially the provisions of the Soviet Civil Code offered some ground for apprehension as to the position of private rights within the civil law of a socialist society, socialist codes enacted in Eastern Europe make it quite clear that they are not intended as instruments of change. Under the Hungarian Code of 1959, the exercise of civil rights and performance of civil obligations must conform to the interests of society. Further, civil law relations must be characterized by mutual cooperation in accordance with the demands of socialist coexistence. And finally: "cooperation shall be effected through strict performance of obligations and by exercising all rights in conformity with the function of such rights."

Section 5 of the Hungarian Civil Code prohibits the misuse of private rights and lists the following instances as constituting typical examples of the violation of this rule: exercise of a right with an objective which is incompatible with the social function of the right; the exercise of a right which might damage the national economy; exercise of a right in a manner interfering vexatiously with citizens; prejudice of their rights and lawful interests, or in procuring undue advantage.[68]

67 Bolgár, "The Magic of Property and Public Welfare," 2 Inter-Amer. L. Rev. 283 ff. (1960); *cf.* art. 226 of the German Civil Code, art. 2 of the Swiss Civil Code, and arts. 135 and 187 of the Polish Code of Obligations.

68 Art. 3 of the Polish Law on General Principles of Civil Law of 1950;

These and similar formulations found in the civil codes of Eastern Europe represent a fairly static set of circumstances aimed at maintaining a balance between the exercise of individual rights and the interests of others, and not at creating a mechanism of change. If the latter were so, the mechanism of social change would be administered by the courts and the lawyers. It is easy to see that this is not the function to which either courts or the legal profession of the socialist countries aspire.[69]

While the civil codes of Eastern Europe do not shape the course of history, they nevertheless bear the marks of social development. In consequence, the institutions of socialist civil legislation offer an important avenue for the exploration of social realities.[70] In particular, the provisions of property law in the Soviet Union and other socialist countries in Eastern Europe allow a glimpse of the elements determining the role and the social position of the individual in a society which is involved in a process of rapid transformation. In this connection, three major pieces of civil legislation, the Hungarian Civil Code of 1959, the Draft of the Principles of Civil Law Legislation of the USSR and of the Union Republics of 1960, and the Draft

---

Czechoslovak Civil Code of 1950, secs. 1 and 3; Bulgarian Law on Contracts of 1950, sec. 2.

Art. 47 of the Polish Draft of the Civil Code stated: "Legal acts aiming at the establishment, change or abolition of a legal relationship produces not only those results which are directly aimed at, but also those which are the consequences of a statutory provision or follow from the rules of social coexistence." Art. 40 (sec. 1) of the same Draft provided that: "... a legal transaction contrary to law, or concluded with a purpose of obviating its provisions or contrary to the principles of social coexistence is null and void." It further stated in art. 54 (sec. 1) that: "Declaration of will must be construed according to the circumstances of the case, and with reference to the rules of social coexistence." Finally, art. 309 (sec. 1) exhorts the debtor to "perform in accordance with the terms of his obligations, in conformity with its social purpose, and principles of social coexistence."

69 Differences in the role of law and of the legal profession in the socialist and open societies in enforcing the policies of social change provide one of the most significant illustrations of the differences between the socialist and traditional techniques of government. In the free societies courts and lawyers are a vehicle of change.

70 *Cf.* art. 1 of the Soviet Draft of Principles of Civil Legislation of the Soviet Union and Union Republics, and also sec. 1 of the Hungarian Civil Code of 1959.

of the Polish Civil Code of 1960, offer an up-to-date review of the state of civil law institutions in the socialist countries.

Polish and Hungarian provisions regarding property differ from the Soviet Draft in this respect; in neither of the former countries was socialist economic order connected with a nationwide nationalization of landed property, as in Russia. Therefore, although the larger farming estates were liquidated, there remains a considerable amount of private farming in both countries. The law, of course, must take account of this situation.

The Soviet Draft is based on the recognition of two types of property, socialist and personal. The Hungarian Code and the Polish Draft, on the other hand, introduce an additional category of individual (private) property, which includes ownership of means of production (land).

The Polish and Hungarian Codes suggest that state property, cooperative property, and property in ownership of other socialist organizations form one category. However, cooperative property poses certain problems both theoretical and practical since the cooperative movement and cooperative property relations in Poland and Hungary are based on individual ownership of land. As a rule, collective farms are formed by pooling the land owned by individual peasants. And while they join various cooperative organizations, they still continue to own such land as their share in the cooperative venture. It is true that their rights as regards this land are circumscribed by the fact that a member of a collective is unable to dispose of it except by testament and then only to the benefit of other members of the collective, but he is still the owner of his land. Unless there is a different provision in the statute of a collective, only crops and trees become the property of the cooperative. Buildings and other fixtures on the cooperative's land may become cooperative property only if its statutes rule so. Consequently, the inclusion of cooperative property in the category of socialist property is a somewhat dubious operation. This is demonstrated by the fact that in 1956, both in Poland and Hungary, a considerable amount of cultivated land was withdrawn from cooperative farming and, without changing owners, was transferred from the socialist to the private category of property.

Personal ownership serves physical persons and cultural needs only. It includes objects which serve the satisfaction of the "personal and cultural needs of the owner and those living with him in common household." Included are such items as a one-family house, a one-family apartment, household articles, clothing, motor vehicles, etc. Here also belong small means of production which serve to satisfy personal needs.

The scope of personal ownership varies according to the economic situation of the person involved. The dividing line runs between rural and industrial environment, according to the situation of the owner within the social and economic stratification of Soviet society. For example, a member of a collective farm may own things denied to a town dweller. Examples are: buildings, animals, poultry, and other objects necessary to engage in the limited production of food on a garden plot. On the other hand, there are things not available to a member of the agricultural sector which a town dweller may own. A successful city dweller may own a house in the city and a summer home in the country. If he can afford it, he may own an automobile; and there is no reason why he should not own a horse, if he likes horseback riding. Yet, the Soviet farmer is expressly prohibited from owning a horse. In Hungary and Poland, however, peasant-owned horses belong to the category of private property. Thus, it is possible in these two countries for a horse to be a socialist horse if it belongs to a cooperative; a personal horse if his owner rides him for pleasure and is not a farmer; or an individual-property horse if its owner is a farmer. In the Soviet Union, where no individual property is legally permitted, a horse could be either a socialist or a personal horse.

The classification of rights of ownership is tied to the gradation of the protection offered by the law to each of these three classes of property. The property of the state as the foundation of the social and economic order calls for the highest degree of protection. The Polish Draft assures this property a "singular protection." Of the property in private (individual) ownership, only the property of the working peasants and artisans "enjoys the support of the state" or "the protection of the state." Personal property is under what the Polish Draft calls a "full protection."

The system of gradation of legal protection under the law is the result of the contemporary situation in the social and economic order in Poland. It still includes important elements of individual ownership of means of production (land), which is under the protection of the law. This is because the protection of private property is an indispensable condition for the prosperity of agriculture and its contribution to the welfare of the nation. The Polish Supreme Court, in its plenary session of February 27, 1960, issued the following directives for the guidance of the courts:

The interest of the people's state in the increase of agricultural production of food in order to improve a continued rise in the supply of food articles to the growing population, and in order to assure the socialist industry the necessary raw materials, requires to take preventive measures against an excessive atomization of the existing farms at the present stage of development of our economy. It is necessary to maintain the largest possible number of farms, which would provide adequate outlet for the labor of a peasant family, to provide it with a main means of support, and assure a constant technical progress in agriculture.[71]

In other words, the degree of protection afforded is the result of the actual interests of the state in the existing state of things, and this dictates a conservative approach which would seem to favor viable individual enterprises. However, the Supreme Court also suggested that, once the government deemed it important to change its policies, the restricted disposal of landed property by inheritance or contract would be removed. Thus, when the Supreme Court directed that judicial policy had to preserve agricultural farms of a certain size, it was not concerned with the protection of individual rights but with the preservation of an agricultural organization which would be able to feed the urban population. Protection of individual ownership is an incidental question and represents only a technique.

These policies are not contradicted by the fact that the long-range policy of the regime seeks to limit the types of property relations in socialist society to only those two types which are at present admitted in the Soviet law, and which are typical of the social and economic order in which all means of production belong to the state. Personal property, which results from individual participation in the

71 Decision of Feb. 27, 1960, 1 CO 34/59, PiP 832–34 (No. 4–5, 1960).

socialist processes of production and services, represents a system of incentives to promote the productivity of labor. As such, it has a positive function and deserves effective protection.

The property of the state is the foundation of the regime. In addition, it is an instrument of its policy of social change whereby it seeks to achieve higher forms of social and economic organization, calling for as effective a regime of protection as is feasible. The realm of socialist property may grow, but never diminish.[72] Private property relations represent an order of things which must eventually be replaced by the new order of things. It deserves legal protection as long as it has a useful function.

The property regime as outlined in the Soviet Principles of Civil Legislation (1960) also contains, though in less visible form, a germ of the incipient change which will further simplify the property regime in the Soviet Union. The Soviet property regime is based upon two types of property, socialist and personal. Socialist property (Article 18) consists of state property (property of all the people) or collective farm property. The latter category of collective, or co-operative, property is limited to the membership of each collective, or of a cooperative association or of the common ownership by several collective farms or cooperative associations. Similarly, personal property appears in two forms, depending on the environment, i.e., urban or rural.

The reason for this distinction becomes clear with the continuing discussion of the reorganization of the types of legal relations in the period of communist social and economic order. They will be characterized by the complete assimilation of these two population groups as to the types of objects which shall be available for them. The rural population, collectively engaged in agriculture, will have to give up the continued use of garden plots and the management of individual household economies, including animals and poultry, which is permitted under the present regulations.

---

72 Sec. 91 of the Hungarian Civil Code of 1959 provides: "Such means of production as not declared state property may be capable also of private ownership. The private property of peasants and artisans working individually—as individually acquired property—enjoys the support of the state. . . . The private property must not prejudice public interest."

Another feature of the future regime of property relations will be the gradual concentration of ownership of durable consumer goods (automobiles, private houses, and perhaps major items of sporting equipment) in the hands of social organizations. Thus, cooperative, and therefore socialist ownership, will be extended, and the institution of personal ownership, restricted. This regime may be introduced as preliminary to a system in which the use of such items, or at least some of them, will be made generally available to the membership of the social organizations through the network of their various establishments. It has been suggested that in order to make the first step in the direction of communism, the present owners of automobiles and houses should vest their property rights in a collective consisting of similar owners. In this manner, a collective use of such consumer goods would be established and personal ownership would cease.[73]

An even greater integration of property relations within the socialist sector would consist of a gradual liquidation of the group ownership of collective farms. One of the modern developments in the Soviet economy is the practice of forming business associations by the collective farms for the purpose of promoting industrial or service (transport) enterprises to serve specific needs of their members. According to the Draft of the Principles of Civil Legislation of the USSR and of the Union Republics (1959), the property of such associations constitutes the property of the collectives. It is, therefore, separate from the property of the state. It was proposed that these *interkolkhoz* enterprises be classified as state property (property of all the people). Furthermore, it was suggested that the so-called indivisible reserve funds of the collective, which provide means for capital investment for collectivized agriculture, should be put under national administration. The purpose would be twofold: to implement a general agricultural policy and to finance other sectors of national economy as well. As these funds are replenished by yearly appropriations from the net income of the collective farms, such a

---

73 *Cf.* "XXI sjezd KPSS i zadatchi pravovoi nauki," SGP 7 (No. 2, 1959); Stepanyan, "Kommunizm i sobstvennost," Oktiabr (No. 9, 1960); Aleksieiev, "O zakonomernostiakh razvitia sovetskogo prava v period razvernutogo stroitelstva kommunizma," SGP 10–20 (No. 9, 1960).

move again would amount to a conversion of important items of group ownership into the outright ownership of the state.[74]

Special protection of socialist property is primarily expressed in the fact that law makes it impossible to transfer objects of socialist ownership to any other ownership. The transfer of property from one socialist juristic person to another has no legal significance, as it always remains in state ownership. Socialist juristic persons "merely exercise right of ownership vested in the state in their name with regard to assets in their management" (Article 122 of the Soviet Draft). Article 19 of the Soviet Draft states tersely:

The state is the sole owner of all state property, regardless of what it is or who manages or uses it. State organizations exercise within the limits established by the law only the rights of possession, use and disposal of state property attached to them in accordance with the aims of their property and the purpose of the property.

According to the Hungarian Code, the state's right to own all property which is not fit for personal ownership is safeguarded by provisions regarding the acquisition of ownership of objects which have no owner (Section 127). Objects which constitute social property, or of which the state or a cooperative have been wrongly dispossessed, can never become the property of another person by prescription. This, however, does not apply to movables capable of personal ownership (Section 121). Article 165 of the Polish Draft of the Civil Code provides that the owner of the land may renounce his property, which then goes to the state. Under the Albanian Code:

Private ownership of land may be terminated by a decision of the competent government agency. Such a decision may be taken either because of an attempted transaction concerning the land, because of neglect in farming it for a period of two years, or if the owner moves to another locality and therefore is unable to cultivate it personally.[75]

Article 201 of the Polish Draft rules that the statute of limitation does not apply to a claim for the surrender of a movable ob-

---

74 Kozyr, "Aktualnyie problemi kolkhoznoi sobstvennosti na sovremennom etape," SGP 60–80 (No. 8, 1960); Aksenenok & Ruskol, "Neobkhodimo dalneisheie sovershenstvovanie pravovogo regulirovania khoziaistvennoi deiatelnosti kolkhozov," SGP 60 (No. 1, 1959).

75 Gsovski & Grzybowski, Government Law and Courts in the Soviet Union and Eastern Europe 1195 (1959).

ject if such a claim is based on "state ownership and is directed against a physical person or a non-state organization." The Soviet Draft rules out all forms of transfer of state property to private citizens unless specifically authorized by the laws in force (Article 20):

State property ... is not subject to alienation by citizens, except in the case of housing and other types of property whose sale to citizens is permitted by the USSR and Union Republic legislation.

A dichotomy in civil law regulations in the sphere of property relations reflects the structure of economic controls in a socialist state. The state holds a monopolistic position regarding the ownership of means of production, while the citizen's property rights are restricted to consumer goods. Some variation from this scheme occurs in agriculture—on a considerable scale in the satellites, and less in the Soviet Union itself.

Since there is a conflict between the actual condition of property relations in the socialist societies and the pattern pronounced by the principles of Marxism, there is an internal contradiction within the legal systems of socialist societies. On one hand, in the interest of current reality, the law takes account of the actual situation and extends its protection. On the other hand, it tends to accommodate social change, which is a matter of social and economic policy, toward a uniform system of social and economic relations based on the total control by the public authority of all means of production.

INHERITANCE

The institution of inheritance in the Soviet orbit likewise reflects the impact of governmental policy upon the provisions of the civil law. It has served in the past as an instrument for the reshaping of property relations according to the socialist model. In those provinces of social life where this has been accomplished, its present shape differs little from the provisions of the civil law in traditional societies. In other provinces of life, where a change is still to be effected, inheritance continues to be used as an instrument of governmental control.

A Soviet decree of April 1917 abolished inheritance altogether, in line with the ideological stand of Marxism, according to which inheritance was a pillar of the capitalist system of economy. Later, in a number of successive laws the institution of inheritance was re-established, and followed, on the whole, the traditional lines of the European Codes.[76] The Draft of Principles of Civil Legislation of 1960 provides only a partial answer to the question as to what future Soviet law will be, as it leaves important details to be filled in by legislation of the individual republics. However, it continues a tendency to liberalize further the provisions of Soviet inheritance. Thus, it rules that the testator shall have the right to "will all or part of his property to one or several persons either included or not included in the circle of heirs by law. . . ." This would be impossible under the law which is now in force, for he must choose his heirs from the circle of persons included in the three classes of statutory heirs. The Draft also provides for a statutory share of inheritance to certain of the statutory heirs, but its size and to whom it will go is to be determined by the Union Republics.

The Polish Draft of 1960 continues the system of the devolution of estates as enacted by the two decrees of 1946. It is highly reminiscent of the Soviet system of inheritance as devised in the Draft of 1960, but it must be stated at once that under the Polish law which is now in force the power of the testator to select the heir freely by testament was never restricted.

The Hungarian Code of 1959, in an obvious effort to preserve national institutions as far as compatible with the socialist order, differs widely both from the Polish and Soviet pattern. Legislation enacted prior to the Civil Code of 1959 had abolished some medieval institutions, including separate inheritance systems either for certain classes or for certain groups of population, had limited the classes of heirs, and had removed all discrimination between illegitimate and legitimate children.[77]

However, the 1946 reform maintained a separate system of inheritance for ancestral property. Thus, in absence of descendants and testamentary disposition, property devolving upon the decedent from his ancestor was to be returned to the line of the ancestor whence it came.

The Code provided for a far broader circle of heirs by law

76 *Id.* at 1171–74.
77 *Id.* at 1300–1.

than did either of the two drafts. The first class of heirs consists of children. Where no issue is left, the surviving spouse inherits the entire estate. Where no spouse is left, parents and their issue, then grandparents and their issue, and finally more distant relatives are entitled to inherit. The main feature of Hungarian inheritance is the life interest of the spouse in the entire estate. Children may, however, seek restriction of this right if the needs of the spouse are met by other inherited assets or by the spouse's property and earnings.

Provisions on the inheritance of ancestral property no longer have practical significance, but are still included in the Code.

The Hungarian Code has no restriction on testamentary disposition as to the selection of heir or heirs, or of their shares, except to the extent of the statutory share which obligatorily devolves upon certain statutory heirs.[78]

The People's Republics in Eastern Europe have never adopted the Soviet pattern regarding the general system of inheritance. In theoretical writings, the shift from the original position of the complete abolition of the institution of inheritance to its re-establishment is explained by the fact that the original abolition was a tactical move in the struggle against the capitalist system. However, once the state became the sole owner of all means of production, there was no need to continue the system. The inheritance of items acquired by the workers of the socialist countries through their own labor promotes thrift and constitutes an added incentive toward raising productivity of labor. In addition, it assists the government program of raising the general standard of living and welfare of the people, increases family cohesion, and strengthens the ties of the socialist community.[79] No less important has been the fact that since nationalization in most of the Eastern European satellites never assumed such drastic forms as in Russia, some degree of protection for the property which was still left in private ownership had to be devised.

General relaxation of the rules of inheritance is not a uniform pattern and indeed favors disposal of property within the urban sector of the economy. For other sectors of the economy, particularly for agriculture, far less liberal regimes continue in force.

78 *Id.* at 1302.
79 Gwiazdomorski, Prawo spadkowe 15 (1959).

In the Soviet Union, the basic unit in the regime provided for peasant's estates is the peasant household. This is an association engaged in joint farming operations and consists of those related by blood and of all those who *de facto* belong to it. As the life of the Soviet peasant family centers around the house and the garden plot which household members farm together, by law the share of the deceased member of the family in the community property is not subject to inheritance but automatically devolves upon its surviving members.[80]

With the exception of Northern Albania, the institution of the peasant household was foreign to the legal tradition of Soviet-controlled Europe. Nevertheless, an institution similar to Soviet peasant inheritance has made its appearance in the satellite countries. In a purely Soviet form, it has been introduced into Rumania and Albania. In other countries, the inheritance of peasant estates is subject to a regime which tends to further the continuation of a household and of the farm as an economic unit,[81] thus achieving the same results as the Soviet system of inheritance.

DAMAGES FOR MORAL WRONGS

Article 140 of the Civil Code of the RSFSR provides for damages only in the event of material wrong. This, in turn, may consist only of restitution or, when this is not possible, in payment of damages. Soviet authors support the position of the Soviet Code by the argument that monetary damages cannot be a substitute for moral wrong. Criminal repression in the socialist state is thought to represent an adequate guarantee of protection of individual rights, and consequently, criminal punishment declared by the court should represent an equivalent for moral wrong. Furthermore, Soviet jurists

---

80 Gsovski & Grzybowski, *supra* note 75, at 1170–71.
81 "Property and Inheritance Rights of Peasant Members of the Collective Farms in Romania," 2 Highlights 15 (1954). *Cf.* Polish Law of July 3, 1957 (DU 39/172); *cf.* also the Directive of the Polish Supreme Court of Feb. 27, 1960 (1 CO 34/59), which introduced a separate regime for the devolution of peasant estates by setting a minimum size of peasant farms, in order to maintain efficient farming units. Nowe Prawo 570–73 (1960); *cf.* also Gsovski & Grzybowski, *supra* note 75, at 196, 1234, 1300, 1380.

declare, constantly improving conditions of life in the Soviet order represent a higher guarantee and a better means of securing the happiness of the individual and recompensing his sufferings—even those resulting from moral wrongs—than any damages which a court could possibly decree from the defendant. In addition, damages are said to constitute a form of income without work, and therefore are contrary to the socialist prohibition of unearned income. But—what is most important—the idea that health, life, honor, or any other aspect of human existence can be expressed in a sum of money is said to be a purely bourgeois idea and contrary to the high respect of socialist society for the human individual.[82]

In fact, Soviet solutions may hardly be deemed a highly advanced answer to the new situations arising from the social and economic changes which have exposed human existence to additional hazards. The imperial law of Russia (Afticle 670 of the Tenth volume of the Code of Laws) had provided no legal basis for the modern concept of damages to compensate for moral wrongs, and the Soviet system followed the old path by adding new argumentation for an old position. In addition, it was realized that in the chaotic conditions of industrial expansion involving a policy of drawing into industrial production vast masses of inexperienced and half-literate peasants, a liberal policy with regard to loss of life, health, or limb by the new workers would place a strain on governmental industries. Thus, Soviet industrialists have maintained the old position because it was cheaper for the state.

Once the Soviet law crossed the western frontiers of the Soviet Union on its civilizing mission of socialism, its position in this respect caused serious doubts. Particularly was this true in a number of Eastern European countries where interwar legislation followed liberal standards evolved in Western Europe.

In the Polish case, the Code of Obligations of 1933 followed the example of the Swiss Code of 1907, which in its Article 40 provided for damages for moral wrongs due both to the victim and to relatives. In the Polish legal system, the Swiss formula was also reflected in a number of special laws which provided for moral

82 Fleishits, Obiazatelstva iz prichinenia vreda i neosnovatelnogo obogash-chenia 18, 29, 224 (1951).

wrongs such as dealing with copyright, protection of industrial property, unfair trade practices, press legislation, etc. In this situation, the adaptation of the new legal concepts involved a conflict between the doctrinal viewpoint and well-rooted legislation as to what was right in the public mind. The matter was complicated by the fact that both the public and the legal profession on both sides of the bar were well aware that the institution of damages for moral wrong was intended to favor the economically weaker classes, and therefore constituted a progressive phenomenon.

In the first years of the new regime, Polish courts continued to award damages for moral wrongs. Later, in a series of decisions, the Polish Supreme Court began to seek means of justifying the practice of awarding damages with the principles of new legality. So, for instance, in the decision dated December 5, 1950, the Court found that in principle damages for moral wrongs were not contrary to the ideological principles of the new order. It stated that, as a matter of fact, the new order provided for a possibility of income without work, pointing to monetary awards and prizes to artists, scholars, leaders of labor, etc.[83] In another case shortly thereafter, the Supreme Court pointed out that pensions, leave pay, and other forms of payment, legal in the Socialist order, bore no direct relation to work performed.

In this case the Court of Appeal propounded a thesis which reflected the influence of the Soviet point of view. It stated:

To award damages for moral wrong resulting from physical or moral suffering would in the first place challenge one of the fundamental principles of the socialist order, namely that work is the basic source of income of a citizen, and that awarding such damages would force the Treasury of the State or a government enterprise, whose income goes to the treasury, to make expenditure contrary to the social order of the present day Poland.

The Supreme Court rejected this point of view. Article 165 of the Code of Obligations, the Court stated, also applied to a socialist enterprise. Otherwise, it continued, another principle of the rules of life in a socialist community would be violated, namely, "that

83 PiP 172 (No. 7, 1951).

there must be no conflict between the interests of individual human beings and those of the collective." [84]

The first breach in the tradition was made by a decision passed by the bench of seven justices of the Supreme Court which considered the question of damages to the members of the family of the deceased. In this case, the Court stated that awarding damages for moral wrong to the members of the family was "contrary to rules of life in a socialist community." [85]

The new line was again reversed after October 1956, when blind imitation of Soviet institutions ceased to be obligatory. The matter of damages for moral wrongs accruing to the members of the surviving family was brought up again and reviewed by the Plenary Session of the Polish Supreme Court on January 1, 1957. The Court admitted that the bench of seven justices had gone too far. It stated that provisions of the Code of Obligations regarding this matter had been kept on the statute book, in spite of the fact that in the meantime a partial reform of the civil law had occurred. In fact, the Supreme Court stated, the Draft of the new Civil Code continued the institution of damages for moral wrongs, thus preserving the traditional Polish attitude. Furthermore, the Court added the following argument from the armory of socialist legality: money is a basic means of the distribution of social product in the socialist economy, and a feeling of satisfaction resulting from the possibility of meeting one's needs in greater measure may follow a monetary award. The Government also thought fit to use the same means on some occasions. [86]

At the background of this ideological storm in the juristic teacup stood the fact that provisions of the Swiss Code of 1907 and of the

---

84 Decision of June 5, 1951, Case No. C 649/50, ZOIC (No. 34, 1952); also PiP 312 (No. 2, 1952).

85 Case No. C 15/51, ZOIC; Case No. 3 (1953); Nowe Prawo 53 (No. 12, 1953).

86 That compensation paid to the members of the immediate family of the deceased admitted by the Code is not contrary to socialist morals is also proved by the well-known fact of payment by the government of certain monies to members of the families of miners who lost their lives in a catastrophe. Decision of Jan. 29, 1957, Case No. 1 CO 37/56, PiP 1141–43 (No. 12, 1957).

Polish Code of 1933 were designed as means of equalization and distribution of the hazards of modern life—favoring the economically weaker in a free enterprise system. Once the state took over the management of the industrial establishment in Poland, some enthusiasts were inclined to the protection of the interests of the new employer on the theory that he represented the interests of all.

In East Germany, the Supreme Court established the principle that the claim to a pension by the surviving spouse, following the accidental death of a wage earner, must be calculated in relation to the economic position of the surviving person. The Court ordered that the property status and actual earnings of the surviving spouse be taken into consideration, as well as his working and earning capacity in case he was not working.[87]

Of the three pieces of civil legislation, only the Polish Draft of 1960 provides for damages for a moral wrong. However, it is restricted to the injured person alone and does not accrue to his family (Article 833, Section 1). Otherwise, restitution of the actual loss may be sought in the form of a periodic payment for the loss of the working ability. Or it may be sought to cover the cost of maintenance due from the deceased to the members of his family, who were a statutory charge on the deceased, and also all those whom the deceased provided voluntarily with means of subsistence.

Under the Hungarian Civil Code of 1959, the only form of damages for personal injury is an annuity due to the injured person or to the members of his family or his kin entitled to claim maintenance from him (Section 357 (2)). Under the Soviet Draft of Principles of Civil Legislation (1960), damages for injury or loss of life are due only where social security benefits do not provide for full compensation, either to him or to the members of his family who were dependent on the deceased or who were entitled to be supported by him (Article 77).

COPYRIGHT

Since the very beginning of the debate regarding the protection of the rights of authors, it has been clear that such could be realized

---

87 Decision of March 3, 1959, Case No. 2 Uz V 7/58, Neue Justiz 391 (1959).

only in a regime recognizing the social implication of creative activity. A work which is not made accessible to the public brings no fruits of his labors to the author. Publication makes the public a partner in the creative process, and its rights deserve recognition. The reporter to the French *Constituante* on the draft of the copyright law stated that: "It seems that from the moment an author has put his work into the hands of the public . . . the writer has made the public a partner of his property rights. . . ."

The legislative solutions proposed and adopted by the legislators of the French Revolution defined this partnership and established a pattern which was to persist until our times. The law of January 19, 1791, and the Decree of the Convent of July 19–24, 1793, recognized the exclusive rights of the author to his work during his lifetime and for some time after his death, and the unlimited rights of the public thereafter.

In the Soviet order, authors' rights appeared again in a different dimension. The regime was intensely interested in controlling intellectual activity as a means of political action. The nationalization of printing facilities and of sources of raw materials for dissemination of intellectual works, as well as the institution of economic planning, called for the definition of mutual relations, not only between the author and the public, but between the author and the regime as well. The political significance of copyright regulations is thrown into sharp relief by the fact that the Soviet model of the copyright law was reproduced in the satellite regimes without serious departure from its main characteristics. Whereas in other provinces of legal regulation socialist governments have been inclined to continue local traditions, in regard to copyright the reception of the Soviet model was complete.

The proper provisions of the copyright law are comparatively simple and quite orthodox. The rights of authors to the products of their literary, scientific, and artistic activity were recognized during their lifetime without limitation and for fifteen years after death. Copyright was declared inheritable.[88]

88 Unesco, Copyright Laws and Treaties of the World (1956): Bulgaria, Law of Nov. 16, 1951, IPNS, July 10, 1956; Czechoslovakia, Law of Dec. 22, 1953, Sbirka No. 115/1953; Poland, Law of July 10, 1952,

The exercise of the copyright and the administration of all related problems were entrusted to a network of social and governmental institutions which participate in the process of planning artistic, literary, and scientific productions, the enforcement of uniform standards of conditions of publishing and production contracts, and in the raising of the new generations of artists, writers, scholars, and scientists. In the socialist society, all of these aspects of intellectual life become a matter of social concern. The purpose of copyright legislation, as the Bulgarian copyright law stated, is to "protect the interests of the authors by harmonizing them with those of the people" (Section 1).

The mechanism which the socialist regimes in Eastern Europe have set up in order to harmonize the rights of authors with those of the society consists of three elements: (1) authors' unions; (2) special funds administered by government or social agencies to promote creative activity in the arts and literature; (3) the supervisory governmental body which determines general conditions of artistic and literary production and the program and policy of promoting various activities in this field. This high governmental agency is either a ministry of culture or a department or an agency subordinate to it. Sometimes a separate agency is attached to the office of the prime minister, which testifies to the singular importance of cultural life in the socialist society.

Authors' protective organizations, including the Writers' Union, exercise wide powers. They have the exclusive right to represent individual authors in their dealings with the publishing houses and other institutions engaged in the production of artistic works and to make publishing and production contracts. They also collect the fees and honorariums, and deduct a fixed percentage from them for the fund to promote artistic activity. Their duty is to initiate legal action to protect authors' rights and to prevent violation of a copyright.

Funds are designed to promote and foster literary and artistic

---

DU 234/1952; Albania, Law of Sept. 24, 1947, GZ 19/1951; Rumania, Decree of June 18, 1956, B.O., June 27, 1956, No. 18, and Aug. 3, 1957, No. 21; USSR, Law of May 16, 1928, Sob. zak. SSSR, No. 27/1928, secs. 245 and 246; *cf.* articles 80–86 of the Draft of Principles of Civil Legislation of the Soviet Union and of the Union Republics.

activity in the fields of belles lettres, music, plastic arts, and in particular to encourage and recruit newcomers to the professions. Authors' protective organizations also participate in the fixing of rates of honorariums and fees by government decree and in working out the yearly programs of artistic and literary production. These various functions are distributed among three elements of the administration of cultural production according to a pattern which varies from country to country. In Hungary, for instance, such functions as the collection of fees and the contractual relations of authors with publishing institutions, which elsewhere belong to the Writers' Union, are handled by the governmental agency (Office for Copyright Protection). In Poland, the Academy of Science is drawn into the administration of cultural production.

The paramount feature of these social and government operations is the planning of culture. As a recent Soviet treatise explained the functions of the various governmental organizations in this field:

The progressive growth of socialist culture constantly urged the establishment of organizational forms and institutions which would direct the activities of the publishing, cinematographic and other enterprises. . . . The Ministry of Culture of the USSR also directs the activity of the unions of the workers of the creative professions. . . .[89]

The technique of control is primarily a system of economic incentives. According to the Directive of the Council of People's Commissars of June 28, 1934, the purpose of the Fund for the Promotion of Literature is to establish a

. . . cooperation with the members of the Union of Soviet Writers by means of improving their standards of living and their material situation, and to give support to the cadres of the new writers by means of creating for them indispensable conditions for their existence. (Section 2).[90]

In regard to the forms of contractual relations between authors and publishing institutions, socialist copyright laws feature short-term publishing contracts. They also contain a general prohibition

89 Antimonov & Fleishits, Avtorskoe pravo 36 (1957).
90 Sob. zak. SSSR 39/311, 1934; *cf.* Antimonov & Fleishits, *supra* note 89, at 38–39.

of permanent acquisition by a publishing institution of the copyright of an artistic work.

Soviet jurists are of the unanimous opinion that under the socialist law the copyright is no longer a property right. The fact that the interests of society in the exploitation of intellectual and artistic production have found an institutional expression has moved Soviet jurists to point to the fact that it is influenced essentially by the government monopoly of publishing and that it is a part of the general process of production. Authors have no right to reproduce and circulate their works except through government channels. On the other hand, government enterprises must obtain agreement to reproduce the works of individual authors.[91]

As to the nature of the copyright under socialism, two theories have been advanced by Soviet jurists. One school of thought favors the view that a socialist author is a worker entitled to fruits of his labor in a socialist society:

As any other toiler, the author has the right to remuneration in accordance with the quality and quantity of his labor, if the product of his labor is used by society. Here lies the difference in principle of Soviet copyright from the copyright of capitalist countries.[92]

Others favor a doctrine which views authors' rights as under a separate category, belonging neither to that of property rights nor to the field of labor regulation. They point out that one of the characteristics of Soviet legal solutions in this field is that authors are guaranteed remuneration for their intellectual or artistic labor. Furthermore, they claim that under socialism, authors' rights are not property rights and their works are not commodities. This is because the law opposes a permanent transfer of the copyright and limits the rights of the publisher to a short period of time only, after which

---

91 Pasherstnik, Teoreticheskie voprosy kodifikatsii obshchesoiuznogo zakono-datelstva o trude 31 (1955); Genkin, "Predmet i sistema sovetskogo trudovogo prava," SGP (No. 2, 1949); Antimonov & Fleishits, "Avtorstvo i trudovoe pravootnoshenie," SGP (No. 5, 1956); Antimonov & Fleishits, *supra* note 89, at 3, 16–17; 2 Grazhdanskoe pravo 264 (1944).

92 Gordon, "Poniatie sovetskogo avtorskogo prava," 1 Uchonye Zapiski Kharkhovskogo Iuridicheskogo Instituta 100 (1939).

the right of reproduction reverts unrestricted to the author himself.[93]

The Draft of the Principles of the Civil Legislation (1960) seems to favor the second theory. Thus, the provisions dealing with copyright were included in a separate section of the Civil Code, and the treatment is separate from the institutions of property.

THE NEW BALANCE

The position of the individual in the socialist society was affected by two movements: by the expansion of the responsibilities and powers of the state and by the change in the character of the civil law. New legal solutions have removed in effect all differences between various functions of the state, either in its sovereign capacity or as owner of property, lumping them into a single category. Civil law in the traditional sense has little application to relations between the individual and the state. It governs partly the process of acquisition through purchase and sale of consumer goods distributed by the state and loan and credit operations with the government banks. The legal nature of these transactions, however, is seriously in doubt. The supply of goods and credit operations are a matter of public policy; and with the expansion of the concept of public officials, even the very act of purchase and sale over the counter engages public authority. Furthermore, conditions of sale and credit are not determined by the provisions of the civil law, but by the terms of the economic plan.

Otherwise, all relations between the state and the individual, in particular those governed by the labor law or other governmental services which constitute the foundations of individual existence in the socialist order, e.g., social security, are under the rule of law which expresses the public policy of the state.

Moreover, legal transactions which regulate economic activity in the socialist economic system do not engage individual responsibility. They take place exclusively between socialist juristic persons representing various levels of public authority. Individual participa-

---

93 Fleishits, Lichnye prava v grazhdanskom prave SSSR i kapitalisticheskikh stran 164 (1941); Antimonov & Fleishits, *supra* note 89, at 59–61.

tion in the economic processes is an act of public or social service. Thus, the very use of civil law terminology in major pieces of legislation, which are called codes of civil law, is more a matter of tradition and convenience than of the nature of their institutions. Except for a few areas of legal regulation such as inheritance or family law, the rest of the civil law belongs to the field of public administration, involving, as in copyright and industrial property legislation, individual participation in the enforcement of public policy.

Individual life was even more profoundly affected by the process of change which transformed mutual relations between the official system of legal regulation of public life in the socialist state and those other sources of social ordering which are characteristic of modern industrial societies. In the traditional system, the law took account of those local habits, customs, and commercial practices which affected the tenor of legal rule to the extent that they were not contrary to public policy. References in the civil laws to general concepts such as good morals, general principles of law, and conditions of trade recognized the autonomous existence of the parallel system of social ordering which formed individual personality and shaped individual existence with reference to standards which were not imposed by the force of the state.

Under socialism, public authority and the rule of the socialist law have permeated all those innumerable forms of human coexistence and social and economic cooperation, with the result that all nonstate sources of social ordering have become carriers of public policy. Rules of life in the socialist community, or rules of social coexistence, as those extra- or para-legal codes or standards of behavior are variously called, are only channels for the integration of all individual and collective life into a single pattern of which the rule enacted by the government is the center. Social organizations, professions, and economic institutions are identified with the state, and the position of the individual members of social and economic institutions is accordingly affected.

The expansion of governmental responsibilities and social change in the West have also affected the perspectives of mutual relations between the individual and collective life. In the mind of the drafters of the Civil Code of France, different criteria of action apply in these two provinces. The legislator has a duty "to discover for each matter the principles which would favor the common weal . . . ," and the judge has the task of "putting these principles into action to adapt and extend them, by a wise and reasoned application, to private situations. . . ." [94]

In modern societies it is no longer possible to see the problems of balance between collective and individual interests in such simple equations. But the axiom that the function of law is to protect individual existence against the encroachment of those who wield power has still remained the important duty of public authority. While the government has assumed new responsibilities in the adjustment of economic and social forces for the purpose of eliminating harmful forms of competition, the restriction or elimination of private initiative is not understood as eliminating the need for the protection of private interests. The question of providing protection has simply moved into another dimension, since the conflict of interests is a fact of life. In new conditions, modern courts and modern legislation have been able to afford protection to individual interests, in their various forms, sometimes merged into the collective form of social cooperation. The response of the socialist state to changed conditions was to assume direct responsibility for the management of social and economic affairs, thus eliminating the need for imposing or affixing liabilities and duties upon individuals. This policy, it is claimed, brings about harmony of the individual and social interests, reducing the problem of legal protection to the problem of managerial responsibility for the efficiency of service.

In opening societies, the function of judicial control has retained its full significance. New powers and responsibilities of public authority call for additional expansion of judicial control, both for government departments and in regard to the action of departmental or private tribunals, which all affect the economic and social position of the individual.[95]

The legal protection of individual rights and interests in open

94 Portalis, Discours préliminaire, Projet de Code Civil présenté par la Commission nommée par le Gouvernement, Le 24 Thermidor an 8, at vii.

95 Denning, The Changing Law 20–37 (1953).

societies is predicated upon the decentralization of governmental responsibilities, which permits operation of public services under the uniform cloak of law.

In *Tamlin* v. *Hannaford,* involving the effect of the nationalization of British railways upon private rights, the British Court held that:

In the eyes of the law, the corporation is its own master and is answerable as fully as any other person or corporation. It is not the Crown and has none of the immunities or privileges of the Crown. Its servants are not civil servants and its property is not Crown property. It is as much bound by Acts of Parliament as any other subject of the King. It is, of course, a public authority and its purposes, no doubt, are public purposes, but it is not a government department nor do its powers fall within the province of Government.[96]

In France, a distinction was made between government-organized private corporations and public corporations having the character of a public agency. Neither of them is free from judicial control. Government interests in the form of private corporations act as private parties, subject to courts of general jurisdiction. In accordance with the doctrine of separation between acts of public authority and those pertaining to the management of governmental proprietary interests, public corporations are controlled either by administrative courts or by courts of general jurisdiction.[97]

In most general terms, the mechanics of the approach of Western societies to the needs of our times consists of a pragmatic correlation of all methods of social and economic action with the rule of law and available methods of judicial control. To the mechanism of control are added new institutions, frequently representing a combination of the judicial and social element. A legal framework for the complicated mechanism of social and governmental action

96 [1950] 1 K.B. 18.

97 "In the welfare state, the private citizen is forever encountering public officials of many kinds: regulators, dispensers of social services, managers of state operated enterprises. It is the task of the rule of law to see to it that these multiplied and diverse encounters are as fair, as just, and as free from arbitrariness as are the familiar encounters of the right-asserting private citizen with the judicial officers of the traditional law." Jones, "The Rule of Law and the Welfare State, 58 Colum. L. Rev. 156 (1958).

is provided by public and private law alike, and formal justice with judicial action in its traditional form of scholarly interpretation of laws retains its place. The result is individual participation in all levels of social and economic activity.[98]

The tendency of the modern phase of Soviet law is to continue the policy of subordination of individual interests to the commands

98 This is particularly well illustrated by the variety of forms and devices to fit in the initiative of public authority to provide services or organize an industry into the national economies of the free society. *Cf.* the following individual contributions to Friedmann ed., The Public Corporation, A Comparative Symposium (1954):

Sawer, "The Public Corporation in Australia," at 10: "In the field of central government, the corporate structure might be followed for two reasons which continue to have importance to the present day. Firstly, the 'Crown' as a legal personality was a most unsatisfactory basis for the organization of any enterprise which might be involved in daily dealing with property and in litigation, owing to the cumbrous procedures connected with Crown property and the strict limitation on Crown liability to legal action. Secondly, an activity identified with the Crown almost inevitably became a political activity, and this might be either bad for the activity or embarrassing for the politicians." *Cf.* also 38–39 and 38 n. 1, citing "Commonwealth Hostels Ltd. v. Bogle," 26 Aust. L.J. 589 (1952); Argus L.R. 229.

Hodgetts, "The Public Corporation in Canada," at 62, 64, 65–70, and 84–86 these remarks: "Parliament and even the responsible minister must show confidence in the corporation by refraining from breathing down the neck of management. On the other hand, the Canadian system of parliamentary government can impose responsibility only on the ministers of the Crown. Hence the public corporation cannot be used as a means of evading ultimate responsibility. Where to draw the line between the claims of managerial autonomy and the claims of parliamentary responsibility remains for Canada a problem that has been seriously posed rather than solved by contemporary use of the public corporations."

Drago, "The Public Corporation in France," at 108–19, and in particular the following statement at 125: "It ought to be added that in accordance with the principles of the *'gestion privée,'* the public corporations can act like private individuals and in that case are subjected to the civil law. As regards the industrial and commercial corporation, the presumption must be reversed; their activities correspond to those of private enterprise and they are therefore governed by private law and subject to the jurisdiction of the civil courts. . . ."

Friedmann and Hufnagel, "The Public Corporation in Germany," at 138, and the following at 141–42: "In the first place it is now generally established that the legal relations between the *Anstalt* and third

and the interests of society, and to eradicate from the psyche of the Soviet citizen the element of assertiveness in regard to the rights of the individual. Social reforms on which communist society is predicated stress coordination, discipline, and conformity. The message of the social order in the Soviet society addressed to the individual is that through collective action the welfare of the individual is to be achieved. The state and public authority appear in the public eye as the benefactors of all.

A report on the Soviet social security system thus described the general meaning of social security in Russia:

Thus, the overwhelming feeling that one gets about the Soviet program is that, like all other aspects of the Soviet society and economy, it is intended to be for the benefit of all persons as a whole rather than to provide for individual needs. . . .

This impression is further strengthened by the fact that the Soviet social security program is non-contributory insofar as the workers covered are

---

parties are governed by public law unless there are clear indications to the contrary. For example, the citizen who acquires a library ticket or who is admitted to a public bath does not enter into a contract but he is admitted to certain facilities by virtue of public law concessions granted by the public authority. This does not mean that he is without remedy but in case of any dispute it is the administrative not the civil courts that will decide." *Cf.* also, at 144–45: "It goes without saying that the legal status of this form of public enterprise differs radically from the *'Öffentliche Anstalt.'* They are legal persons of private law. They are, like every other commercial company, fully liable in contract or in tort. Their property transactions are governed by private law, and any legal dispute concerning them comes before the civil and not the administrative courts. The public character of their activities lies in the economic and political field; it is not reflected in its legal form. Again, the internal organization of these enterprises was, of course, that of the commercial company. . . .

   "A predominant purpose of the establishment of public enterprises in the form of commercial companies was the emphasis on technical expertise, rather than civil service administration."

   Friedmann, "The Public Corporation in Great Britain," at 165–66: "Shortly after the nationalization of a number of basic industries by the Labour Government, the present writer suggested a division of the most important public corporations into two types: the industrial or commercial corporation, on the one hand, and the social service corporation on the other. Later a third type, termed a supervisory public corporation was added." *Cf.* also at 185.

concerned. The entire cost is met by contributions from the employing enterprises and from the general revenue—a point often repeated in Soviet sources and by Soviet representatives at international meetings. That the workers are in fact "grateful" for this financing basis is indicated by the comment that is so often heard: "The government is providing all these social benefits for us free of charge." [99]

In fact, the report goes on to say, whatever the financing arrangements of social security in the Soviet Union, in the final analysis its cost comes from the national economy and, strictly speaking, from the workers' pockets. In terms of controls, this attitude provides an important channel of psychological influence over the mind of the masses.

Another example of integration of the Soviet man with the official apparatus of the government is the Soviet institution of complaints, which is the main means of public defense against the arbitrary action of the governmental authority. Its general usefulness for the regime consists in the check it provides against the irregularities in the operation of the governmental institutions. The control which a complaint initiates is a matter of internal process and is exercised with reference to general provisions regulating governmental action, rather than in response to a demand for the protection of individual rights. Its general form (the absence of the personal involvement of the complaining individual) will tend to de-emphasize the element of individual participation in the action aiming at the preservation of public order.[100]

99 Social Security in the Soviet Union, Draft of the Report by the U.S. team that visited the USSR, 8–9 (1959).
100 *Cf. infra* at 235 ff.

Chapter v

SOCIALIST LEGALITY

SOCIAL CHANGE AND THE REFORM OF SOVIET LAWS

In 1917, Russia was a country deeply rooted in the pre-industrial era. Not only was its economy predominantly agricultural, but it was backward in terms of the techniques of production and social relations as well. The comparatively recent abolition of serfdom had failed to sever the bonds between the lower and higher strata of society which characterized the medieval forms of life. And the incipient growth of the industrial economy, although contributing significantly to the process of social and economic change in Russia, was as yet unable to affect the style of life of the large peasant masses which constituted the bulk of the population.

The revolution, however, violently disturbed this pattern. Indeed, Russia began to experience a period of great social mobility, as the masses moved both from the countryside to the cities and up and down the social ladder.

The physical movement of the human masses was coupled with a great ideological upheaval involving a revision of basic concepts regarding the role of the individual in the social order. Involved were conflicts of various doctrinal formulations on the historical predictions of Marxism and a political struggle involving purges and the physical liquidation of opponents, including those who at one time occupied highest positions in the government of Revolutionary Russia and in the ideological and moral leadership of the new order.

At the same time, the regime was tackling the enormous task of transforming the illiterate peasant mass into an industrial labor force. It was necessary to train the new workers in basic industrial skills and urban ways of life and to educate industrial, social, and business leaders on a grand scale. The forced expansion of the Soviet economy, beginning with the Five-Year Plans, was made possible only through this immense transfer and training of the labor force. This process was nearly complete by the end of the thirties, and in the late forties and early fifties the process of adaptation of the masses of peasantry from the countryside to urban surroundings and exacting industrial employment was well advanced. The Soviet labor force began to resemble in behavior, attitude toward work, mode of life, and common interests their counterparts in the industrial economies of other countries.[1]

This development in the growth of the Soviet labor force was paralleled by a number of refinements taking place in Soviet industries. These latter were reflected in the methods of achieving progress in labor productivity and in greater perfection in the end result of the productive processes.

An expert in Soviet labor relations has suggested that there have been three periods in that country's improvement of the efficiency and productivity of labor. When Soviet industry was primitive and economic expansion still a matter of large-scale construction, military discipline was the most efficient regime for coordinating the efforts of workers, the majority of whom were peasants. Thus, shock work was said to characterize the first Five-Year Plan. Since 1935, however, when the foundations of the Soviet industrial plant had been laid and the equipment in Soviet factories was becoming more sophisticated, the method of sheer intensification of mass labor was no longer useful, and a new method featuring individual performance was needed. To serve this new need, Stakhanovism was invented. Such, together with a number of similar competitive schemes, remained the chief method for raising the productivity of the labor of factory crews for almost two decades. It was an improvement because raising the productivity of labor was predicated upon the improvement of the production processes and upon the mastering of techniques.

1 About 25 million people moved from rural to urban areas during the period 1926–1939 alone. *Cf.* Eason, "Population and Labor Force," in Soviet Economic Growth 114 (Bergson ed., 1953).

After World War II, Stakhanovism was no longer satisfactory. At this point, emphasis was shifted from record-breaking to individual initiative, to the intelligent employment of modern factory equipment, and to the extension of automation methods in various fields of industrial production.[2]

In the first period, after an initial phase marked by the regime's endeavor to win the masses to its side, the emphasis of Soviet legislation was on the stabilization of social conditions in the Soviet economy and enforced government control of the labor market. Its aim was to raise the discipline of labor. It struggled against the rapid turnover of labor, labor migration between industrial centers, and against absenteeism, all of which were causing enormous losses in Soviet industries.

The Soviet regime was handicapped by the deplorable state of the cities and by a shortage of urban accommodations and consumer goods—even of staple foods. To meet those conditions, economic incentives were replaced by a system of military discipline as the basic approach to the management of labor. The 1933 decree introduced the "labor book." Under the 1940 decree, a worker was prohibited from leaving his employment without the permission of the management, under penalty of two to four months of imprisonment for noncompliance. A system of penalties was established for unexcused absence from work. A worker could be moved from employment to employment or even to another enterprise. The government established a system of trade schools and training centers where young workers were trained in industrial skills. They were admitted either on their applications or on the basis of draft, again under a regime characterized by army discipline.[3]

After 1951, the labor regime was somewhat modified as sanctions became less severe. Finally, the decree of April 25, 1956, acknowledged the fact that a new regime for industrial relations had become possible because:

2 Gliksman, "Recent Trends in Soviet Labor Policy," 79 Monthly Labor Rev. 772 (1956).
3 Schwarz, Labor in the Soviet Union, 95 ff. (1952); Guins, Soviet Law and Soviet Society 150–81 (1954); Kulski, The Soviet Regime 404 (1954); Gliksman, *supra* note 2, at 767–75.

Labor discipline at enterprises and institutions has been strengthened as a result of the growth of the working people's consciousness and the rise in their living standard and cultural level.[4]

Thus, it was implied that the presence of economic stimuli removed the necessity for harsher methods of discipline. The reform of 1956, however, did not produce the emancipation of the worker in the same sense as occurred in the West. The regime of control was continued in force. Subtler methods of regimentation were introduced. Severe penalties were replaced by differentiation in social insurance and pension benefits according to the employment record, thus favoring those who stayed with their jobs. Furthermore, discipline through a system of penalties, including those imposed by the courts, was replaced by public censure organized and administered by the workers.[5] More recently, an amelioration in general conditions of the industrial worker was enacted, introducing two important improvements in the worker's status. The Presidium of the Supreme Soviet enacted the Decree (January 25, 1960), subsequently approved by the Supreme Soviet on May 7, 1960, which removed inequalities in sick pay benefits due to the interruption of employment:

[W]orkers and employees who have left their previous jobs of their own free will are to be paid temporary benefits in all cases on a common basis, regardless of the amount of time they have worked on new jobs.

[W]orkers and employees dismissed on their own will retain uninterrupted seniority, if they begin work within one month after the day of their dismissal.[6]

One can still distinguish sectors of economic life in the Soviet Union where, owing to local difficulties, the organization of new industries is undertaken in conditions resembling early methods, and the recruitment of new workers and their movement into new areas of expansion assume the shape and atmosphere of military campaigns. But on the whole, the stability of labor has been achieved, production processes have been mastered, and alternate methods of social control to enforce the discipline of labor have been developed.

4 Vedomosti (No. 10, 1956).
5 Gliksman, *supra* note 2, at 775.
6 Vedomosti (No. 4, 1960).

The consequence of these achievements has been the enactment of more humane labor legislation.[7]

A similar process of relaxation by the regime has taken place in other fields of Soviet law. Thus, police powers have been circumscribed and their activities in the field of the administration of justice placed under the control of the public prosecutor. Control from the center over local authorities has been relaxed, the institution of inheritance liberalized, and progressive reform of criminal law undertaken.

The general change in the methods of enforcing government policies in the Soviet Union and other socialist states of Eastern Europe has called for new qualities in the system of rules governing life and legal commerce in Eastern Europe. As Professor Fuller observed when confronted with a specimen of Soviet legal thought:

Most definitions of law mistakenly try to make it equivalent to an authoritative ordering of social relations, but this does not expose its real essence. The ideal type of an authoritative ordering would be a military company marching in perfect step, ready to follow every command of its captain. Yet such a phenomenon is not only not legal in nature, but actually stands at the opposite pole from law. This is true generally of mere relationships of power. Slavery, for example, requires no legal form. If the relation of master and slave is in any sense legal, it is only because the master can exchange the slave for other goods, or because the law recognizes some semblance of a right in the slave against the master. Law appears as a distinct social phenomenon not when we have one man standing over another, but only when we have men standing toward one another with rights and duties.[8]

The rule of law represents a technique which operates by a clear assignment of roles in legal relationships, and this is the quality of which the Soviet legal system was almost completely deprived during the life of Stalin. The bulk of the legal regulation of that period consisted of *ad hoc* commands. Sometimes issued in abstract form, they never served as standards of permanent conduct. As an editorial in the leading Soviet legal publications stated:

7 Barton, "The Current Status of the Soviet Workers," 9 Problems of Communism (No. 7, 1960).
8 Fuller, "Pashukanis and Vyshinsky: A Study in the Development of Marxian Legal Theory," 47 Mich. L. Rev. 1160 (1949).

Law called for the new normative acts, and they were issued and frequently they were found to be in conflict with the articles of the codes in force, which officially were not amended, and also with other earlier normative acts. The mass of such careless, frequently contradictory legal material obstructs its application to concrete cases.[9]

When in 1956 the Twentieth Party Congress called for the return to the rule of law in the Soviet Union, it had two aims in view. In the first place, the abuse of power was to be discontinued. In the second place, the laws of the Soviet Union were to be reorganized into a clear system of rules. However, this was not understood as a change in the basic premises of the Soviet regime. The rule of law in its new meaning would still be subordinated to the needs of the national economy which would continue to be administered by the government according to the plan. Furthermore, the leading role of the Communist Party within the social and governmental apparatus was reaffirmed.[10]

Thus, the role of the Soviet legal experts was limited primarily to a systematic organization of the body of Soviet law with a view toward making the law a more useful standard for the guidance of the citizens and law-enforcing authorities. Only secondarily were Soviet lawyers called upon to devise more perfect legal solutions for the purpose of achieving technical improvement rather than a more progressive rule. While it is in the tradition of the European jurist to work for the reform of the legal rule on the basis of an independent scientific analysis of social reality, in the Soviet Union the professional authority of the jurist is highly circumscribed. In-

9 SGP 3 (No. 1, 1956); Orlovskii, "Zadatchi pravovoi nauki v svete reshenii XX sjezda KPSS," 26 Vestnik Akademii Nauk 5 (No. 8, 1956).
10 Hazard, "Le droit soviétique et le dépérissement de l'État," in 8 Travaux et conférences, Université Libre de Bruxelles 26 (1960); Romashkin, "Razvitie funktsii sovetskogo gosudarstva v protsesse postroienia kommunizma," SGP 12, 15 (No. 10, 1958): "Victory of socialism and communism is possible not in the result of dying off of the economic-organizing function, but in the expansion of that function. It is quite clear that while moving towards communism, the role of the planned direction of the national economy will acquire a growing significance. While progressing towards communism, grows and will grow the directing role of the communist party, which appears as a leading and directing force of the Soviet state, as the nucleus of all organizations of the toilers, both state and social."

deed, the formulation of the basic policies of the Soviet state and of the legislative program is within the exclusive jurisdiction of the Party.[11] Thus, the role of the socialist jurist is not that of an independent social or legal reformer.

Within these limitations, however, socialist jurists hold a monopoly over the technique which alone is able to produce the advantages of orderly government and the enforcement of social and economic policies with least resistance and greatest economy of effort. Within these limits, the socialist jurist is responsible for the results of the legal reform in the Soviet Union and Eastern Europe.

The return to socialist legality, to use the official language of the communist leadership, had two aspects. The first step was the re-establishment of legal order on the basis of the laws in force; the second was the reformation of the laws themselves and the raising of the general standards of government operations and legal commerce.

Socialist lawyers have reaffirmed in new form the axiom that legality means observance of certain procedural forms:

Socialist law and procedure endeavors to remove systematically from the positive law those provisions which are superfluous, insisting at the same time on a scrupulous enforcement of these rules which it continues in force as indispensable. . . . Too liberal an interpretation of the rules of procedure may easily lead . . . to a violation of the rules providing for the indispensable formalities, and thus result in a confusion which would undermine the principles of the socialist law of procedure.[12]

As the rule of law consists also in the observance of forms, one can detect among Soviet lawyers a conviction that socialist legality significantly depends on familiarity with legal techniques. Soviet lawyers, whether in practice or in academic circles, urge the importance of legal education and of refined legal thinking for the proper functioning of legal institutions. In the first instance, anxiety is expressed concerning the familiarity of the lawmakers with legislative techniques. Soviet lawyers urge that this inadequacy be remedied by expert assistance of trained lawyers. In the second instance, a low

11 Hazard, *supra* note 10, at 26–28.
12 Decision of the bench of seven justices of the Polish Supreme Court, of April 16, 1955, I.C. 20/55, PiP 677 (No. 10, 1955).

level of legal training is deplored among those called upon to enforce the laws of the socialist state.[13]

While in most of the satellite countries law courts are staffed by lawyers, in the Soviet Union even the recent reform of the judiciary failed to introduce the requirement of legal education for judges. The only steps toward assuring a higher degree of expertise on the bench were the extension of the tenure of office of elected judges from three to five years and the reorganization of the People's Courts by integrating one-judge courts into locality courts. In the latter instance, judges were assembled physically in one building on the basis of districts, localities, or wards for which these courts were competent. This created opportunities for handling the general business of the court by a more experienced member of the bench and for consultation and advice among the judges as to cases which they were called to decide.

In the beginning of 1960, Dean Karev of the Moscow University Law School demanded that a candidate for judicial office have legal training. He also revealed on this occasion that 55.4 per cent of the people's judges had legal training acquired in Soviet universities, that 37 per cent had legal training of the high school type, and that only a small number of people's judges had no legal training. The latter had acquired practical experience on the bench.[14]

Another aspect of the work of the legal profession in socialist countries drives home the axiom that legality in the operation of government must proceed under conditions in which certain formal standards of action are met. These standards are necessary in any legal order, irrespective of the social order or political regime.[15]

Essentially, these standards are not only the rules of operation of government, but constitute, as well, basic rules of judicial method which during the Stalinist period lost currency. The Polish Supreme

13 "Za povyshenie roli pravovi nauki v kodifikatsii sovetskogo zakonodatelstva," SGP 3 (No. 1, 1956); Nabatov, "Strogo okhraniat prava grazhdan," Sots. zak. 19–23 (No. 12, 1960); Ilyin & Mironov, "O forme i stile pravovykh aktov, SGP 65–73 (No. 12, 1960).

14 Karev, "Dalnieshee sovershenstvovanie sovetskoi pravovoi sistemy," SGP 61–71 (No. 2, 1959); *cf.* Strogovitch, "Nekotorye voprosy sudoustroistva," SGP 72–83 (No. 7, 1959).

15 *Cf. supra* at 104; Polish Supreme Court, directive ruling of February 12, 1955, PiP 290 (No. 7–8, 1955).

Court, in a decision passed by the full bench of the Civil Chamber, formulated the following directive for the lower courts:

[P]opular legality means the duty of the citizens to respect the laws in force. While imposing this duty on the citizens, it is not permitted to obscure the actual meaning of the law and to expose citizens to unexpected situations.[16]

This decision was passed after a long period of arbitrary repeal by the Polish courts of the laws which were deemed typical of the bourgeois social and economic order.[17] This practice, however, jeopardized the position of individuals and undermined the very foundations of legal commerce. In order to break away from this trend, the Court declared that:

It is a basic postulate of legality that, inasmuch as it is possible, the law which was not formally repealed be given full effect, even if there is a need for the reform of that law. Until this reform is introduced, strict observance of those provisions which are still formally in force, is the duty of all....[18]

Another principle of the orderly processes of government which socialist jurists have endeavored to bring to the attention of Soviet administrators and government officials is the concept of jurisdiction and the formal legality of each act of a governmental authority. This means a considerable restriction of the freedom of higher authorities to tamper with the decisions of lower agencies. By this means it is sought to give effect to the laws providing for the distribution of authority and responsibility. As a Soviet lawyer wrote:

In our opinion a decision of a lower Soviet may be changed only in the case of the violation of the law. The Constitution of the Union guarantees the rights of the Soviets directly elected by the population as agencies of self-government in their territory, by ruling that Soviets make their decisions within their jurisdiction determined by the law. Socialist legality is based on the principle of expediency, which is correctly interpreted. In other words, a higher Soviet has no right to deal with matters or change decisions which were already made by the lower Soviet within its jurisdiction. A decision of the lower Soviet has legal

16 PiP 290 (No. 7–8, 1955).
17 Grzybowski, "Continuity of Law in Eastern Europe," 6 Am. J. Comp. L. 44 ff. (1957).
18 PiP 291 (No. 7–8, 1955).

force if it is within the jurisdiction fixed by the law, functions or rights of the lower Soviet. In practice higher Soviets, and especially their executive committees, frequently change the decisions of lower organs also for reason of expediency which is a violation of the principle of socialist legality and of the rights of the lower organs. And so for instance in a number of provinces of the Russian SFSR and Byelorussian SSR, the organs of the regions deprive village Soviets of the right to dispose of surplus funds, resulting from higher revenue than estimated in the budget.[19]

Another important development in the general tendency to give some substance to the principle of self-government in various fields of social activity—which is supposed to be the fundamental principle of the Soviet political order—was the directive passed by the plenary session of the Supreme Court of the Soviet Union in December 1959 in the matter of "Judicial practice in civil cases involving collective farms." The Supreme Court gave effect to the March 1956 Resolution adopted by the Central Committee of the Party and of the Federal Government concerning "the statutes of agricultural collectives and further promotion of the initiative of their members in the organization of the Collective's industry and its administration." The resolution recommended and advised the collectives to assume direct responsibility for changes and amendments of their statutes according to local conditions. The Plenary Session of the Supreme Court had made it clear to the lower courts that, in deciding civil cases involving the activities of collective farms, courts ought to take into consideration that it is within the competence of the collective's members to make decisions as to the disposal of collective's products and property, and to direct its activity in accordance with the Soviet law and decisions of the Party and government

. . . that the statute of the agricultural collectives with its amendments, properly registered with the executive committee of the region represents the basic law of the kolkhoz activity. . . . The courts in their cases ought to apply the laws in force and the statutes of the collective farm concerned.[20]

19 Tikhomirov, "Nekotorye voprosy dalneishego razvitia miestnykh organov gosudarstvennoi vlasti SSSR," SGP 82 (No. 1, 1960).

20 Bardin, "Novoe postanovlenie plenuma Verkhovnogo Suda SSSR 'O Sudebnoi praktike po grazhdanskim kolkhoznym delam,'" SGP 12 (No. 6, 1960).

A Soviet jurist drew the attention of the officials of social organizations in charge of public functions to the fact that these activities, in contrast with the internal affairs of the organization, must conform to the provisions of the Constitution "which envisages the uniform subordination of all organizations and citizens to the law of the Soviet state." [21]

The significance of this discussion, which is barely sketched here, is that socialist jurists worked for the reconstruction of the foundations of the legal order from materials which were already available in the statute books of socialist legislation. New life had to be put into institutions which under Stalin had served to provide a façade for administrative practices which were far from being normal governmental procedures. The effort of Soviet lawyers is directed toward the precise distribution of social functions so as to provide for a framework in which social discipline may be achieved by a method in which individuals, government authorities, and socialist organizations are placed not "standing over another" but "toward one another" with rights and duties.

The work of Soviet jurists is part and parcel of a large program of social reform. It began in 1956 with the repudiation of some of the basic features of the Soviet regime under Stalin. Finally, the Twenty-first Congress of the Communist Party in 1959 declared that Soviet society had reached the halfway mark on the road of its historical progress and had passed into the period of communist construction.[22] Thus, the legal reform begun after 1956 has acquired a new dimension and is geared now toward improving the general standard of the Soviet legal system and to the devising of new techniques for fostering the emergence of the new society.

REFORM OF CRIMINAL LAW

The efforts of Soviet jurists to reform the Soviet legal system are motivated by the conviction that its institutions must meet cer-

21 Mitskevitch, "Razshirenie roli obshchestvennykh organizatsii v period razvernutogo stroitelstva kommunizma," SGP 32 (No. 9, 1959).
22 "XXI siezd KPSS i zadatchi sovetskoi pravovoi nauki," SGP 3–11 (No. 2, 1959).

tain requirements valid for all types of lawmaking. The patterns for modern laws are the result of centuries of scientific inquiry. A refined legal system, which alone can meet the needs of modern society, cannot deviate from certain generally accepted standards. This position, although formally concerned with technical aspects of lawmaking, is not without its ideological content. Legal reformers of the West, striving for the solution of practical problems, have always seen their task in terms of social policies. Such, it should be noted, are also declared to be the purposes of law enforcement in socialist societies. So, for instance, the purpose of criminal law is not only to punish crimes. In addition, its function is to eliminate criminality and to provide a method for the effective rehabilitation of the criminal, thus implying a judgment as to what social needs are. It follows, therefore, that Soviet imitation of the models of Western lawmaking implies also adoption of the ideological positions which motivated those who devised them.[23]

This is particularly true with regard to the field of criminal legislation. Since the time of Beccaria and Montesquieu, it has been realized that only through the scholarly reform of criminal legislation and the efficient and prompt enforcement of scientifically determined penal policy could the desired two purposes be achieved. In the first place, criminal activity would tend to diminish; secondly, a humane system of punishment might be introduced. The French reformers realized that harsh punishments contribute to the brutalization of the social psyche and tend to make matters worse. The history of European legal thought has equated a liberal system of government with a humane penal policy. In this scheme of things, the basic object of the inquiry into the causes of crimes has been the person of the offender as against the background of social conditions, in general, and special situations leading to the emergence and formation of criminal psychology. Methods of crime prevention and a program of rehabili-

---

23 An illuminating account of the currents of ideas in the socialist world at the present time is to be found in Hazard, *supra* note 10, at 26 ff.; *cf.* also, Ehrlich, "Uwagi o praworządności socjalistycznej, PiP 233–52 (No. 8–9, 1958). Ehrlich asserts that it is necessary to take account of the continuity of political ideas and that socialist legality and political institutions must expand social and humanitarian values formulated in the earlier social formations.

tation were thus formulated with regard to the individual concerned, not with regard to social conditions as such.[24]

The initial Soviet position, which motivated some of the basic ideas of the Soviet criminal code, stemmed from the general inclination to regard social conditions as the prime object of legal regulation. Pashukanis, who contributed largely to the "ideology" of the criminal legislation of his time, saw the axis of the reform movement in Soviet society in the departure from the contractual principle in criminal law. This, in his opinion, permeated the institutions of criminal law in the West. It was expressed, according to Pashukanis, in the fact that the offender knew "the amount of freedom which he pays as a result of the court arrangement." Instead, he suggested that the penalty be converted into a measure of expediency for safeguarding society and correcting a socially dangerous personality. Thus, socialist law needed no definitions of crimes, nor did the measure of social protection administered by the courts need strict and precise formulation, because that would again restore the contractual principle in criminal law. And so, criminal legal science was also unnecessary.[25]

Although Soviet criminal codes, as they emerged after a number of amendments, have failed to incorporate the basic ideas of the ideologists of the Soviet legal order, they certainly evidence little attention on the achievements of criminological thought in the West. As a result, they were inferior products in terms of legislative techniques. The RSFSR Code of 1926, which finally has assumed the position as model of criminal legislation for the Soviet Union, failed to provide a basis for an orderly administration of justice in the Soviet society. Constantly amended by inexpertly prepared insertions, the Code quickly became a shapeless mass of penal provisions, lacking a central idea and even a formal order. It has also failed as an expression of a theoretical formulation.

Responsibility for this state of affairs is divided. On one hand,

24 Grzybowski, "Criminal Law of France," in Essays on French Law, 47 ff. (1958).

25 Pashukanis, "The General Theory of Law and Marxism," in Soviet Legal Theory, 221–25 (1951); see *supra* at 46 in regard to the views of Krylenko and Kurskii; *cf.* Starosolskyj, The Principle of Analogy in Criminal Law: An Aspect of Soviet Legal Thinking (1954).

Soviet jurists who experimented with lawmaking were not professionally prepared to draft a new code. Their successors, who added to the Code's provisions, had little concern for the central ideas of the Code or even its terminology. The general climate of the legislative work was initially characterized by lack of experience, a lack of concern and patience with technical aspects of the lawmaking, and an inclination, even among the leading jurists of the new elite, to look at things from the political rather than legal point of view.

The central piece in the 1926 Criminal Code of the RSFSR was the analogy clause (Article 16), which permitted the imposition of criminal liability for a socially dangerous act not expressly proscribed by a criminal statute. Criminal liability was imposed under that article of the Criminal Code which most nearly approximated such an act.[26]

This provision was in direct opposition to the principle, "nullum crimen sine lege, nulla poena sine lege," which since the French Revolution has been the fundamental rule of modern criminal law. Its juristic implications were perhaps most expertly formulated by the Permanent Court of International Justice in the case of certain Danzig decrees, which provided for the prosecution of acts "deserving of penalty according to the fundamental conceptions of penal law and sound popular" feeling, which was a Nazi formula for the Soviet revival of analogy in criminal law. The Court stated:

A judge's belief as to what was the intention which underlay a law is essentially a matter of individual appreciation of the facts; so is his opinion as to what is condemned by popular feeling. Instead of applying a penal law equally clear to both the judge and the party accused, as was the case under the criminal law previously in force in Danzig, there is a possibility under the new decrees that a man may find himself placed on trial and punished for an act which the law did not enable him to know was an offense, because its criminality depends entirely upon the appreciation of the situation by the public prosecutor and the judge. Accordingly, a system in which the criminal character of an act and the penalty attached to it will be known to the judge alone, replaces a system in which this knowledge was equally open to both the judge and the accused.[27]

26 *Cf.* Starosolskyj, *supra* note 25.
27 The Permanent Court of International Justice, Ser. A/B, No. 65, 53.
   Cf. sec. 2 of the German Criminal Code as amended on June 28, 1935.

While the analogy provision was not the only cause of the harsh practices of Soviet courts, it was symbolic of the general attitude of the Soviet and satellite courts to the problems of law enforcement. The RSFSR Code of 1926 was imitated in detail by the other Soviet republics, and, after Soviet influence spread in Eastern Europe, also in a number of Eastern European countries, where analogy clauses and other features of the Soviet criminal law made their appearance in socialist legislation.[28]

The Soviet criminal code and its analogy clause has had a devastating effect on the level of legal practice and on law enforcement wherever Soviet institutions have made their appearance. This was due to the fact that the Soviet architects of the new legal concepts were guilty of a basic miscalculation in constructing a legal system of ill-fitting parts, borrowed from foreign political and legal doctrines with little discrimination as to their origin or understanding of their real functions.

The idea that courts ought to have great powers in meting out punishment was not a Soviet innovation. It was and still is current in legal thinking in the West, and is motivated by the need of the strict adjustment of punishment to the circumstances of each individual case and the personality of the offender. According to the founders of the sociological school of criminal law, vast judicial powers postulated high expertise on the bench. Professional judges, well trained in law and in the basic techniques of criminal policy and assisted by the auxiliary services of modern penology, were authorized to apply judicial pardon or extraordinary reduction even below the minimum statutory limit. The central purpose of the vast judicial powers was to make law enforcement humane by eliminating the element of vengeance. Soviet criminologists have extended judicial powers even further and have entrusted them to a bench of laymen. By insisting on the objective criteria of crime, they have rendered the adjustment of penalties according to the degree of guilt impossible.[29]

28 *Cf.* Grzybowski, "From Contract to Status, Some Aspects of the Reception of Soviet Law in Eastern Europe," 2 Seminar 60 ff. (1953).
29 Pound, "Individualization of Justice," 7 Fordham Law Rev. 153 (1938); Hall, "Nulla Poena sine Lege," 47 Yale Law J. 165–93 (1937); Solnar, "Maintien ou abandon de la règle nulla poena sine lege," 17 Revue de droit pénal et de criminologie 744–50 (1937); Donnedieu de Vabres,

The death of Stalin made the reform of criminal law feasible; and in December 1958, fourteen laws were adopted which instituted a new trend in the criminal legislation of the Soviet Union.[30]

The new laws fell into three categories. First, there were three statutes containing the basic principles of criminal law, the organization of courts, and judicial procedure in criminal matters. These statutes required additional legislative action by the constituent republics. The second group consisted of those statutes which came into force directly and uniformly throughout the Union without any additional action by the individual republics. Two principal statutes constituted this category—one pertaining to crimes against the state and another concerning military crimes. A statute abolishing the punishment of deprivation of electoral rights and another on changes in the election of the people's courts—which was connected with the new basic principles of the organization of courts—belonged to the same category. Another law which went into effect immediately was the Statute on Military Courts. The final category was made up of six statutes containing formal and transitory provisions for the interim period before the new regime in the Soviet administration of justice was fully established.

Some of the enactments of December 1958 constituted basic reforms affecting due process of law. Others, though less fundamental in scope and significance, were nevertheless of great practical importance. In the first category of reforms, the issue of punishment

---

La crise moderne du droit pénal, la politique criminelle des états autoritaires 156 (1938). The only exception in the general adoption of the principle of the nonretroactivity of penal laws, except when more lenient than the law under which an offense was committed, represents the legislation of the Nordic countries. Danish criminal codes of 1866 and 1930, contrary to the general European practice, have stated the principle of the analogous application of the criminal statute to crimes not defined in the written law. Art. 1 of the Code of 1930 rules that: "only acts punishable under a statute or acts of entirely similar nature shall be punished. . . ." In fact, however, legal science has limited the application of the analogy clause thus formulated to situations in which western European courts also resort to the analogy technique. *Cf.* Hurvitz, "L'analogie dans le droit danois," Revue de science criminelle et de droit pénal comparé (n.s.) 1–5 (1950).

30 For details see Grzybowski, "Soviet Criminal Law Reform of 1958," 35 Ind. L.J. 125–28 (1960).

by analogy was central to the whole range of questions involving the nature of judicial process in the Soviet Union. Its significance, involving basic attitudes toward the function and role of the state in relation to the individual, clearly exceeded the somewhat narrow limits of criminal law and judicial procedure.[31] Article 3 of the 1958 Basic Principles of Criminal Legislation of the USSR and the Constituent Republics signified the victory of the traditionalist tendency. It stated that "only persons guilty of committing a crime, that is those who intentionally or by negligence have committed a socially dangerous act specified by the criminal statute, shall be held responsible and shall incur punishment."

Modern criminal law is based on the proposition that the purpose of punishment is primarily to correct and only in exceptional cases to eliminate. As a consequence, liability to punishment, as well as its type and severity, are related to the form and nature of subjective guilt which modern criminologists consider the surest guide to the personality of the offender. Absolute liability (objective criteria of responsibility) is little known to European criminal law. The commission of a punishable act requires either intent (*dolus* in its various forms, *directus, indirectus, eventualis, preterintentional*) or negligence (*culpa*). As a rule, a punishable act must be committed intentionally. If the offender is guilty of negligence he is liable to punishment if the law expressly provides for it.[32]

As legislative techniques developed, types of guilt were related to the classification of offenses. Crimes and misdemeanors as a rule require intent. In expressly provided circumstances, a misdemeanor may be committed through negligence, while petty offenses (police

---

31 *Cf. supra* at 185–86.
32 Art. 19 of the Danish Criminal Code stated: "As regards the offenses dealt with in this act, acts which have been committed through negligence on the part of the perpetrator shall not be punished except when expressly provided for..." The Norwegian Criminal Code of 1902 stated the same principle in a somewhat different manner (art. 40): "Whoever acts without malicious forethought is not subject to punitive provisions of the present statute, unless it is expressly provided for, or undoubtedly results that the omission is punishable." Italian pre-Fascist code also stated (art. 45) that a person is not subject to punishment if he did not intend (*non abbia voluto*) the result which constitutes a criminal act, unless the law provides otherwise.

transgressions) are liable to punishment without regard for the type of guilt (absolute responsibility), except when the law rules otherwise. A full statement of the various forms of guilt seems to have been included for the first time in the Russian Code of 1903, and its classification has become almost a rule in modern codes.[33] The Yugoslav (1927) and Polish (1932) Codes have repeated it almost without change.[34]

Even these fairly detailed provisions have not satisfied European scholars, and one may note efforts at a closer definition of the conditions under which the law should punish crimes committed by negligence. The Swiss Code of 1937 (Article 18) rules that an offense committed by negligence is punishable only when the

... perpetrator, out of carelessness contrary to his duties, has not foreseen or taken into account the consequences of his behavior. Carelessness is contrary to duty when the perpetrator has not exercised caution to which he is obligated either by the circumstances or his personal situation.

The Greek Criminal Code of 1952, which included in its provisions a short theoretical treatise dealing with various aspects of guilt and forms of criminal acts, introduced a small addition to the generally accepted limitation of criminal responsibility for acts considered punishable but committed without direct intent. Article 15 of this Code states:

33 Art. 48 of the Russian Code of 1903 ruled that an offense should be considered intentional not only when the offender desired its commission but also when he was aware of the possibility of the result, which constitutes the criminal nature of the act. An offense is committed by negligence not only when the offender failed to foresee it, although he could or should have foreseen it, but also when, having foreseen the possibility of the result, he lightmindedly supposed that he could prevent its occurrence.

34 Provisions of the Italian Code of 1930 (art. 42) represent another type of formulation of the same set of ideas: "No one may be punished for an act of omission, or omission deemed by the law to be an offense, unless he has committed it with criminal intent, except in cases of crimes of transferred intent or crimes without criminal intent which are expressly contemplated by the law. The law determines the cases for which an agent is otherwise accountable as a consequence of his act of commission or omission. In regard to contravention, each person is answerable for his knowing and willful act or omission, whether it be with or without intent."

When the law requires that a specific consequence should occur as an element of a criminal act, the non-prevention of that consequence shall stand for causation only when the offender was under special duty to prevent that consequence.[35]

The general meaning of the provisions of modern criminal codes concerning types of guilt in their relation to the classification of offenses and the type of punishment is that while guilt by negligence extends the scope of responsibility regarding the type of criminal act, at the same time it restricts the class of persons criminally responsible for a negligent act or omission (special duties, violations of orders, etc.) and reduces the severity of punishment.[36]

The reform of 1958 has failed to change Soviet criminal law as to the determination of criminal responsibility according to the degree of guilt. The new law defines as criminal any socially dangerous acts (of commission or omission) directed against the Soviet social and political order, the economic system, etc., if so specified by the statute.[37] In addition, it defines criminal intent and negligence in much the same manner as the Russian Code of 1903, but fails to repeat the latter's general reservation that unless otherwise expressly provided for by a criminal statute, a prohibited act is punishable only when committed with intent.[38] Contrary to modern practice, the Soviet statute lumps all punishable acts into a single category of socially dangerous acts. Although on occasion a distinction is made between more dangerous and less important crimes, a systematic grouping of offenses into classes according to their seriousness is avoided. In this manner, it is left to the judge to distinguish between intent and negligence; and unless expressly provided in each

35 As to the position of Ferri on the question of responsibility for intentional or nonintentional crimes, *cf*. 31 La Scuola Positiva 20–21, 135 (1921); *cf*. Cuban Code of Social Defense, arts. 18–20.

36 E.g., ch. XXXIII of the Polish Code of 1932 on crimes causing public danger. According to the provisions of the Code of 1932, intentional crimes are punishable by imprisonment from 6 months to 15 years, while negligent commission of such crimes calls, as a rule, only for detention (from one week to one year) or a fine.

37 Basic Principles of Criminal Legislation of the Soviet Union and of the Union Republics, art. 7 (1958).

38 *Id*. arts. 8 and 9.

definition, the court has to give similar weight to intent and negligence.

Lack of differentiation between negligent and intentional offenses permits the measurement of punishment according to the objective criteria of social danger involved and not according to the personal relationship of the offender to the prohibited act. That this is to remain a feature of criminal legislation of the Soviet state in the future is already apparent from the two federal statutes on antistate and military crimes. Regarding crimes which by their nature may be committed only intentionally, these statutes contain statements making intent a constitutive element of the crime definition. Sometimes the definitions of intent are somewhat vague, and give little concrete instruction for the court to go by ("weakening the state," "undermining . . . a branch of economy"). Thus, an unusually wide latitude of interpretation of the true purpose of the crime defined in the statute is permitted. In other cases, however, the statute fails to make clear the nature of guilt which renders an offender punishable.[39] But in addition to those two groups, a considerable number of crime definitions are couched in terms which make it clear that a serious penalty is threatened for the commission of an act which may be the result of either intent or negligence.[40] Both the statute on antistate crimes and that on military crimes list a large number of offenses of this type. After a list of crimes, which either by their nature or by direct statement must be committed with intent, the statute on military crimes lists a large group of offenses which, although threatened with serious punishment, may also be committed by negligence. The mere loss of secret documents is punished by imprisonment for from two to five years. Article 24 of the same statute provides a stiff sentence of from six months to ten years for a careless attitude toward service duties, a vague and all-embracing statement permitting a criminal prosecution for any dereliction of duty. The two statutes still leave many questions unanswered; but there is little hope that

39 E.g., Soviet Statue on Crimes against the State, art. 8 (propaganda of war).

40 *Id.* art. 13 (loss of documents), art. 21 (violation of rules of international flights), art. 22 (violation of rules of safety of traffic and exploitation of transport).

in other parts of the criminal codes, which still await enactment by the republican legislatures, a new approach to the question of guilt may be expected.

The attitude of the Code of 1926 is quite orthodox in regard to crimes which are traditional and specially connected with crimes against the life, health, freedom, and honor of a person or against private property. A distinction between intentional and unintentional crimes is clearly made in the definitions and is properly reflected in penal sanctions.[41] The type of guilt is not specified when only intentional crime is possible.[42] Furthermore, there is no reference to criminal liability for negligence when failure to take action is criminal owing to specific obligations and duties resulting from the offender's qualifications or position. In such a case, a modern code would make it clear that negligence is punishable.[43]

In defining crimes which constitute an attack on the new order, there is either no reference to the type of guilt, or it is described in different terms from those used in the general part. Article 58[14] on sabotage speaks of conscious nonexecution or intentionally careless execution of duties. Sometimes no clear distinction is made between an intentional and negligent act,[44] which is also the case with respect to crimes particularly dangerous to the governmental order.[45] Sometimes a reference to negligence signifies that all forms of prohibited activity or inactivity from which damage results are punishable irrespective of the type of guilt.[46] The obliteration of the dividing line between intent and negligence is particularly striking in the definitions of economic crimes.

Additional light is thrown on Soviet legislative solutions of the question of negligent and intentional crimes by the extent to which this technique was followed by satellite criminal legislation

---

41 Arts. 138 and 139 (murder and negligent homicide); arts. 142–47 (intentional and negligent bodily harm).

42 Art. 162 (larceny).

43 Art. 176 (a captain's failure to give assistance to a ship involved in a collision with his own ship, if such assistance could be rendered without serious danger to his own ship, crew, or passengers).

44 RSFSR Criminal Code of 1926, art. 58[1].

45 *Id.* art. 59[3] (violation of rules of international aviation).

46 *Id.* art. 74[2].

in Eastern Europe. Of five criminal codes enacted there since 1945, two—the Hungarian Code of 1950 and the Albanian Code of 1952—have adopted, in one form or another, the Soviet formulation of intent and negligence. The Hungarian Code differs from its Soviet model, stating plainly in Article 11 that "crimes committed by negligence shall be punished except when the law declares that only an act intentionally committed shall be punished." The statement of the Minister of Justice, submitted with the bill to the parliament, explained that:

[T]he law declares that as a general rule crimes committed by negligence are punishable, except when the law states that only an act intentionally committed shall be punished. This represents a more satisfactory defense of the society, because the social danger of negligence is frequently equal to that of intent, and sometimes even surpasses it.

Other satellite codes, however—the Bulgarian Code of 1951, the Czechoslovak Code of 1950, and the Yugoslav Code of 1951—state that crimes committed by negligence are punishable only when so provided by law.

The Soviet approach to the question of guilt falls far short of the general European standards which, before the revolution, provided a model for the reform of Russian law. It denotes a total lack of concern with the personality of the offender as a factor in determining the nature and severity of punishment, and turns the administration of justice in penal matters into blind retribution.[47]

On the other hand, the reform bears eloquent witness to the effort to make Soviet criminal law more humane. Under the old rule, juveniles were equally responsible with adults after reaching the age of fourteen. In a number of limited, most serious crimes, the age of responsibility had been lowered to twelve years, with no restriction to the kinds and types of penalty applied, including the death penalty. Under the 1958 General Principles of Criminal Legislation, minors under fourteen are not liable to criminal prosecution. Those over fourteen and not more than sixteen are criminally liable only for the most serious offenses, such as murder, rape, serious bodily harm, etc. Between sixteen and eighteen they are criminally

47 Basic Principles of Criminal Legislation of the Soviet Union and Union Republics, art. 10.

liable as adults, with the limitation that if the youthful offender can be reformed without the imposition of penalty the court may so refrain. However, if the offense represents a great social danger, the court must apply coercive educational measures. What these measures shall be is left to the legislation of the individual republics.

The new regulations on the treatment of juveniles thus represent a considerable improvement, although they are far from models of moderation. The general tendency of modern codes is to substitute educational measures for punishment as a matter of principle and not as a matter of exception. Indeed, the provision is made that even after the age of full responsibility is reached, the court may apply judicial mercy or educational measures.[48]

The system of penalties provided in the 1926 Code was extremely complicated. In 1958 the number of penalties was reduced from eighteen to eight, retaining, however, the most important and traditional punishment in Russia, exile and expulsion. The maximum prison sentence has been reduced from fifteen to ten years; and in cases where previously, under the Code of 1926, a maximum sentence of twenty-five years imprisonment could be imposed, the maximum is now fifteen years. The death penalty is now imposed only for treason, espionage, subversion, terroristic activities, banditry, and murder, and in time of war, for the most serious military crimes. In no case is the death penalty mandatory. It should be mentioned, however, that treason covers a number of activities, among which is the refusal to return from abroad, for which the death penalty seems excessive.[49]

There are special provisions concerning the penalties for juveniles and pregnant women. The death penalty cannot be imposed on juveniles under eighteen or on women who are pregnant either at the time when the crime is committed or the sentence is rendered, and such sentence cannot be carried out on a pregnant woman. The

48 In the Polish Code of 1932 and the Greek Code of 1952 the age of responsibility began at 17 years, and educational measures or judicial mercy to the youthful offender could be applied until he was 20 or 21 years old respectively.

49 Basic Principles of Criminal Legislation of the Soviet Union and of the Union Republics, arts. 21–22; Law on Crimes Against the State, art. 1.

maximum prison sentence for a juvenile under eighteen is ten years. Juveniles serve their prison sentences in separate labor colonies. Exile and expulsion cannot be imposed upon juveniles under eighteen or upon pregnant women.[50]

One of the disappointments of the reform is the preservation of the penalty of the general confiscation of property. In the Principles of 1958, this appears as an additional penalty for the most serious crimes against the state or crimes committed for mercenary motives. A leading Soviet jurist, in an article which appeared in this country, has confidently forecast its repeal.[51] Obviously this part of the reform failed because of the last-minute tug of war in the drafting committee. There is no record of the discussions of the committee, however, which makes it difficult to establish the reason for the retention of this penalty in the arsenal of repressive measures. The confiscation of an offender's entire property was introduced as a typical measure to combat counter-revolutionary activities, and its presence suggests that however optimistic the official image of the ideological unity of Soviet society may be, it still needs bolstering up by exceptional measures. The Principles of 1958 continue a practice which the French bourgeoisie hoped to consign to the unreturnable past in the *Declaration de droits de l'homme et du citoyen*. Together with expulsion, exile, and long term imprisonment, the general confiscation of property constitutes a measure which is testimony to the pessimistic attitude of the penal policies in socialist society and suggests *sui generis* elements of civil death.

In contrast, the abolition of the penalty of deprivation of the right to vote strikes a somewhat bizarre note. One would suppose that in a socialist society which, according to the official line, is the first in history to realize the complete equality of citizens, the exercise of political rights would be one of the most cherished privileges, fully deserved by only the most loyal citizens. Obviously this is not so, if the deprivation of such right has no deterrent value.[52]

50 Basic Principles of Criminal Legislation of the Soviet Union and of the Union Republics, arts. 22–23.

51 Karev, "The Forthcoming Reform of USSR Criminal Law," Harv. L. Record (May 1, 1958).

52 Polianski, Izvestia, Dec. 27, 1958.

At the foundation of the provisions guaranteeing a fair trial stands the conviction that, in the system of the separation of powers or of checks and balances, the courts constitute the branch of government specially designed to protect the rights of the individual. Under the Soviet rule of unity of powers, citizens are said to need no special protection against the agencies of the people's government. In theory administrative authorities of a socialist country have no policy but that determined by the well-understood interests of the people. However, this assumption has not worked with the perfection expected, and Soviet legislators have felt obliged to proclaim anew the principle of judicial monopoly in imposing serious penalties. Article 4 of the General Principles of Procedure in Criminal Matters formally states that no person shall be put in the position of a defendant otherwise than in virtue of, and in a manner prescribed by, the law. Article 7 of the same law states that the "administration of justice in criminal matters belongs exclusively to the court. Nobody may be declared guilty of committing a crime and be subjected to penalty except by court sentence." The same principle is restated in the General Principles of Criminal Legislation, which asserts in Article 3 that criminal punishment may be imposed only by a court sentence.

Legislative formulas adopted in the December 1958 laws, restricting the exercise of judicial power exclusively to the proper courts of justice, were seriously affected and put in doubt by the policy of transferring some of the governmental responsibilities and public functions into the administration of social organizations.[53] But by no means is this the only instance of administrative trespass into judicial functions which survived the reform of 1958.

The Principles of Judicial Procedure in Criminal Matters of 1958 have re-established the traditional terminology indicating the difference between a police and formal investigation, the latter being obligatory in trials of more important crimes (crimes against the state and military crimes). In modern European criminal procedures such investigations are controlled, after the French pattern, by the court and are conducted by a judicial officer who enjoys all the privileges and has the status of an independent judge. The strict connection between formal investigation and the disposal of a case

53 General Principles of Criminal Procedure, art. 15 (1958).

is indicated by the fact that Soviet legislators have included herein the law on judicial procedure. But while judicial control of an investigation assures all the guarantees of a fair trial, the element of judicial guarantees is lacking in the Soviet procedure. Here the real difference between police investigations and formal investigative proceedings is that the latter are conducted by the more experienced agents of the security police or the public prosecutor.

The principle that pretrial investigations are controlled by the public prosecutor has also been uniformly adopted by the socialist states in Eastern Europe, although actual solutions in implementing the principle of procuratorial control differ from country to country. In some of the satellites, courts have been given a role in controlling the legality of the proceedings in regard to certain specific points, such as the legality of temporary arrest. In this respect, the Yugoslav Code of Criminal Procedure is of singular interest. The first Code of Criminal Procedure enacted in 1948 was an imitation of the Soviet pattern. After experimenting for five years with this type of judicial procedure, the Yugoslav Code of 1953 vindicated the validity of some fundamental principles of law for all social orders. As it was originally enacted, the Code of 1953 was a combination of two approaches. The distribution of jurisdiction was conceived, according to the general interests of the administration of justice, not only to expedite the investigation of crimes, but also to preserve certain fields of criminal investigation exclusively for the jurisdiction of the public prosecutor and the administrative authorities, especially the investigators of the Ministry of the Interior. In this category of proceedings, the public prosecutor controlled the informal investigations and could address himself variously to the county court, to the investigating judge, to the district court, or to the police, with a request to investigate a case or a phase of it or to perform a function in the proceedings (Article 141). The Law of December 26, 1959, abolished this dichotomy by giving the investigating judge of the district court the overriding authority to assume, at any time, the conduct of any pretrial investigation (Article 161), thus restoring the principle of the full judicial character of the pretrial proceedings.

There are areas where the Procedural Principles of 1958 constitute a definite improvement over those of the Code of 1923. Article 14 introduced an important innovation by incorporating into Soviet criminal procedure the Roman law principle "ei incubat probatio qui ait non qui negat." Thus, the Article stated that "neither the court, the prosecutor, nor the investigating agent has the right to impose the duty of furnishing proof on the defendant." In this connection, two other issues are important: the presumption of innocence and the status of the defendant.

The presumption of innocence is dealt with in Article 43, which states:

A conviction cannot be based on suppositions, and may be decreed only when in the course of trial the guilt of the accused in committing the crime has been proved.

In regard to the second issue, the Principles of 1958 are less clear. In one place, they put the depositions of the defendant in the same category as those of a witness or of an expert, calling them testimony (*pokazania*). In another, the procedural principles state that the defendant has the right, but not the duty, to give explanations in connection with the charges against him. This suggests that the defendant may either participate actively in the proceedings or remain passive, and that his position differs from that of a witness.[54]

The rights of the defendant circumscribe the powers of the court and the prosecution, and their exercise is subject to definite rules which, in the final analysis, constitute the essence of legality. Soviet criminal procedure still falls short of generally accepted standards in this respect, although in the 1958 reform, a definite attempt was made to bring Soviet procedure in criminal matters closer to the established practice. This is especially evident in appeal proceedings. Contrary to the Code of 1923, the Principles of 1958 limit the right of the higher court to impose stiffer sentence only when the appeal is lodged by the prosecution or by the injured party. At the same time, the higher court always has the right to go beyond the appeal if, in reviewing the case, it comes to the conclusion that a milder sentence would be more appropriate.[55]

Generally speaking, the reform has produced more cohesion

54 *Id.* art. 21.
55 *Id.* arts. 44–45.

between the various parts of the Soviet legal system and in the machinery of criminal justice. In addition, it has removed some of the inherent contradictions by reinstating a number of the principles which are basic for any system of justice. It has also corrected some of the misconceptions and plain mistakes born of the endeavor to produce a socialist order equipped with institutions differing fundamentally from those of free societies. Thus, the humane aspects of the new provisions are not to be overlooked, although there is perhaps a greater distance between practice and the legal rule in the Soviet Union than in any other public order.

However, some of the most important aspects of the Soviet penal policy have not been affected by the reform. The General Principles of 1958 provide no machinery for permitting the individualization of criminal cases in order to make proper use of the large punitive powers with which the law has equipped the Soviet courts. The most important element in the determination of criminal responsibility, the element of guilt, has remained blurred, and there is no direct connection between the degree of guilt and the penalty. Elsewhere, modern legislators have employed great ingenuity in order to assure as full and purposeful a realization of criminal policy as possible. This example has not been followed in Soviet law which still contains little more than high-sounding slogans having no coverage in the detailed provisions of the law.

The same conservatism prevailed in regard to the principal features of the administration of justice. It is still dominated by the person of the government attorney, who combines in his office the role of prosecutor of crimes and guardian of legality with the duty to enforce government policies and to protect the law. The prosecutor appears in the dual role of party before the court and supervisor of court practice. Furthermore, the government attorney represents the only element in the complicated machinery of the administration of justice in which the principle of professional proficiency has received consistent recognition.

Two aspects of the reform are particularly disappointing. In the first place, the conduct of pretrial investigations is left in the hands of the public prosecutor and police authorities.[56] This conservatism is

56 *Id.* arts. 28–35.

the more surprising in that there is a definite tendency in other socialist countries of Eastern Europe to return the conduct of pretrial investigations, which are obligatory in all the more important crimes,
to judicial officers. These officers act as judges and are subordinate
exclusively to the court, before whom a government attorney has only
the position of a party. The other disappointing feature is that little
has been done to improve the professional qualifications and the
performance of Soviet courts. No requirement of legal education or
practice, which would have extended the principle of professionalism
into the administration of justice, has been established. The serious
effect of the absence of trained personnel in the administration of
justice is apparent from the low level of judicial work in the Soviet
Union.[57]

As early as 1927, Ferri, the founder of the Italian Positive School
of Criminal Law, having come into immediate contact with the Soviet
Criminal Code, complained about the verbosity and propagandistic
passages in the Soviet statutes. Theoretical or political expositions
are not needed in a well-written law. The same is also characteristic
of the 1958 judicial statutes. Faced with untrained judges who have
never been exposed to organized instruction in law, the Soviet legislator feels compelled to lecture on the rudiments of the theory of
criminal law. The low level of legal preparation prevailing in the
Soviet Union makes it doubtful whether the use of modern legislative
techniques is at all possible and practicable. The modern tendency
toward simple phraseology and succinct definitions is based on the
assumption that the bench, the prosecution, and the defense consist
of highly trained jurists, familiar with the theory of modern criminal
law and fully conversant with the various penological theories. In
countries with modern codes, judges must first refer the definitions
of individual crimes to the provisions of the General Part which determine the principles and purpose of the punishment of crimes, and
secondly to legal theories learned from their professors which constitute the ultimate terms of reference in order to fill a gap or clarify
a doubtful point.

57 For a comprehensive treatment see Gsovski & Grzybowski, Government, Laws and Courts in the Soviet Union and Eastern Europe ch.
15 (1959).

STANDARDS OF CRIMINAL POLICY

Reform in Soviet criminal law has taken place in two areas. On the one hand, Soviet lawyers, in drafting Soviet statutes, introduced basic concepts of orderly and purposeful criminal policy. On the other hand, they found it necessary to clear the ground of fundamental misconceptions which were largely responsible for the harshness and low level of Soviet criminal justice in practice. As a leading Soviet jurist noticed at the moment when the new Soviet criminal statutes were being debated, one of the Stalinist cliches which had influenced the tenor of judicial action was demolished. The idea that the more socialist society moved toward communism, the harsher would be the forms of criminal repression against the offenders of the rules of socialist law was no longer recognized as valid. The other notion was based on the conviction that all crime constituted a remnant of the capitalist order, and that as socialist construction made progress, crime became more and more rare. Exceptional manifestations of criminality would then call for even stronger measures in order to hasten the arrival of the millennium.

With the theory of the capitalist devil exploded, Soviet jurists were forced to abandon the sheltered theoretical position which absolved them from making researches into the real causes of crimes in socialist society. One leading jurist wrote with exasperation that Soviet legal science had done little to inquire into the causes of crime or into the effectiveness of the educational measures which the Soviet State was employing. The mere fact that there was among criminal groups a large number of youthful criminals, who were the product of the new social order, put a question mark over the validity of all stereotyped explanations.[58]

This call for objectivity and attention to those facts and circumstances important for the disposal of criminal cases was reflected in an appeal for what the public prosecutor of the Moscow region called the raising of the level of culture of the pretrial investigations. Such was thought to be an indispensable condition for the realization of the postulate that only those whose crimes which were proven should be subject to criminal repression:

58 Romashkin, *supra* note 10, at 14–16.

Tendentiousness, lack of objectivity, prejudicial inclination to produce a criminal charge in the examination of criminal cases (*obvinitelnyi uklon*) lead to serious mistakes. When we talk of the prejudicial inclination to prove a criminal charge we have in mind such activities of the inquisitorial, procuratorial and judicial authorities which lead to unfounded accusations or illegal imposition of harsher penalties. Sometimes this prejudicial tendency is revealed in cases involving innocent persons.[59]

The term culture has many meanings in Soviet parlance. In our present connection, it seems to signify a civilized approach to the administration of justice together with a proper understanding of the purpose of the prosecution of crimes. It means due respect for human dignity, elimination of lynch-law attitudes, striving to set an example by punishing an accused only after proper examination of all the circumstances of the case, and endeavoring to discover whether there is a legal foundation for the charge.

Soviet legal periodicals have begun to publish various instances of such attitudes. So, for instance, a young man was found guilty and sentenced to ten years of deprivation of freedom for taking without authorization a ride in an army truck. His act was found to be a crime of causing damage to government property (decree of Presidium of the Supreme Soviet of July 4, 1947), though there was no evidence that the accused intended to dismantle the truck of its parts or that he planned or actually had damaged it in any manner.[60]

In another case, a people's court in Uzbekistan sentenced a dining room supervisor for causing a shortage of goods which were said to constitute government property. Owing to the defendant's negligence, some of the fruit which was in her care was spoiled. The public prosecutor lodged a protest against the sentence, which had pronounced the defendant to be guilty of negligence without explaining what this negligence consisted of. Obviously, the Soviet court confused two ideas, one of negligence in the usual sense of the word, as a case of spoilage of fruit, and the other as denoting a state of mind, which caused criminal action or omission punishable in law.[61]

Frequently, harsh justice is the result of the poor professional

59 Urakov, "Povisyt kulturu sledstva," Sots. zak. 12–16 (No. 7, 1960).
60 Sots. zak. 86–87 (No. 2, 1960).
61 *Id.* 89–90 (No. 7, 1960).

preparation of Soviet judges, sometimes even on the bench of appeal instances, and their consequent inability to relate the facts of the case to the provisions of the law or the doctrines of legal concepts. Ideas and institutions, such as acting under emotional stress, self-defense, and reduced criminal responsibility, have no concrete meaning to Soviet judges who until quite recently worked in a regime which stressed prompt and formal crime repression calling for little refinement in judicial action.[62]

Another area where the mechanical enforcement of the criminal statute has wide currency is that of prohibitions of certain trades and industries. In this regard, courts frequently dispose of cases without a proper examination of all the circumstances of the case, of the nature of criminal offenses as defined in the law, and of the purposes of criminal policy. Sometimes, high prison sentences are imposed for making articles for sale permitted by the law or from raw materials available on the open market. On occasion, criminal repression has struck at persons for whom sewing and producing items of clothing, underwear, etc., was the only possible means and source of support. In one case, a widow with three young children was sentenced to prison for making infants' clothing. Prison sentences have been imposed for making articles which are a legitimate object of private industry or for using small amounts of certain metals which cannot be used in private production. At the same time, certain consumer articles made of those metals (nails) are available on the market. A Soviet jurist has vigorously criticized these provisions, stating that they lead to an obvious misinterpretation of the law and, in most instances, deserve no place in the statute book.[63] Confronted with cases of this nature, the appeals of Polish lawyers striving for the humanization of the socialist law become both urgent and realistic.[64]

While these various matters, which contribute vitally to the tone and climate of the life of the law in the Soviet Union, deal with peripheral issues of the Soviet penal provisions, Soviet lawyers have attempted some basic reconstruction of juristic concepts. After the

62 *Cf*. procuratorial protests in Sots. zak. 79–80 (No. 12, 1960).
63 Kozak, "Otvestvennost za zaniatie zapreshchonymi promyslami," Sots. zak. 36–38 (No. 3, 1958).
64 Hazard, *supra* note 10, at 26 ff.

analogy clause was removed, another central institution which highly colors Soviet practice of criminal law, i.e., the institution of social danger, came under consideration. Appearing in the Soviet Codes and also in the 1958 statutes, it persists as a constitutive element of crime definition.[65]

Article 7 of the General Principles of Criminal Law stated that:

As a crime shall be considered, if it is so specified by a criminal statute, any social dangerous act (of commission or omission) attacking the Soviet social or political order; socialist system of economy, socialist property; persons; political, labor, property and other rights of citizens; as well as any other socially dangerous act attacking the socialist legal order, if so specified by a criminal statute.

The doctrine of social danger is one of the oldest concepts in criminal law. It formulates a basic reason for the prohibition of certain acts under the sanction of penalty, as each society protects those ideas, institutions, or assumptions which are fundamental in any legal order. Its role is to provide the reason for the legislative enactment of a legal prohibition of certain acts. The difference between the traditional law and the socialist legal concept begins at the moment when courts come into the general picture of law enforcement. In disposing of individual cases, courts are not primarily concerned with the aspect of social danger. Rather, they focus their attention upon the personality of the offender and other specific circumstances of the case.

A Soviet jurist has attacked the doctrine of social danger in connection with recent plans for drawing in and engaging Soviet social organizations in the process of law enforcement and the struggle with criminal activity. He pointed out that the conviction that a criminal act must produce a single type of reaction in the form of court punishment has been replaced by a new approach. Now, the reaction of society to a criminal act may take any of the three forms. In the first place, the court may declare that a guilty person may be subject to educational measures which will engage social action as a chief measure of social defense. Secondly, in certain categories of offenses, the case itself may be transmitted to be dealt with by a social organization, which takes the place of the court. Thirdly, there is a possibility of

65 *Cf. supra* at 185–86, 191 ff.

dealing with the case and of applying educational measures without formal sentence being passed either by the courts or social organizations. A multiplication of methods for disposing of criminal cases calls for a new approach to criminal activity and a careful study of the individuality of the offender. Such alone can provide a guide to the selection of the best method.[66]

Thus, after forty years of experimenting with criminal justice, Soviet jurists have discovered the importance of the teachings of the sociological school of criminal law, which has inspired the institutions of modern criminal law.

Soviet jurists complain that in the Soviet Union itself little work has been done to provide the bar and the bench with a proper understanding of the issues involved. Again, the period of Stalinism seems to be responsible for the lag in this field. Prior to Stalin's supremacy, there were serious efforts to build up a theoretical basis for the criminal policy of the Soviet state. The official doctrine of law enforcement and of the nature of judicial decision left no room for legal refinement in Soviet courts. Courts were to be people's courts, guided by their feeling of what was right in a socialist order. They were to enforce a simple penal policy which distinguished between the enemies and supporters of the regime. Soviet jurists, more realistic than the architects of the Soviet legal order, have concentrated their attention on the study of the personality of the offender. Already in 1921, an Institute for the Study of the Personality of the Offender was set up in Petrograd (Leningrad). Shortly afterwards, similar institutes were created in Moscow, Kiev, Minsk, Saratov, and Rostov-on-Don. In 1925, Commissariats of Justice, Health, and Internal Affairs of the RSFSR acted jointly to create an Institute for the study of the causes of criminality and the personality of the offender in Moscow. In time, as Stalin's grip on the Soviet regime tightened, formal aspects of the criminal policy attracted attention. In 1931, the name of the institute was changed to the Institute for Criminal Policy and Correctional Labor, reflecting thus, in a truly classical Soviet manner, a new interest of the regime—the collective aspects of social life. In due course,

66 Utevskii, "Voprosy ugolovnogo prava v projekte zakona," SGP 116–19 (No. 1, 1960).

all the institutes and studies of the personality of the offender in the provinces were abolished.[67]

The new policy had a profound influence on the state of legal science in the field of criminal law. Law books and treatises on criminal law of the Stalinist period reduced the problem of the personality of the offender exclusively to the formal aspects of guilt, accepting without demur the fact that, in most important crimes, absolute responsibility was being practiced.[68]

Revived interest in the individual aspects of criminal responsibility and attention to the personality of the offender were not purely academic quests. They were the natural consequences of the policy of Soviet authorities, which, since the decisions of the Twenty-first Congress of the Communist Party of the Soviet Union, had called for a closer cooperation between society and the administration of justice. The Resolution of the Congress drew attention to the fact that greater emphasis should be placed upon the application of preventive and educational measures as a means of crime prevention, thus eliminating opportunities for formation of criminal individualities.

In the implementation of the Resolution, the Supreme Court of the USSR and the Procurator General of the USSR each issued in July 1959 instructions to courts and subordinate personnel of the procuratura regarding judicial practice in imposing court sentences on offenders. Both indicated that in order to implement these directives of the Congress the policy of individualization in imposing sentences should be followed. The criminal policy of the Soviet statutes, the instructions insisted, is based on the rule that all aspects of the case must be examined, including all mitigating and aggravating circumstances and the personality of the offender. This new policy is to provide a guide for differentiation between various cases. Further, it is directed to the discontinuance of the mechanical and automatic imposition of the penalty of deprivation of liberty for each criminal conviction, replacing it by social supervision and other educational and correctional measures. The purpose of criminal prosecution, both

---

67 Utevskii, "Novye formy i metody borby z prestupnostiu i lichnost prestupnika," Sots. zak. 14–18 (No. 2, 1960); *cf.* Romashkin, *supra* note 10, at 14.

68 Romashkin, *supra* note 10.

resolutions state, is to reform the individual and prevent criminal activity. In this connection, the usefulness of the actual carrying out of the sentence, or even of the act of sentencing, should be separately examined and gone into. Similarly, a system of conditional sentences and of paroling those who have partly served their sentences, deserve leniency, and have merited a conditional release from prison should be established. The question of the treatment and prevention of juvenile crime also came under special attention. In order to enforce a proper policy, it was thought social organizations should be brought into the process of the administration of justice.

The instructions of the public prosecutor insist that this policy should be reflected, in particular, in pretrial investigations. Here all questions of expediency regarding various correctional, educational, and prophylactic measures should be probed and concrete steps suggested in connection with the investigation of the case itself. This latter should always include an investigation of the personality of the offender.

Among others, the prosecuting and investigatory agencies were instructed—perhaps for the first time in the history of the Soviet administration of justice—to examine the expediency in each case of preliminary detention and to apply it only to cases where preliminary detention was absolutely indispensable in the interest of the administration of justice. The instruction recommends that formal prosecution of offenses in courts should be limited to those cases where the social danger of the crimes committed is considerable. Otherwise, the question whether the case should be disposed of through social organizations rather than by the courts should be gone into as early as possible.[69]

These instructions and the response of Soviet jurists have introduced a new dimension to Soviet administration of justice. One of the important tendencies which the instructions of the Supreme Court and

---

69 Postanovlenie No. 3, Plenuma Verkhovnogo Suda SSSR, 19 Iunia 1959: "O praktikie prymienienia sudami mier ugolovnogo nakazania," Sots. zak. 13–15 (No. 9, 1959); "Prikaz Generalnogo Prokurora SSSR," No. 43, 20 Jula, 1959, "O praktikie organov prokuratury po privlecheniu k ugolovnoi otvietstvennosti i o usushchestvleniu nadzora za pravilnym prymienieniem mier ugolovnogo nakazania," Sots. zak. 16–19 (No. 9, 1959).

of the Prosecutor General demonstrate is the attempt to introduce some of the atmosphere of judicial procedure into pretrial investigation. This, of course, is an indispensable condition for the realization of the new postulates in the administration of criminal justice. Hence, the insistence on the impartiality of the investigating authorities, on the clarification of all circumstances which would support not only the accusation but also the defense, and on the making of pretrial investigation a stage at which the case could be disposed of without necessarily reaching the stage of the open trial.

Recent Soviet legal thought aims at getting the administration of justice out of the official routines. It seeks to endow it with flexibility in the application of the necessary techniques and broadening the significance of findings regarding the personality of the offender. Thus, the administration of justice is not to be limited exclusively to the question of the severity of the criminal repression or the form of the educational and correctional measures, but is to be employed in determining the question of the criminal responsibility itself. The fact that there may be a clue for the determination of guilt or its degree in the general behavior of the accused has already been affirmed in some of the decisions of the Soviet Supreme Court.[70]

Post-Stalin developments in the field of criminal prosecution and the reaction of the Soviet legal profession to new opportunities to advance the cause of legal science, and in this connection the level of Soviet lawmaking and court practice, all bear the signs of great intellectual ferment. Discussions which take place seem to indicate that the Soviet legal profession is fully aware of some of the basic shortcomings of the Soviet laws, even in their reformed editions of December 1958. Whenever opportunity offered, Soviet jurists insisted on a broader understanding of the new provisions in order to reach a higher level of refinement in the administration of justice. Of great assistance in this situation has been the new trend which differentiates between various categories of offenses in order to permit disposal of cases involving minor transgressions by social agencies. This provided an opening for an attack, although in an oblique form, against some of the consequences of the doctrine of social danger on which the Soviet practice of absolute responsibility relied.

70 Motovilovker, "Dokazatelstvennoe znachenie dannykh o lichnosti obviniaemogo," Sots. zak. 32–35 (No. 9, 1959).

At the same time, there are serious obstacles to the efforts of Soviet jurists to lift Soviet law and court practice to that level of administration of justice enjoyed generally in modern societies. In the first place, the 1958 statutes are still unable to accept the postulate of a uniform application of the principles of criminal responsibility to all categories of crimes. Rather, they still single out certain crimes which are not only threatened by harsher penalties, but are judged according to standards tending toward absolute justice. As long as this attitude prevails, Soviet jurists are helpless as they are unable to take a stand independent of political authority. As long as this state of Soviet criminal legislation is perpetuated, the effects of the doctrine of social danger in individual cases will limit the effectiveness of the doctrine of individualization.[71]

Another major obstacle in the Soviet jurist's struggle for making the judicial process in the Soviet Union an efficient tool of criminal policy is that judicial technique itself is below the accepted standards.

Its major feature is that, in accordance with the Western European tradition, pretrial investigations in the Soviet Union are also a part of the judicial process. But it is only a bastard child of this tradition, as only in form and not in substance do the pretrial investigation and the open trial constitute a single whole. In the traditional pattern, the unity of proceedings in these two stages is reflected in the unity of principle by which they are governed. Preliminary investigations are conducted by a judge, and both the defense and the prosecution have the right to participate in it. The secrecy of the proceedings is offset by the right of appeal to the court, and generally all acts of preliminary arrest and detention by the administrative authority are only preliminary to the judicial review of reason for arrest within a short and preclusive period of time (automatic habeas corpus).

In the Soviet Union, even after Stalin, there has been no judicial control of preliminary investigations. Further, there is no judicial examination of reasons for arrest, the defense has no right to participate, and the prosecution, with its unavoidable prejudice, dominates the proceedings.

Furthermore, in the Western European tradition, evidence obtained in the course of preliminary investigations must be examined again in the open trial. As a matter of principle, police investigations

71 Utevskii, *supra* note 66, at 116–17; Utevskii, *supra* note 67, at 14–18.

and evidence produced in the course of preliminary investigation have no probative value in the trial court.

In the free world, the tendency is to extend the rules applicable to the open trial to the proceedings in the pretrial investigations, thereby extending the protection of individual rights. Under the Soviet system, on the other hand, administrative action in pretrial investigations not only is free from controls characterizing judicial process, but tends to influence materially the open trial in its most important aspects. This is due to the fact that evidence collected in the course of pretrial investigations constitutes evidence in court; and furthermore, that depositions of the defendant in the course of a pretrial investigation constitute such evidence.[72]

This situation has a profound influence on the course of the open trial. It voids the constitutionally guaranteed rights of the defendant to legal defense. The defendant may exercise his right only in the open court, not in the pretrial investigations. However, in the Soviet system, pretrial investigation far outweighs in importance the open trial. It is there that issues are joined, evidence examined, the defense line is formed, and most, if not all, evidence inculpating or exculpating the defendant, including his own depositions and testimony, is gathered. Thus, the position of defense and prosecution is a very unequal one. Professional advice, matching the expertise of the prosecution, which may at times be higher than that of the court itself, is available to the defendant only in the latter stages of the proceedings. In the course of the pretrial investigations, the defendant—generally under arrest—has no right to communicate with the outside world with regard to the case against him or to question witnesses or experts.

The case against Francis G. Powers, the pilot of the U-2 plane who was tried by the military collegium of the Soviet Supreme Court, is a typical example of the consequences of this state of affairs. On several occasions, the prosecution pointed out to the defendant that his depositions in the open court differed from those in the pretrial investigation. Furthermore, the court in sentencing him lumped together all the evidence which was produced in the open proceedings and that which was produced only in pretrial proceedings as sources

72 General Principles of Criminal Procedure, art. 16 (1958).

of information which convinced it of the guilt of the defendant. It appears from quotations of various documents in the Powers dossier that at least six volumes of such documents were involved. These were far more extensive than the slim pamphlet which covered the proceedings in the open court. It is matter of speculation what other "evidence" the dossier contained.[73]

As a result of this basic debility of Soviet rules of procedure in criminal matters, various institutions modeled on those of civil law countries are simply empty and useless paraphernalia of a process which has little meaning. To give an example from the Powers case, the defendant was asked at the outset of the proceedings whether he had any objections regarding the person of his defense counsel, who was appointed by the court, and whether he agreed to grant this same lawyer access to the files of the case. After an affirmative answer the court proceeded with the examination of the case. This little ceremony presupposed that the Soviet lawyer was not familiar with the six-volume dossier of the case and that, in spite of this fact, he was able to participate actively in the trial, without even having opportunity to converse with his client.[74]

The Soviet answer to this type of criticism is that the judicial control of legality has been replaced by procuratorial control. In the Soviet federal system this concentration of legal control is vested in a central organization which owes its allegiance to the federal regime, and is said to provide a better instrument for the preservation of uniform standards of legality and a greater guarantee of correct law enforcement.

To this argument two exceptions may be raised. The necessity for a procuratorial system of control over legality arose from the extravagant and, on the whole, unsuccessful effort to establish a purely popular system of justice; Soviet complaints against their own courts are the best witness of the results of this policy. Soviet people's courts, and frequently even higher courts, demonstrated little understanding of their functions; nor were they able to grasp finer points of law. Certainly, Soviet courts have failed as guardians of

73 *Cf.* Grzybowski, "The Powers Trial and the 1958 Reform of Soviet Criminal Law," 9 Am. J. Comp. Law 425–40 (1960).
74 *Ibid.*

civil liberties and as barriers to the abuse of power by the administrative authority.

While Stalin's regime lasted, the presence of the Procurator General of the Soviet Union, with his enormous network of offices, various means of information, and his vast powers to institute proceedings in the judicial and administrative branches of government, was certainly no substitute for independent courts as a guardian of legality. Nowhere in the Soviet literature is it claimed that the procuratorial service systematically attempted to enforce standards of justice. The reason for this is quite simple: the procuratorial organization is administrative in principle and is not independent.

Yugoslavia experimented with many aspects of the Soviet legal system. After an initial period of a full-scale imitation of the Soviet system, it was discovered that the interests of the administration of justice were best served by a return to the traditional pattern. The reform of criminal procedure of December 26, 1959,[75] shifted the control of all stages of criminal proceedings from the procuratorial offices, which are still charged with the general prosecution of crimes, to the courts. This is apparent in all those cases where the rights of the individual are involved in pretrial investigations. In its present shape, Yugoslav criminal procedures distinguish between two types of detention, according to the authority which decides to deprive a suspect of liberty. Anybody may apprehend a suspect at the scene of the crime in order to take him to the county court, to the police, or to the investigating judge of the district court. The police or a county judge may detain a person for three days only. Detention may be prolonged by a decision of the judge or the county court for valid reasons if more time is needed for the investigation. Arrest by the police or the county judge may be extended for an additional twenty-four hours in order to bring the suspect before the investigating judge of the district court.[76]

In more serious cases, the decision to impose arrest upon a person may be issued only by the investigating judge in the course of a formal pretrial investigation (Article 190). An investigating judge may arrest a suspect without a formal pretrial investigation only if,

75 Sl. L. 1953, as amended by the Law of Dec. 26, 1959, Sl. L. 5/1960.
76 Arts. 182 and 188 of the Code of Criminal Procedure.

within three days, he obtains from the public prosecutor a motion to institute a formal pretrial investigation. If the public prosecutor refuses this demand, the suspect must be released (Article 184). In addition, Yugoslav law rules that detention in the course of pretrial investigation is limited to a fixed period, after which the suspect must be released.

The increased role of the judicial function in Yugoslavia is part of the general pattern of the decentralization of authority and of various forms of self-government introduced into the public life of that country, including management of the national economy. Legality has been divorced from the tasks of administration and of the economic management of the country.

In other socialist countries, in addition to the procuratorial control of pretrial proceedings, some of the criminal procedures provide for statutory possibility of two standards of proceedings, depending upon the type of matter involved. Criminal procedures of Eastern Europe contain clauses indicating that special governmental interests may cause the investigating authorities to use the provisions regarding temporary detention for purely punitive reasons. So, for instance, the Bulgarian Code of Criminal Procedure (Section 92 (a)) rules that preliminary detention is mandatory in all cases of offenses against the political, social, and economic aspects of the regime. Furthermore, the Bulgarian legislators strengthened the power of the investigating authorities to restrict the liberty of the offender by providing that preliminary detention may also be imposed for important governmental reasons (Article 93 (a)).

Polish Criminal Procedure rules that preliminary detention may be applied if the social danger of the offense, owing either to its kind or to its prevalence, is considerable (Article 152 Section 2). According to the Rumanian Code of criminal procedure, the investigator has the right to detain the suspect whenever so indicated in the interest of public order and general security (Article 200 (8)). There is no mandatory detention in Hungarian criminal procedure, but the Code states that if a criminal act belongs to the category of crimes directed against the People's republic, detention may last twice as long as preliminary detention in ordinary crimes (Sections 98, 99 (3)).

With few exceptions, therefore, in the majority of Eastern European criminal procedures preliminary detention may be used as a form of criminal repression. In certain situations the socialist state desires to strike at the possible offender even before his guilt and criminal responsibility are established. According to the traditional pattern, detention imposed in connection with a type of offense was justified by the reasoning that the severity of a possible punishment might induce the offender either to hide from justice or to interfere with its course by some other method. The present practice in Eastern Europe blurs this line of thought and makes criminal procedure an instrument of political action.

These various practices and applications of the rule of law to achieve special protection of governmental policies of the moment disturb the course of justice which is, or should be, centered on the implementation of the policy defined in the rule of law itself. Otherwise, it becomes political justice. Institutional guarantees of the subordination of the administration of justice to the demands of governmental policy are further aggravated by the practice of enacting exceptional statutes, which introduce drastic measures in order to stamp out abuses of power or offenses which, at a given moment, are declared as specially dangerous to the regime.

Special legislation providing for the death penalty and for other special measures for embezzling, theft, or dishonesty in dealing with government property is an ever recurring phenomenon in Soviet life. It has frequently been used as a shock device to strengthen standards of integrity among those responsible for handling or managing governmental property. The Decree of the Presidium of the Supreme Soviet of May 6, 1961, which introduced a death penalty for large scale embezzlers of government property in the Soviet Union, represents one of these measures. By such means the general pattern of law enforcement regarding the type and scale of punishments provided for in the general laws of the country is greatly disturbed. It must be said that they are not marked by great leniency against those who offend government or social interests.[77]

Soviet reform of the criminal law and penal policy was further set back by the article of Prosecutor General of the Soviet Union

77 Izvestia, May 6, 1961.

Rudenko, which provided a theoretical explanation of the Decree of May 6, 1961. Rudenko argued the necessity of the harsher penalties for the embezzlers of government property by reviving the Stalinist doctrine on stepping up the severity of criminal repression as Soviet society moves forward on the road to the millennium, although it was declared to be no longer a cornerstone of Soviet criminal policy.[78]

Thus, the general picture one obtains from contemplation of the life of law in the Soviet Union seems to suggest that it is influenced by the constant change of official opinion, purporting to be the expression of general convictions on some of the fundamental institutions of the Soviet order. There is constant revision of views on the role of the courts, on the function of penalty, on the purpose of law enforcement, and on the significance of courts' paying attention to the social and political needs of Soviet polity. Since the May 1961 decree, it seems that the policy of individualization and circumspection in the use of penal sanction is again being frowned upon. Courts are criticized for leniency, while only a few months ago they were criticized for their severity. Socialist legality now means the harsh prosecution of offenders, while a short time ago it was interpreted to mean particular attention to avoid meting out punishment in cases where guilt was dubious and to see the case in the terms of the individual situation of the accused.

As a result, the very standards governing the rule of law, the function of administration of justice, the guarantees of human freedom, and the limits to powers of the state are in constant jeopardy. An objective attitude toward those concepts which in more traditional circumstances constitute the very foundations of collective and individual life is almost impossible for a member of socialist society.

Indirectly, these constant changes of policy jeopardize the prospects for re-educating the Soviet man. This is because the institutions of Soviet life appear as relative values and not as constants, raising no doubts in the minds of the majority. In this situation, the prestige of the law cannot be great, respect for the courts cannot be firmly rooted, and the concept of socialist legality, which means so many things, has little practical content.

78 *Id.*, May 7, 1961.

UNITY OF SOCIALIST CIVIL LAW

The program of legal reform in the Soviet Union and in the satellite states included the enactment of new civil codes which sought to provide a new basis for legal commerce involving property relations in the socialist society. Legislative work and theoretical thinking on the subject of the form, scope, and content of civil legislation and its place within the general framework of the socialist legal order was stimulated by the fact that the new political conditions, which made legal reform possible, have also removed the stigma of unorthodoxy from the theories of the early Marxist theoreticians who were deeply concerned with problems of civil law.

According to Pashukanis, revolution per se will not destroy civil law and replace it automatically by some other higher type of regulation:

As state enterprises are subordinate to the conditions of turnover, the bond between them is molded in the form of arrangements and the form of technical subordination. Accordingly, the purely juridic—that is to say, the legal—form of regulating relationships becomes possible and necessary.

Gradually however, after the bourgeois civil law, inherited from the previous socio-economic formation, had expended its utility, new relations between the economic units of the socialist order would be established. These, argued Pashukanis, would be based on a new type of regulation, i.e., administrative regulation, leading finally to a total disappearance of legal rule and to the emergence of the new economic order based on economic links between social functions.[79] In other words, the realization of the program of socialist construction was linked to the transformation of the nature of legal rule.

The theories of Pashukanis, who was an official leader of Marxist juristic thinking, have produced considerable response among Soviet lawyers. They have come up with various schemes indicating an imminent transformation of the civil law of the Soviet state into what was called the economic law—a system of administrative regulations governing relations between Soviet agencies of government in charge of the national economy of Russia.

79 Pashukanis, *supra* note 25, at 165, 169, 179–80.

In particular, Stuchka conceived the pattern of transition from the civil law order into the economic law as the struggle of two systems. They were forced to coexist within the Soviet society for a time, i.e., as long as the Soviet economic system contained some elements of the private economy and some belonging to the socialist order. The anarchic character of the private economic relations was primarily reflected in the institution of contract of sale and purchase, while the planned character of the socialist economy as its vehicle had a channel of administrative regulations.[80]

Thus was devised a legal system governing property and contractual relations of which the Civil Code was only a part of the legal order. This idea produced a considerable number of works, of which perhaps the most representative was produced by the first systematic treatise on the economic law of the RSFSR, which began with the analysis of the civil law in force.[81]

The first of the five-year economic plans was greeted by this school of thought as the sign that their prophecies were beginning to take practical shape. Transformation of the Russian economy into a socialist system, in which only collective forms of economic activity were to survive, was understood to mean that the whole basis for civil law relations would disappear. It was thought then that contractual relations between government enterprises would be barred. As a result, two sets of business relations would be reflected in a dual system: those based on contracts between private individuals— a marginal legal situation, and those based upon administrative regulations between units of the socialist economy. The Civil Code would thus cover almost exclusively transactions between individuals while

---

80 Stuchka, 3 Kurs sovetskogo grazhdanskogo prava 10 (1931); *cf.* also Basic Principles of Civil Legislation of the USSR, a draft edited and prefaced by Stuchka (1931); also Amfiteatrov, "Osnovnye cherty zakonoproekta o dogovorakh (1934); Hazard, *supra* note 10, at 62 ff. Although Stuchka and other writers of the epoch have never acknowledged their indebtedness to Jellinek, their theories were a direct borrowing from the writings of this influential and widely read legal writer. *Cf.* in particular Jellinek, Der Kampf des alten mit dem neuen Recht 8–9 (1907); also Jellinek, 1 Ausgewählte Schriften und Reden 396 (1911); *cf.* Grzybowski, *supra* note 17.

81 Goighbarg, "Khoziaistvennoe pravo RSFSR," 1 Grazhdanskii kodeks (1924).

administrative economic law, based on central economic plans, would govern the socialist sector.[82]

This school of thought was violently condemned by Vyshinskii. As long as Stalin's regime continued, nothing more was heard of the schemes of gradual transition from the bourgeois legal system into a system of law which would reflect more truly the socialist management of the national economy of the Soviet Union. Theoretical difficulties were solved by the declaration that all Soviet law was socialist law and that the Civil Code in force was a socialist code and an indispensable part of the Soviet legal system. Soviet lawyers were told to get busy with the practical problems of legal rules of socialism and to forget about theories of socialist law.[83]

The decisions of the Twentieth Congress of the Communist Party of the Soviet Union (1956) to prepare and enact new codes of law in all provinces of socialist law revived the discussion of the systematic organization of the Soviet legal system. Also revived was the question of the duality of regulations pertaining to property relations and business transactions.

The tenor of the discussion which followed is perhaps illustrative of the barrenness of intellectual life under Stalin. It demonstrated the absence of fruitful and significant ideas despite enormous experience in the field of economic relations. As the problem of the new codes came to the fore, the Soviet Union, for nearly four decades, had experimented with socialist economic forms. In addition, new socialist communities in Eastern Europe had come into existence and had been developing new economic forms as well as new forms of economic transactions between socialist states and enterprises on an international scale. Nevertheless, Soviet jurists found little to inspire them in the contemporary reality and turned rather to the ideas which were formulated in the beginnings of the Soviet State.

This trend was obviously encouraged by the rehabilitation of Pashukanis and Krylenko, the originators of the concept of economic law and of a legal order based on an administrative regulation of

82 1 Gsovski, Soviet Civil Law 433 (1948).
83 Vyshinskii, The Law of the Soviet State 53 ff. (Babb transl. 1948); Grzybowski, *supra* note 17, at 73.

the economic activity in the socialist society. After twenty years in Siberia, one of the leading jurists of the initial years of Revolutionary Russia, Gintsburg, regained his freedom.[84]

But it was also apparent that the freedom of intellectual speculation which the Soviet jurists gained was limited, and they could hardly give free rein to their imagination by expressing preferences and offering suggestions regarding systematic arrangements of the Soviet legal system. The Yugoslav experiment with socialist law was condemned, and its patterns for socialist legal relations and theoretical solutions were rejected. Between the two extremes of the solutions adopted by Stalin's regime and the pattern of transition developed by Pashukanis and his school was all the room that was left for the exercise of the minds of Soviet jurists. The astounding fact that there was no discussion of the actual regime in the management of socialist industries or of organization of socialist agriculture once the program of legal reform was announced could perhaps be explained by the fact that such a discussion and suggested programs of reform would have offended the policy makers. And so discussion centered around problems of great theoretical attractiveness, although with little practical profit.

Even contemporary changes in the administrative methods and new organization of industries in the Soviet Union following the reform of 1957 have attracted little attention from Soviet legal scholars. Changes taking place before their very eyes did not register as indicative of social needs, nor as a manifestation of a process calling for a reformulation of the legal rule.

This is even more surprising since the debate on reform was initiated by the realization of the disjointed and amorphous state of the Soviet legal system. While criminal and civil law were in a poor state of organization, the real problem existed in the field of administrative regulations, concerned with management of the Soviet national economy. There can be no doubt that Soviet lawyers were aware of this state of affairs. That there was no great debate concerning these issues was due primarily, or so it seems, to the fact that these matters belonged to the central issues of the Soviet system of govern-

84 Hazard, *supra* note 10, at 62 ff.

ment, and that suggestions and discussions in this connection might involve fundamental axioms as to the nature and method of the socialist government.[85]

Thus, the main issue of the debate on reform was the problem of the systematic arrangement of legal rules. Followers of the early school of legal Marxism suggested that instead of the division of law into public and private, a trichotomy be adopted, consisting of the following groups of legal rules: the law of the state, economic law, and civil law. The first group would include rules to regulate the organization of government machinery and its public services, including judiciary and procuratura. The second would cover all aspects of economic activity of the state. Civil law would be exclusively concerned with the individual but would include some constitutional and political aspects of the legal position of the citizen, such as electoral and other political rights.

These suggestions for the reform of the Soviet legal system were the result of the conviction that regulations dealing with the management of the national economy have little if anything to do with the circulation of consumer goods, property relations, and other fields of law governing individual life. The rights of a Soviet citizen have been thus segregated into a separate category. In terms of concrete legislative proposals, partisans of the new category, economic law, proposed to limit future civil codes to property and nonproperty relations involving individuals only. Consequently a socialist civil code would be restricted to relations between individuals, those between

85 Tadevosyan, "Nekotorie voprosy sistemy sovetskogo prava," SGP (No. 8, 1958); Genkin, "K voprosu o sisteme sovetskogo sotsialisticheskogo prava," SGP (No. 9, 1956); Shargorodskii & Joffe, "O sisteme sovetskogo prava," SGP (No. 6, 1957); Aleksieiev, "O teoreticheskikh osnovakh klasifikatsii otraslei sovetskogo prava," SGP (No. 11, 1958); Bratus, "O nekotorykh chertakh istorii sovetskogo grazhdanskogo prava," SGP 86–104 (No. 11, 1957); Pavlov, "K voprosu kodifikatsii sovetskogo grazhdanskogo zakonodatelstva," SGP 39–49 (No. 8, 1959); Denisov & Bernstein, "Osnovy grazhdanskogo zakonodatelstva i 'khoziaistvennoe pravo,'" SGP 48–60 (No. 5, 1959); Aleksieiev, "Differentsiatsia grazhdanskogo pravovogo regulirovania v sotsialisticheskom obshchestve," SGP 75–84 (No. 2, 1960); Laptev, "K voprosu o khoziaistvennom prave," Voprosy Ekonomiki (No. 12, 1959); Romashkin, *supra* note 10; *cf.* also "Osuzhdenie voprosov sistemy sovetskogo prava i sotsialisticheskoi zakonnosti," SGP 117–28 (No. 11, 1958).

individuals and socialist enterprises and economic institutions, and would include family law and such institutions as copyright and patents.

Simultaneously, a separate code would include the totality of rules dealing with planning, administration of the economic enterprises of the state, and their business relations.

The argument of the partisans of the new systematization is that the present system continues an artificial division of the rules pertaining to a single field of social activity, i.e., the operation of the economic system of the country under two classes of rules, one dealing with those relations which are based on the administrative subordination of economic enterprises to higher authorities of economic management, and the other on the contractual relations between them. The weakness of the present order is thought to be its predication upon a formal difference between the modes of regulating social relations, and not on their qualitative characteristics. Civil law, it is argued by the partisans of the economic law, is concerned with the satisfaction of the personal needs of citizens, while the economic law is a means of organizing the economic activity of socialist enterprises and organizations. The economic law should deal with the hierarchy of the economic administration, including economic councils and the legal position of economic enterprises. It should be directed toward their internal organization, economic planning, commercial basis of their operation, planned contracts, and government arbitration in settling disputes between socialist organizations.

Opponents of the economic codes have brought out serious arguments against segregating the rules regarding management of the national economy in a separate legal category. They have pointed out that not all the rules regarding the activities of economic enterprises have the same character. So, for instance, there is a difference between business transactions among socialist enterprises and administrative regulations regarding relations between the planning and supervisory authority and the enterprise itself. While in the first class of relations there are rights which have their basis in a contract which cannot be unilaterally changed, in the second type of relations this concept of rights does not apply. Thus interenterprise relations and business transactions have similar characteristics to those involving individuals or socialist organizations and individuals. As such they may be subject to uniform treatment within a systematic arrangement in a single code of civil law regulations.

Another objection is that proposals for the economic code disrupt the unity of the institution of property. The conservative trend among Soviet jurists insists on the preservation of the idea of the civil code in its present form and scope and argues that there is no valid reason for the segregation of property relations concerning the individual from the rest of the legal regulations concerning property relations between socialist enterprises. Civil law rules regarding property between individuals and socialist enterprises represent a channel for including property relations involving individual existence into the general over-all planning activities of the state. Property relations between socialist enterprises represent a basis for property relations between individuals, as their economic activity is indissolubly tied to the satisfaction of social needs.

Furthermore, both the Party and the government are planning for a progressive relaxation of the centralized management of the national economy. Decentralization of administrative responsibility tends toward increasing the independence and initiative of economic enterprises regarding their business activities. In fact, civil law provisions regulate all those relations which are characterized by the absence of administrative subordination, and the equality of partners is the basis of operations. The tendency is to restrict the method of administrative handling of problems of the national economy and to favor a growing use of the channels of the civil law. This does not mean, say the defenders of the present scope and form of civil law regulation, that the traditional approach favoring the form of contractual relations tends to disrupt the mechanism of planning by separating the plan from the planned contracts. While the plan represents a statutory obligation, it is put into effect by a contractual method, such constituting a better means of establishing relations between equal partners.[86]

86 Bratus, "Khoziaistvennyi dogovor kak grazhdansko-pravovaia forma planovogo razpredelenia produktsii," SGP (No. 2–3, 1953); Bratus & Lunts, Voprosy khoziaistvennogo dogovora 11–12 (1954); Bratus, "O normowaniu prawnym stosunków majątkowych w ZSRR," PiP 630–43 (No. 4–5, 1960).

A slightly different position was taken by a Soviet jurist who has proposed that the new Soviet civil code should take account of the changes in the property relations in the socialist economic order. In fact, he claimed that there is no longer one system of the civil law relations and that, therefore, several laws ought to be enacted. All of them, however, would still pertain broadly to the branch of civil law. Thus, he proposed to differentiate between the civil law of the socialist economy, the civil law of collective farming, the civil law of physical persons, and the civil law of foreign trade.[87]

In spite of the theoretical attractions of the early theories of socialist law, the traditional trends seem to have carried the day, although not without some hesitations. Three major pieces of legislation which have made their appearance in the Soviet Union (Draft of Principles of Civil Law Legislation in the Soviet Union and Union Republic), in Hungary (Civil Code of 1959), and in Poland (Draft of the Civil Code) express the principle of the unity of the civil law. Thus, the tradition of the civil law countries of the West has been continued. The Soviet Draft (Article 1) states that its provisions cover property and related nonproperty relations, with the exclusion of those based on the administrative subordination of one party to another or to the budget relations. The Polish Code (Article 1) states that it regulates civil law relations between physical persons, between socialist and nonsocialist organizations, and between the physical persons and these organizations. It repeats the reservation contained in the Soviet Code by stating that the Code applies between state organizations only inasmuch as these relations are not differently regulated either by the laws in force or by the regulations issued by the supreme authorities of the state administration. The Hungarian Code (Article 1) contains a similar regulation.

The report attached to the Polish Draft reveals that the members of the codification commission did not quite see eye to eye on the various aspects of the scope and function of the civil code in a socialist country. They were doubtful whether management of the national economy, owing to the nature of its regulations, constituted a proper subject for inclusion within the civil code. Consequently, they did not propose to deal with the organization of the socialist economic

87 Aleksieiev, *supra* note 85, at 79.

units, quasi-corporations created by the government for the management of various industries and services.

In each of these civil law codifications, the law on obligations (contracts) constitutes the core of their provisions and raises important problems of technique and theory, due primarily to the fact that most legal commerce in a socialist state is handled by governmental, cooperative, and social institutions of all types.

The Polish approach took account of the fundamental difference between the dealings and transactions of socialist organizations and those involving individuals or individuals and socialist organizations. Thus, in order to preserve the unity of civil law but at the same time to recognize the special position of the socialist economic units, general provisions of the civil law were given a subsidiary role regarding the relations of socialist juristic persons. They apply only when other more specific provisions regulating economic cooperation and legal commerce between socialist units are absent.

In the Hungarian Civil Code no such reservation has been enacted. However, separate provisions for legal relations between socialist institutions are made whenever applicable. Thus, for instance, provisions on contracts deal separately with socialist contracts within the general framework of provisions covering all types of contractual relations.

The Polish Code failed to provide in detail for the mechanism of contractual relations between socialist institutions. However, in the general provisions a special reservation was made as to the spirit in which contractual relations between the socialist enterprises ought to be entered into (Article 343):

[S]ocialist organizations are obligated to cooperate both in concluding contracts as well as in their execution, taking into account the influence of their action on the execution of the contract by the other party, on the satisfaction of the needs of the economic life, efficiency of production commerce, and on safeguarding the national economy from losses.

In addition to this general regulation and the initial reservation that the Code applies only in the absence of more specific rules, the Code made it clear that agreements between socialist business partners must follow government regulations as to form, content, and choice of partners in their business activity (Article 342, 344).

The degree of influence of higher authority on the execution of contracts between socialist partners is especially visible in business deals connected with assignments of the national economic plan. Polish and Soviet drafts have kept the rules of the distribution of planned assignments between socialist enterprises outside the civil code. It was impossible, however, to avoid reference to administrative regulations of higher authorities in charge of economic management regarding the institution of contractual obligations between the parties, the effects of the nonfulfillment of contractual obligations, and the decisions of higher authorities regarding the change or abolition of planned assignments.[88]

The scope of modern efforts at devising patterns for a socialist code discloses the fact that civil codes in socialist countries are profoundly affected by the internal conflict, characteristic of the Soviet legal order, which pertains in the precarious position of individual rights and the stability of social structures. Nevertheless, the usefulness of a code of law predicated upon the free exercise of will in legal commerce is beyond doubt. The perspective of forty years of operation of the socialist economy in Russia has put a question mark after the theories of the Pashukanis school. Its ideas on the nature of legal rules within the socialist economic order have had some foundation in reality only in the initial years of the regimented and government-directed transition from free enterprise to the government-owned and -controlled system of economic institutions and planned economy. Centralization of planning and the neat organization of economic activities according to administrative schemes, with economic ministries on top, was a proper method and could produce desirable effects as long as investment, organization, and expansion and deployment of the industrial establishment were stressed, at the expense of service and consumption. However, once the economic machine reached a certain level of expansion, it was discovered that the very size of the economic mechanism and the multiplication of its parts called for a different method of cooperation in performing services and satisfying human needs. In this situation, methods characteristic of the market economy were the only answer.

The solutions which finally prevailed were based on the simple

88 *Cf. supra* at 85 ff.

reality of the nature of economic operations. Theories of the partisans of the economic law had to be relegated to limbo, because in spite of the centralized direction of the national economy, the contract has maintained its function in the socialist economic system. As a Soviet jurist wrote in 1959, when the question was debated again:

Efforts to separate regulations of the circulation of goods between the socialist organizations, from the regulation of circulation between organizations and citizens (and also citizens) amount to denying the unity of economic circulation in the Soviet society. Previously some justification for such a denial was supplied by the view that means of production in the internal exchange are not goods. But at the present time Soviet economists have come to the conclusion that in view of the unity of the socialist economy, even the means of production are goods produced and circulated within the governmental sector, although there is no change in the person of the owner.[89]

Theories on the place of the civil law contract within the framework of the Soviet legal system raise serious theoretical objections which cannot be answered by a dogmatic dictum, e.g., that goods disposed in the trade between socialist units are goods in spite of the fact that the contract of sale and purchase produces no change in the person of the owner. It is realized that the contract theory is tied to the theory on the position of the juristic persons in the Soviet order in terms of their concrete rights. Their business independence is emphasized at the expense of the doctrine that socialist juristic persons represent only various forms of the activity of the state, which remains the sole owner of the means of production. Those who favor the concept of the unity of the civil law and the contractual form of business transactions in the socialist sector of economy would insist on distinguishing those activities of the state which engage the action of governmental agencies from those which are exercised through the operation of juristic persons.[90]

The heart of the matter is that complexities of economic life in socialist societies tend to favor business independence of the

89 Denisov & Bernstein, *supra* note 85, at 54; *cf.* also Ostrovitianov, "Tovarnoe proizvodstvo i zakon stoimosti pry sotsializme," Kommunist 92 ff. (No. 13, 1957).

90 Denisov & Bernstein, *supra* note 85, at 57 ff.

juristic persons, at the expense of the idea of the centralized management of the national economy, as the business of public authority. In a new form the distinction between various functions of the public authority, those subject to the rule of the public law, and those under the rule of the Civil Code is finding its way into the Soviet legal system.

In Yugoslav legal theory, which was evolved after a total reorganization of the economic mechanism of the country, the concept of national ownership of the means of production became a purely theoretical proposition. As a Yugoslav lawyer wrote:

[N]o organ of society may be the general bearer of social property. Each institution is the bearer but of determinate rights as issuing from social ownership. This does not mean that property as property is divided into a supreme property and the lower categories of property as in feudal law, but that the different social organs have different rights in the management of social property.[91]

Socialist codes of the most recent vintage still maintain the unity of the ownership of the means of production. Article 18 of the Soviet Draft of Principles of Civil Legislation stated:

Socialist ownership has the form of state ownership (property of all the people), or the form of collective farm cooperative ownership (ownership by an individual collective farm of cooperative association, or common ownership by several collective farms or cooperative associations).

In practice, however, these differentiations have little practical significance. Indeed, it seems that property relations in terms of the permanent assignment of control of various economic assets to various parts and elements of Soviet government apparatus have not yet reached that degree of stability which would permit a serious analysis of reality in order to produce a doctrinal formulation. In addition to a great movement in various forms of the immediate control of economic assets by socialist corporations, there is constant change in assigning responsibility for organizing industrial activity to various levels of government (federal, individual republics, provinces, etc.). The only real element of significance for legal forms of economic ac-

91 Gerskovic, "On the Basic Institutes of Property Law," *The New Yugoslav Law* 27 (Jan.–June, 1955).

tivity are the powers of various institutions to participate in their own name in the system of socialist transactions.[92]

Another aspect of the economic operations which militated against the doctrines of Pashukanis in contemporary conditions in Russia and in the satellite countries is the fact that such notions would tend to strengthen the rule of bureaucratic management in the national economy. It was not only a question of the realization of political postulates, i.e., of direct participation of the workers' organizations in the management of their factories. In addition was involved the question of economic efficiency which, in the final analysis, decides the issue.

These two questions provided the chief motivation in the demand for the reform of economic management and the rule of law in Poland after October 1956. In order to put a limit to bureaucratic rule and to establish an efficient bulwark to administrative arbitrariness, it was proposed to distinguish between various types of enterprises and to apply a varying degree of decentralization in their administration. Decentralization, however, was to stop short of their virtual return to private, although collective, ownership. In this system civil law would regain its pristine role and application. It was argued that, although the government would continue to control all industrial enterprises and that trade and distribution would continue to be an almost exclusive preserve of government monopoly, this fact would not preclude the rule of civil law and the regime of contracts in their commercial relations. Indeed, it was agreed, if anything, that the rule of civil law in the government sector of economy was even more indispensable, because by its very size government participation in the administration of economic resources affected the life of everybody. Polish lawyers at that time saw the only alternative to untrammelled rule by bureaucracy in decentralization and in the return of regulation of business transactions by the civil law.[93]

---

92 In an article published in 1958, Professor Pyontkovskii attacked the view that subjective rights have no place in the Soviet legal system: "K voprosu o vzaimootnoshenii obiektivnogo i subiektivnogo prava," SGP (No. 5, 1958).

93 Buczkowski, O właściwą rolę prawa cywilnego w gospodarce uspołecznionej," PiP 249–62 (No. 8–9, 1956); Brus, Prawo wartości a problematyka bodźców ekonomicznych 88 ff. (1956); Mayzel, "O umowach

While the defenders of the system of contractual relations in the socialist economic sector favor an expansion of civil law institutions, they are quite firm in their conviction that Soviet civil law is not the private law of the West. A leading Soviet expert in this field stated that:

[T]he term "civil law," as well as a number of other terms, has lost its pristine meaning. Soviet civil law represents that branch of law which concerns property relations tied to the commodity exchange relations irrespective of the participants. The political, procedural, rights of citizens from employment relations do not enter there, but belong to the field of civil law financial relations, agrarian relations, and also relations arising from the membership in the agricultural and other cooperative organizations.[94]

In this sense, the civil law of the Soviet Union has lost its traditional function. It has become part of the legal system which is concerned primarily with public service, administered in a manner which has borrowed from the patterns of Western Europe, developed in the Soviet law.

Defenders of civilistic forms in business relations or the socialist economy have also pointed out that the preference for these forms was brought about by processes which are characteristic of the period preceding the moment of transition from socialism to communism. Civil law signifies relations based on cooperation, while economic law emphasizes administrative forms of ordering. Thus, civil law forms are closer to the ultimate form of social institutions characteristic of the highest form of social existence:

What meaning has the above-described objective process, if it is considered in terms of the perspectives of the development of Soviet society in the period of construction of communism? . . . one must keep in mind the fact that in contrast with the administrative law, in civil law the main role belongs not to the organizing activity of the governmental agencies, but to regulations founded on juristic equality of . . . parties. And therefore, the expansion of the sphere of application of civil law at the expense of the sphere of direct organizing activity of the agencies of Soviet state

dostawy pomiędzy jednostkami gospodarki uspołecznionej," PiP 378 ff. (No. 8, 1956); *cf.* Grzybowski, "Polish Workers' Councils," 17 Journal of Central European Affairs 272–86 (1957).

94 Bratus, "O normowaniu prawnym stosunków majątkowych w ZSRR," PiP 631 (No. 4–5, 1960).

represent a sui generis stage in the process of the development of the Soviet law, which is characterized by the narrowing of the realm of direct governmental coercion.[95]

The problem of the historical significance of the re-establishment of the rule of civil law is a somewhat esoteric issue. What is real is that the economic situation calls for departure from the administrative methods in the economic life of the socialist countries. Yugoslavs have referred this process to an earlier historical moment, that of the transition from capitalism to socialism. A Yugoslav lawyer, supplying a political rationale for the administrative and legal reform in his country, thus described the stages of transition from the capitalist to the socialist society. He pointed out that in the last stages of capitalism, the control of means of production was in the hands, not of the capitalists, but of the managerial class, consisting of the "economic bureaucracy both of the private monopolies and the contemporary state developing in the direction of state capitalism." He continued:

The experience of socialist development in the world has indicated that even after the winning of power on the part of the working class, a special social stratum is being created which stands between the direct producers and means of production. The same practice has further shown that, at this early stage of socialist development too, the direct producers are still separated from the means of production. The social stratum in question, and which still separates both the essential factors of any production in the initial stages of socialist development, is made up of the members of the economic administration of the proletarian state. Such a condition is necessary directly after the Revolution . . . but after a time such a condition begins to lose its necessary and progressive character . . . and leads to a system of bureaucratic dictatorship and this system in its deepest substance in no way differs from any other class rule. . . . Consequently: as long as there will subsist such a social stratum, which will stand between both the essential factors of every system of production, whether in the form of legal owners of means of production or in the form of state bureaucracy, exploitation also will subsist.[96]

95 Aleksieiev, "O zakonomernostiakh razvitia sovetskogo prava v period razvernutogo stroitelstva kommunizma," SGP 16 (No. 9, 1960).

96 Goricar, "Workers' Self-Government in the Light of Scientific Socialism," New Yugoslav Law 3–4 (April–Dec., 1957); Yugoslav theories were condemned by the Soviet jurists because they were based on the theory that the process of the withering away of the state and law in

LAWS OF SOCIALIST COMMERCE

In effect, a number of causes have contributed to the fact that political amnesty for the theories of Pashukanis has not been transformed into his posthumous victory. Such would have meant the continuation of the rigid regimentation of economic life, very much in the pattern of Stalin's regime. That, of course, was no longer politically possible. It was out of tune with the general economic situation in the Soviet Union and other socialist countries, where further economic progress depended on the decentralization of authority. Finally, it was inconsistent with the great expansion of trade with other members of the socialist bloc and also with the free world, both in its neutralist part as well as that organized in the Western alliance. All of these developments called, not for the first time in the history of the Soviet Union and other socialist states, for stabilizing the rules of trade in some general formulas.[97]

Internally the most important development was the administrative decentralization of economic management, practically throughout the entire area of the Soviet bloc in Eastern Europe. Administrative reform in the Soviet Union in the course of 1957 contributed fundamentally to the expansion of the contractual forms of economic cooperation between Soviet economic units. As Professor Bratus wrote at the end of 1957, barely a few months after the reform, it was apparent that "the scope of purchase and sale contract has now

---

a socialist society begins immediately after the overthrow of the power of the bourgeoisie. *Cf.* Romanshkin, *supra* note 10; also Hazard, *supra* note 10, at 27.

97 The responsibility for building up a new legal system under the revolutionary regime in Russia was laid at the door of the capitalist states with which the Soviet Union had concluded commercial treaties and agreements. Kurskii told the congress of workers of the administration of justice that when the question of the agenda for a congress in Genoa was being discussed, Lloyd George had said that Soviet Russia would have to establish a known system of legal norms which would permit other countries to have permanent relations with her. Kurskii added as an aside: "We shall see what these juridical norms shall be and who in the last analysis will dictate them." He admitted, however, that commercial treaties had raised some problems because they put forward demands for specified guarantees of property and persons. Hazard, *supra* note 10, at 150.

been considerably enlarged as regards the legal relations between the socialist economic organizations." [98]

No less important was the impact of foreign trade. Professor Bratus, the chief spokesman of the civilist orientation in the ranks of Soviet scholars, was convinced that:

> To accept proposals of the partisans of the economic law, would result in serious difficulties in the field of foreign trade transactions with the capitalist firms. . . . It would be impossible to apply to a foreign merchant . . . those rules, which determine property relations of the Soviet citizens as the owner of the consumer goods. It would be also impossible to apply to foreign transactions the rules of the so-called economic law which is to serve relations between the Soviet socialist organizations. . . . When a foreign deal is referred to the rule of law competent in the place of the contracts, such rules of the civil law are applied as a given state applies with regard to its physical and juristic persons. Otherwise a discrimination against the foreign partner would take place, which in turn would result in the creation of a special legal regime for the trade organizations of the Soviet Union, which would upset the foundations of the economic cooperation of the USSR with the capitalist countries.[99]

Developments in the Soviet Union and in other socialist countries have inspired hopes that this was a first step toward the gradual relaxation of the administrative rule in business relations, and that the system of planned contracts, "masquerading as civil contracts and until recently unchallenged, is now to some extent giving way to truly civil contracts, and due recognition is given to the law of value." [100] A Polish jurist, an expert in the field of commercial law, drew further comfort from the fact that Soviet economists have changed their position and now stress the commercial character of commodities and recognize the validity of the law of value for the circulation of commodities.[101]

98 Bratus, "O nekotorykh chertakh istorii sovetskogo grazhdanskogo prava," SGP 86–103 (No. 11, 1957).

99 Bratus, *supra* note 94, at 642; Aleksieiev, "Differentsiatsia grazhdanskogo pravovogo regulirovania v sotsialisticheskom obshchestve," SGP 79 (No. 2, 1960).

100 Piotrovski, "The Great Importance of Commercial Law for Peaceful Economic Collaboration of All Nations," The New Yugoslav Law 6–8 (July–Dec., 1958).

101 See proceedings of the Soviet Institute of Economy of the USSR Academy of Science (September 1957), Voprosy Ekonomiki 103–11 (No. 11, 1957).

Furthermore, in a number of Soviet bloc countries, in Yugo-slavia, and also for international trade within the Soviet bloc itself, a type of regulation was adopted which provided some general rules regarding important aspects of commercial relations between govern-mental institutions engaged either in internal or foreign trade rela-tions. In 1954 the State Court of Arbitration in Yugoslavia adopted a commercial code under the name of General Usages of Trade for the adjudication of disputes arising from business transactions of Yugoslav business organizations. In mid-December of 1957 the Council of Mutual Economic Assistance at its session in Moscow adopted "General Terms of Goods Deliveries Between the Foreign Trade Concerns of the Member Countries" for the regulation of for-eign trade between the member countries of the Soviet bloc in Eastern Europe. In Czechoslovakia, a law on "Business Relations between the socialist organizations was adopted on October 17, 1958." [102] Finally, in the Soviet Union itself, a resolution of the Council of Ministers of the USSR of May 22, 1959, enacted a regula-tion on the deliveries of capital and consumer goods to govern the simplified system of contractual relations between economic units after the reform of 1957.[103]

In inter-bloc trade, a more precise definition of the mutual rights and obligations of the parties and of the terms of performance was the result of a considerable reassertion of equal position in the economic cooperation of the members of the bloc with the Soviet Union. Terms of delivery or general usages of trade constitute a system of rules which have their analogy in the commercial codes of the capitalist countries. As such they are *sui generis* civil law statutes adopted to business relations between that category of juristic persons which is closest to the merchant class of the free world. But here their resemblance ends. They contain no rules regarding the organization of juristic business entities. As in the socialist legal sys-tem, these matters belong to the public law. Owing to the standardiza-tion of business relations in the socialist world, only sale-purchase and contract of construction are described. Finally all those con-tracts and arrangements which provide for guarantees and security of commercial relations are eliminated. Performance of contracts and

102 Sbirka, No. 26/67, 1958, consolidated text Sbirka, 26/68, 1958.
103 *Cf. supra* at 91 ff.

terms of performance, as well as terms of payments, are guaranteed by over-all provisions regulating foreign trade. Clearing arrangements make provisions superfluous in case of bankruptcy, and also of liens and sureties.[104]

The presence of the new regulations introduced a new element into the activity of the government arbitration boards in the socialist countries, converting them into a kind of commercial court. In addition to the provisions of the economic plans and other administrative regulations which regulate business relations between various economic institutions, the boards have for their guidance a set of general rules for the performance of contracts which they must apply in the interpretation of the terms of commercial and other business deals between the partners. With respect to these aspects of the litigations concerned with the business activity of Soviet and other socialist enterprises, their function is identical with that of the civil courts dealing with commercial disputes in the civil law countries of the West. Otherwise, government arbitration boards have retained their original character and function as administrative bodies participating directly in adjusting, by administrative action, the cooperation of the economic units. The reform of economic administration in the Soviet Union and other satellite countries, although relaxing the controls and supervision of higher economic authorities, has failed to change fundamentally the regime of the planned economy in which business operations are geared strictly to the plan.

The only exception in this picture was Yugoslavia which reorganized the economic administration according to a pattern which gave full control of business operations to their individual workers' collectives. This made it possible to re-establish the normal system of adjudication between the business organizations of Yugoslavia. Following the economic reform of 1950–1953, the Judiciary Act of 1954 transformed Yugoslav government arbitration boards into a system of economic courts which have assumed functions similar in essence to commercial courts in the civil law countries of Western Europe. As the presiding judge of the Supreme Economic Court of Yugoslavia explained:

104 Piotrowski, *supra* note 100, also Piotrowski, "Na marginesie proponowanych zmian w polskim prawie rodzinnym," PiP 739 (No. 11, 1960).

The reason for converting the State Court of Arbitration into economic courts lies in the changes which were made in Yugoslavia in the system of economy and planning. The new economic system, whose hallmarks included the economic-juridical independence of economic enterprises, the management of factories and enterprises by the working collective and the fixing of the economic organizations' rights, has made it possible for economic organizations to appear independently on the market, which fact, in turn, has had its effect of expanding the role of law in regulating mutual property relationships and strengthening the role of law in that domain.[105]

In this situation, the work of the courts of arbitration has assumed a new function, and has turned into a "purely judicial organ."

The interesting feature of the new Yugoslav arrangement is that the Soviet type of adjudication through arbitration boards was retained in those industries which have remained in the direct administration of the Department of Defense. Such is directed to decide controversies between military and economic organizations, military institutions, or authorized commands which have continued for specific reasons under the bureaucratic regime.[106]

ENFORCEMENT OF PRIVATE RIGHTS

A distinguished American jurist has thus characterized the law of modern societies:

... there had resulted a degree of antinomy between the classic system of private rights and the concept of public service, closely supervised or even provided by administrative organs of the state. Private rights in essence pertain to individuals; the public services to great impersonal public utilities or organs of government. The former are enforced by sporadic litigation in independent tribunals; the latter supervised or conducted by administrative officers subject to more or less restricted judicial review. . . .[107]

In the Soviet polity this antinomy is no longer in evidence. Individual life has been so closely integrated with the activities and vast responsibilities of the public organizations that litigation in independent tribunals is no longer important in securing the frontiers

---

105 Goldstajn, "The Economic Courts," The New Yugoslav Law, 32–37 (July–Dec., 1954); *cf.* Gsovski and Grzybowski, *supra* note 57, at 820–23.
106 Gsovski & Grzybowski, *supra* note 57, at 821.
107 Yntema, Crossroads of Justice 162 (1957).

of individual liberties. Courts are still competent to provide solutions to conflicts arising from family relations and to ajudicate in disputes arising from petty transactions between individuals, private quarrels, or conflict of interests. Rights arising from contracts of work or government employment belong to the jurisdiction of the courts of general jurisdiction, and courts still deal with claims to a share in inheritance. But these rights are precarious. The institution of inheritance is not necessarily a constant feature of socialist order, and the institution of the family was subject to scrutiny as to the role it would play in the new society. In the vast area where the roots of individual existence are planted, however, individual rights have only a secondary mission. Thus, there is no channel for the adjudication against the government of claims arising from their exercise for the benefit of individual existence. Rights are determined in general constitutional clauses and concretized in administrative regulations. The general atmosphere in which the vast mechanism of the socialist state developed and in which the spirit of its laws took shape was such that some forty years after the Soviet State had come into existence, a leading Soviet jurist complained:

Until quite recently such an important function in the activity of the socialist state as the protection of rights and legal interests of the citizens was not considered an independent function. This thesis was based on an incorrect interpretation of the well known statements of I. V. Stalin ... who stated that "the main task of the revolutionary legality in our time consists concretely in the protection of socialist property—and in nothing else." Without doubt, protection of socialist property is an important function of the Soviet state. However, limitation of the tasks of the socialist legality exclusively to the protection of socialist property means nothing else but the neglect in the protection of rights and legal interests of the citizens.[108]

108 Romashkin, *supra* note 10, at 9. Kaminskaia, "V chem znachenie protsessualnikh garantii v sovetskom ugolovnom protsesse," SGP 52 (No. 5, 1950): "If we say that Soviet law protects the interests of the Soviet citizens we mean those interests which are identical with the interests of the state and we may not think of anything else. Certainly, the Soviet state and its legislation cannot guarantee the interests of those citizens to live the life of parasites." *Cf.* Vyshinskii, Voprosy teorii gosudarstva i prava 72, 83 (1949); Trainin, "Nekotorye vivody dla nauki prava iz diskussii po voprosam biologii," SGP 2 (No. 2, 1949); Fedkin, "O rukovodiashchei roli VKP(b) v razvitii sovetskogo sotsialisticheskogo prava," SGP 11 ff. (No. 6, 1950).

In addition, the indifference of the Soviet state to the problem of rights is not the only reason for their poor enforcement and lack of concern with that aspect of legal commerce in the socialist order. The formulation of individual rights is such that legal processes have no function in their implementation. One of the techniques of the integration of individual life into the social processes has been that individual rights became formulated so as to be capable of implementation primarily through social action, e.g., right to work, protection of family, or equality of sexes. Two Polish lawyers have pointed out that such a formulation frequently means that a full implementation of rights depends upon the level of economic development:

For the poor countries, a narrower formula of the civil rights is more advisable particularly as regards these points which deal with the so-called social rights, in order to establish some correlation between their formulation and a reality. It is also indispensable to remove all sorts of "democratic privileges" in the areas which do not belong to the sphere of civil rights. In this sphere, real liberty is better than phony equality—the freedom of the citizen to acquire certain property according to his financial possibilities, and not according to the official prices with rights to acquire factually limited to a small circle of persons. Official prices constitute one of those shams of democracy: prices so low that (theoretically) everybody has a material chance to acquire a thing or a service. But what of it when there is not enough of them for everybody? In such situations it is preferable that the price of such objects be fixed according to supply and demand.[109]

In this situation, the implementation and content of individual rights is not a matter of the concrete legal situation but of governmental policy. In consequence, judicial review became disqualified from playing a hand in the process of the supervision of government's performance, and the control of governmental activities in this respect was entrusted to the procuratura. In addition to its functions in the field of the prosecution of crimes and the protection of the interests of the state in private litigations, it was charged with a general supervision of all governmental institutions below the ministerial level from the point of view of the observance of the laws and regula-

---

109 Opałek & Zakrzewski, Z zagadnień praworządności socjalistycznej 98–99 (1958).

tions in force. In practice, procuratorial agencies respond to individual complaints against governmental actions which impair the rights of Soviet citizens.

This aspect of the activities of the procuratorial agencies came to the fore after the demise of Stalin. *Socialist Legality,* a periodical issued by the Procurator General, carries in each number a section devoted to the protests lodged by the procuratorial officers against the violations of the law not only in judicial cases but also in regard to the action by various administrative agencies.[110]

Procuratorial actions reveal the intimate connection between administrative decisions and the rights of citizens arising from general conditions provided in the laws in force regarding various categories of employment.[111] So, for instance, a protest was lodged against a ministerial instruction which gave the foremen, senior foremen, and chiefs of plants the right to impose certain penalties exceeding the disciplinary powers given these officers under the law.[112] In another case, a protest was lodged against the instruction of the chief of an educational program which ordered the subordinate administration of education in Kursk to replace all instructors without higher education with instructors with higher education, as the law does not require higher education from this category of instructors.[113]

Similarly, a procuratorial protest was made against an instruction of the USSR Ministry of Finance concerning certain persons in possession of houses and building plots. Involved was the operation of certain regulations imposing special taxes on those who had taken posession of such house and plots without proper authorization.[114] The procuratura also protested an instruction of higher authorities which would deprive candidates for higher examinations of their earnings during the time of such examinations;[115] an instruction barring employment of a dismissed worker in another enterprise under the same administration;[116] an order to reduce the wages of

110 Gsovski & Grzybowski, *supra* note 57, at 547–57; *cf.* also editorial: "Pravo grazhdanina na zhalobu," Sots. zak. 4 (No. 7, 1960).
111 Gsovski & Grzybowski, *supra* note 57, at 554.
112 Sots. zak. 5 (No. 5, 1958).
113 *Ibid.*
114 *Ibid.*
115 *Id.* at 94 (No. 4, 1958).
116 *Ibid.*

workers for incomplete production; [117] an order fixing without proper authorization an age limit for certain positions in the research institutes of the Ministry of Health; [118] and an instruction which prohibited employment of persons living in other localities.[119]

Another aspect of the right to work was dealt with by a protest against an instruction which barred the employment of drivers who failed a driver's test in other jobs in the same institution.[120] A procuratorial protest dealt with the refusal of an executive committee of a province in Uzbekistan to continue grants in aid to a mother of many children who left a *kolkhoz* for another locality without the permission of the committee. The protest contended that this decision violated the right to freedom of movement of this woman.[121] In another case, the procuratura objected against delegation of authority to the subordinate agency.[122]

The characteristic feature of this type of redress is that individual complaint is only a means of obtaining information of the departure from the rules of law. Proceedings are then initiated which aim not so much at safeguarding individual rights as at the correction of a mistaken line of policy. Individual involvement in the preservation of the correct line of policy by government authorities in accordance with the laws in force is reduced to a minimum. The element of the violation of private rights pertaining to a specific individual citizen of the Soviet polity is not essential for the performance of the function of supervision. As a matter of fact, it is difficult to detect the element of a violation of rights in the case which concerned the validity of the instruction that in future only people living in the locality where a government institution was located be considered for employment.

Thus, in the final analysis, the concern of the procuratorial services with individual rights originates not so much in the content of the rule of law, which deals also with general conditions of service regarding personnel policy, but from the decision of the

117 *Id.* at 108 (No. 7, 1958).
118 *Id.* at 87 (No. 7, 1960).
119 *Id.* at 87 (No. 5, 1960).
120 *Ibid.*
121 *Id.* at 89 (No. 7, 1959).
122 *Ibid.*

Twentieth Congress which ordered a stricter protection of individual rights. The decision of the Party Congress could influence the general tone of the work of government agencies in the performance of their official duties, but could not change the function of individual rights in the socialist legal order. It is not in the nature of this order to consider individual rights as absolute values.

In a Polish case in which a worker sued a government enterprise for damages (one month's pay) because of improper dismissal, it was alleged that, contrary to the regulations, the factory manager alone signed the notice of separation. The Polish Supreme Court gave the following opinion:

[I]t is necessary to examine whether claimant's demands are not an abuse of his rights . . . It must be borne in mind that the Polish People's Republic is a state of the working people, in which every citizen has a duty to protect social property. . . . It follows that one of the rules of social co-existence in a people's state is that a citizen has no right to counterpoise fully his rights to the interests of his enterprise as being totally alien to his own. Obviously this is not to mean that individual interests should be subordinated to the interests of all, but to mean a wise compromise between the two.[123]

To adjust the rights and claims of the disputants in a civil suit is a legitimate function of the modern judge. According to modern civil codes, its classic example is judicial power to distribute more equitably the hazards of modern life, not according to principles of liability, but according to the economic position of the parties. The appearance of this institution is one of the symptoms of the relativity of the institution of property in our society. The decision of the Polish Supreme Court indicates that the rights of the workingman, which in our world are a matter of public policy and remain unaffected by contract, have also become relative.

123 Decision of November 23, 1958, Case No. 4 CO 18/58, PiP 1085 (No. 12, 1959).

Chapter VI

THE QUESTION MARK OVER THE SOCIALIST RECHTSSTAAT

THE NEW PHASE

The work of the Soviet jurist is done in the shadow of the thesis that its ultimate purpose is to contrive a disappearing act for both the state and the legal order. The prophecy that state and law will one day no longer be the attributes of our life lies beyond the range of the present study. It is brought in here only inasmuch as it provides the ethos of Soviet planning and as it influences the forms of Soviet institutions, preferences for the forms of social action, and the legislative techniques to effect governmental and social reforms. While it is useful to establish connections between political aims and a legal measure, its effects must be examined in the context of its social role, irrespective of the political aspects of its origin. Once the rule of law has been enacted, it represents its own complex of problems occurring in response to the unique characteristics of legal action.

The issue of the withering of state and law lay dormant during Stalin's regime. After the Twentieth Party Congress in 1956, the immediate task was to repair the damage caused to the Soviet ship of state by the "cult of personality"—a brand name for policies and governmental techniques which relied on use of force and dictatorial forms of government with little respect for the legal rule and democratic processes. The socialist state was to give meaning to the rule of its own law. Since the Twenty-first Congress of the Party in 1959, the reform of the legal system has acquired a new sense because, as the Congress stated, the time has come to reorganize all phases of Soviet life. The time is thought to be ripe because of the contemporary upsurge of economic forces in Soviet society on which the dawn of communism is predicated. This declaration has put on the action calendar of the day the question of the withering away of the state and law.

The socialist state, which followed the destruction of the capitalist order, retained certain characteristics of the bourgeois state, which were deemed indispensable under socialism. Among these were remnants of bourgeois law, including techniques of legal action and the use of force by the state. These features of the socialist state were scheduled to disappear under communism.[1]

Lenin established certain objective conditions for the arrival of communism, independent of the levels of socialist productive forces. These consisted primarily in the ability of Soviet society to exercise controlling and organizing functions without the state and formal legal rule. The need for the state and law would be eliminated because the vast majority of members of the society would acquire skills required for performing government and administrative functions. Furthermore, they would acquire the habit of performing these functions without remuneration and in addition to their normal duties in the economic processes. Then these functions, which are now in the hands of the administrative departments, agencies, and special governmental services, would be discharged by the society itself. The result would be a perfect state of law enforcement and a biological unity between the social structure and the exercise of governmental functions.[2]

In general perspective, the reforms initiated after the Twenty-first Party Congress were a continuation of the reforms which followed the demise of Stalin. The regime of the Georgian dictator was characterized by a high concentration of administrative powers in the hands of the Union government. The gradual unloading of the accumulated powers was followed by a radical reform of the economic administration, which shifted all administrative functions from the center to-

1 Aleksieiev, "O zakonomernostiakh razvitia sovetskogo prava v period razvernutogo stroitelstva kommunizma," SGP 10 (No. 9, 1960).
2 Lenin, *The State and Revolution*, 33 Soch. 155; *cf.* Chapter IV *supra*, text at note 9a; the full theory of this process was worked out by Engels in *Anti-Düring*.

ward the republics and the regions administered by the councils of national economy.[3] Decisions of the Twenty-first Congress attached an ideological significance to the process which was already taking place and mapped out a further program of decentralization. Decentralization, in this phase, went beyond the mere framework of the bureaucratic mechanism of the Soviet state, but engaged its representative and social institutions.

In the first place, the Congress recommended further decentralization of authority and a further shifting of governmental functions to the lower levels of governmental authority. Secondly, it was decided to draw social organizations into the processes of government and to devise methods which would make them directly responsible for the maintenance of law and order and for the exercise of judicial and certain other functions of government.

The decisions of the Twenty-first Congress expressed the conviction that, as Lenin predicted, more perfect law enforcement would

3 At the time of Stalin's demise, administration of the national economy of the USSR was almost exclusively tied to decision from the center. According to the distribution of responsibilities for the management of various branches of national economy, only some 30 per cent of industry was in charge of the individual republics, while the rest was run by the Union. This process was reversed, and by 1956, after the initial unloading of responsibilities for various industrial branches, only some 45 per cent of the national economy was still run by the industrial ministries of the federal government, while the rest was classified as industry of local character and importance. As such it was under the direct and exclusive administration of the individual republics or local soviets.

These measures were only preliminary to more basic reforms, and, after a good deal of cogitation and discussion, the Supreme Soviet of the USSR approved during the session May 7–10, 1957, the law on Further Improvement of the Organization of Industry and Construction in the Soviet Union. The main feature of the reform was to replace branch administrations run from the center by the territorial administrations under economic councils (sovnarkhoz) set up by the individual republics forming the Union. The entire territory of the Soviet Union was divided into 104 economic administrative units, each headed by an economic council. Vedomosti, sec. 275 (1957); *cf.* SGP 4 (No. 4, 1959); Kommunist 27 (No. 13, 1958); Khrushchev's speech to the Supreme Soviet of May 7, 1957, Pravda, May 9, 1957; for detailed description of the organization and operation of the councils of national economy *cf.* Petrov, Sovety narodnogo khoziaistva (1958).

thus be assured. The direct participation of society could play an important role in combating breaches of socialist law and order. "Our public organizations," said Khrushchev, "have no less adequate capacities, means and forces for this than the militia, the courts and the prosecutor's office." [4]

Less than a year later, Khrushchev reported to the Supreme Soviet as follows:

Guided by the decisions of the Twenty-First Congress, the Party and the government are constantly effectuating measures for the further development of socialist democracy drawing the wide masses of the working people into the administration of the country's political, economic and cultural affairs. Extension of the rights of Union Republics, local authorities and public organizations and reorganization of industrial management have produced valuable results. The activity of the masses, politically and on the labor front, is growing and their creative initiative developing.

More and more functions are being entrusted to public organizations, and they are playing a bigger part in economic and cultural development and in strengthening socialist legality. One evidence of this is the recent decision of the USSR Council of Ministers and of the Party Central Committee to abolish the USSR Ministry of Internal Affairs and transfer its functions to the Republics and local authorities. This is done not only to reduce the size and cost of our administrative apparatus but chiefly to further develop socialist democracy and enhance the role of public organizations in combating infringement of our laws, and to extend the powers of local authorities.[5]

The process of decentralization, which resulted in an impressive reduction of the central apparatus of the government of the union, was paralleled by the transfer of some governmental functions into the administration of social organizations. Even before the Twenty-first Congress, the administration of sports and physical culture was made the business of the social organizations (trade unions), and the Congress recommended that a similar step should be taken for the administration of health and cultural affairs.[6]

4 XXI sjezd KPSS o razvitii i ukreplenii sovetskogo sotsialisticheskogo gosudarstva (No. 4, 1959); Denisov, "O sootnoshenii gosudarstva i obshchestva v perekhodnyi ot kapitalizma do kommunizma period," SGP 29–40 (No. 4, 1960); cf. XXI sjezd KPSS i zadatchi sovetskoi pravovoi nauki, SGP 4–5 (No. 2, 1959).
5 Supplement to the New Times, No. 4, January 1960.
6 XXI sjezd KPSS i zadatchi sovetskoi pravovoi nauki, SGP 4–5 (No. 2, 1959).

Decentralization of governmental powers and the creation of new channels for law enforcement represent only two sides of the same process, directed at drawing broad social strata into direct participation in government. At the present stage, the level of individual skills and habit of participation in governmental functions does not permit the individual involvement of Soviet citizens. This must still be done by way of their membership in social organizations, on the basis of directed action.[7]

The transition to communism, or at least the first phase of it, will not result in the relaxation of formal social ties. Quite to the contrary, as the Resolution of the Twenty-first Congress of the Party warned:

[A] definite dialectical link is inevitable between a socialist state formation and law, on the one hand, and self-administration by the people and social norm of a communist society on the other; it consists of the preservation in a different form of some of the elements constituting the activity of the state and content of the norms of law.[8]

Soviet jurists interpret this statement as indicating that the centralized character of the Soviet state will not be affected by the process of change, neither at present nor in the future. Communist society is not planned to be a structure of free individuals who act according to a certain pattern because of internal compulsion and acquired behavioral pattern. Communist society will still be a centralized society. As a Ukrainian jurist wrote:

The view that the system of self-administration in a communist society is a decentralized system is a revisionist and anarcho-syndicalist distortion of Marxist-Leninist teachings on the socialist state and structure of society in the highest phase of communist society. Both a socialist state formation and self-administration in a Communist society are understood by the classics of Marxism-Leninism as a democratically centered organization.[9]

Soviet leaders and jurists are anxious to forestall any premature ideas regarding a rapid change in the methods and forms of govern-

---

7 *Ibid.*
8 XXI sjezd KPSS o razvitii i ukreplenii sovetskogo sotsialisticheskogo gosudarstva 14 (No. 4, 1959).
9 Radyanskie pravo 18 (No. 4, 1959).

ment, such as turning the Soviet state into a system of loosely connected organizations, each responsible for its own area of competence. Khrushchev, describing the process of transition from socialism to communism, used language which left little doubt as to the fact that the process of transition means a greater cohesion of both governmental machinery and social structures.[10] Transition from the socialist state into communist society will be a gradual process, characterized not so much by the organization of new means of exercising governmental powers but by the changes in the nature of governmental functions. Organs of state administration will acquire the character of social organizations, and their function will acquire a social character, while rules of social behavior, which they will enforce, no longer will be legal rules:

[T]he withering away of the state by no means implies the disappearance of all . . . authority and administration.

The withering away of the laws does not mean the disappearance of standards of social behavior, personal freedoms, and social duties of the peoples. It would be an unforgivable vulgarization to represent the matter in a manner according to which as the laws wither away under communism, all the rules governing social relations and personal rights and freedoms of citizens disappear, too. They will remain under communism, but they will lose their political and legal character.[11]

Soviet jurists and leaders have restated in a new form Stalin's doctrine that, as Soviet society comes closer to the realization of the goals of social reconstruction, the functions of the state and law will expand. They sound a note warning that resolutions of the Twenty-first Congress indicate that state direction of the national economy will increase, that the government of the Soviet polity will continue to provide for the defense of the country, and that its educational and organizing functions will expand. In particular

10 ". . . year 1960 will go down in history as the first year of the extensive building of communist society in our country. . . . The past year has been a further strengthening of the social and political system, the continued development of socialist democracy and the heightening of the organizing and educational role of the Communist Party." *Supra* note 8, at 15.

11 Romashkin, "Razvitie funktsii sovetskogo gosudarstva v protsesse postroienia kommunizma," SGP (No. 10, 1958).

...shall continue and shall grow such functions of the socialist state as the function of the brotherly cooperation with other countries of socialism, the function of the preservation of peace. Until the full victory of Communism, shall be preserved protection of social property and social order and the supervision and the measure of work and measure of satisfaction of social needs.[12]

Not until several conditions are met will state and law disappear, but even then not wholly. Before that happens, a high level of production and high cultural level of the entire society will have to be reached. Differences between the forms of life in the urban and agrarian environment, and between physical and intellectual work must be abolished. Survivals of capitalism in the minds of the people, and the danger of external aggression must be liquidated, and the entire society with all its members must fully conform to the rules of life in a socialist community. Only then will the socialist state have no function and no responsibility. However, administration of things and productive processes will continue, but will lose its political function.[13]

The general picture of this process is an almost total identification of social organizations with the governmental apparatus, and the integration of social and governmental actions into single patterns of activity not only within a single area of life (e.g., economic activity) but also within the same governmental function (administration of justice, police functions, etc.). Social organizations become government agencies organized on a different principle:

The activities of the social organization in the administration of the affairs of the society, as distinct from the "intra-union" administration of voluntary societies... must be carried out within the framework of the Soviet Constitution which envisages the uniform subordination of all organizations and citizens to the law of the Soviet state.[14]

Conversely, the elements of public administration acquire the characteristics of social organizations of the voluntary associations in the discharge of public functions. Khrushchev, referring to social organizations, called the Soviets the largest and the most important among them.[15] *Kommunist,* the ideological paper of the Communist

12 Mitskievitch, "Razshirenie roli obshchestvennikh organizatsii v period razvernutogo stroitelstva kommunizma," SGP 26 (No. 9, 1959).
13 *Id* at 33.
14 *Id.* at 32.
15 Khrushchev, Rech na sobranii izbiratelej Kalininskogo izbiratelnogo okruga goroda Moskvy 7 (1959).

Party of the Soviet Union, anticipated Khrushchev's statement by writing in 1958 that the Soviets will not disappear from the future Communist society, but "as society draws closer to Communism, they, gradually, losing their class political character may merge into a system of self-administration in a Communist society." Further, they will not only merge, but may even occupy the central, leading position.[16]

Thus, some form of fusion between social and governmental organizations is planned in which the Soviets will occupy a controlling position with two facets—one representative of the administrative aspect of the Soviet governmental machinery and the other indicative of its essential association with the society which it represents. In the new scheme of things which is taking shape as a result of governmental and party decisions, both sides of Soviet activities have gained considerable importance.

Owing to the process of decentralization, the Soviets have obtained a firmer grip on local industries which serve to satisfy local needs. In the areas of its original jurisdiction, interference by the higher echelons of the administrative apparatus seems to have been restricted to cases of clear violations of the rule of law in force.[17] On the village level, the Decree of September 12, 1957, introduced an important reorganization of the village Soviet. By increasing its size and assigning additional personnel, the exercise of some basic functions of government on the local level became possible.[18] Another development, which enhanced the role of the local Soviets, was the assignment of administrative punitive powers to the militia commission of the local Soviet, beginning with the township Soviets within their territorial units.[19]

Moreover, a significant change occurred in the style of the work of the local authorities. Until now, decisions of the Soviet, consisting of the elected members, were implemented through the instrumentality of administrative personnel employed by its executive commit-

---

16 Kommunist (No. 11, 1958); *cf.* Aleksieiev, *supra* note 1, at 12–16.
17 *Cf. supra* at 180–81.
18 Zimin, "Novoe polozhenie o selskom sovete deputatov trudiashchykhsia RSFSR" SGP 3–11 (No. 1, 1958).
19 Mitskievitch, *supra* note 12, at 27.

tee. Now, the emphasis is on the direct action of the various commissions consisting of the elected members of the Soviet. These now practice direct action in cooperation with social organizations or through the so-called activists in various areas of administrative responsibility.

Since 1959, the number of deputies in the Soviet has increased considerably. Thus has been permitted closer and informal cooperation of the Soviets with trade unions, youth organizations, housing and street committees, people's militia, committees for the affairs of minors, etc., which themselves are active in their various areas of social action. These latter also cooperate with the Soviets in order to realize specific programs in the field of public security, education, social welfare projects, the administration of housing, and the liquidation of crime and juvenile delinquency.[20]

The over-all purpose is to exploit the influence, social ramifications, and manpower which various social institutions have at their disposal. There are at least three patterns of cooperation between social and governmental institutions. Social organizations perform specific services (e.g., rehabilitation of criminals). They are in charge of governmental functions, which are also handled at a different level, by the governmental agencies. Finally, social organizations, particularly those which participate in the economic functions of the socialist system, assume general responsibility for the affairs of a social group, thus bringing the situation very close to the medieval pattern of distributing authority.

SOCIAL ORGANIZATIONS AND GOVERNMENTAL FUNCTIONS

The involvement of social organizations in the administration of justice, resulting from the reforms initiated by the Twenty-first Congress, had its precedent in the early days of the Revolution. Trade unions with special responsibilities in the factories of Russia had established their disciplinary tribunals. These were limited initially to disciplining the workers, but tended to expand their functions until they began to compete with the jurisdiction of the people's courts,

20 *Ibid*

which finally caused their liquidation.[21] A somewhat longer career was enjoyed by comradely courts which, organized in the army (1917), ultimately spread later to the factories (1919). Their purpose was to maintain the morale of the army and of factory crews in the fulfillment of their duties. In 1928 (August 28) the basic law on the organization of the comradely courts in factories and in governmental and social establishments was enacted. Then in 1930, village courts were set up, and in 1930 and 1931, similar institutions were established in housing organizations.

The purpose of these organizations was to deal with minor offenses originating mainly in private accusations. Their jurisdiction was based on the fact that parties were employed, or lived, in the same village, factory, or in the same house. Such minor problems, arising out of conflicts between neighbors or coworkers, have little general significance. Neither did they constitute a danger to the preservation of peace. Thus, the state could profitably leave them to be handled by quasi-judicial bodies. However, as Soviet society moved toward total monopolization of public authority by the central government, the activities of the comradely courts began to dwindle and in the late thirties were practically halted.[22]

An editorial in a Soviet legal periodical found the cause of the disappearance of this form of social participation in governmental activities in the fact that comradely courts lost contact with the social milieu which produced them:

The drawback of the regulations concerning social courts, introduced thirty years ago, was precisely this, that direction of their work was the responsibility not of the Soviets or trade unions, but of the people's courts. This fact transformed comradely courts into a supplementary element in the state judicial system, and limited their contact with the broad social masses.[23]

21 Hazard, Settling Disputes in Soviet Society, The Formative Years of Legal Institutions 182 (1960).
22 "Obshchestvennye sudy—vazhneishaia rola borby z perezhytkami proshlogo," SGP 4–5 (No. 5, 1959); Savitskii & Keyzerov, "Razvitie pravovykh form organizatsii i dejatelnosti tovarishcheskikh sudov," SGP 37–46 (No. 4, 1961); Hazard, Le droit soviétique et le dépérissement de l'État 4–5 (1960).
23 Obshchestvennye sudy, *supra* note 22, at 10; Mitskievitch, *supra* note 12, at 26.

It is useless to speculate whether comradely courts had a chance to survive Stalin's regime merely by dint of a different affiliation. However, it is also true that the present policy of the regime is to foster the expansion of governmental functions of a general nature within social groups which owe their existence to their functions in the economic units, i.e., collective farms and workers' organizations on the factory level.

Of the two, farming collectives are more important in terms of the human mass involved, as somewhat more than 50 per cent of the Soviet population lives and works in the countryside. By the very nature of things, village communities, closely identified with the economic organization which almost totally absorbs the life of an average member of the collective, represent an ideal social environment for self-government activities. Under Stalin these tendencies suffered from the fact that centralized economic administration gave little independence to the collective's authorities, which voted charters and statutes according to the single model prepared by the ministries and adopted economic plans and deliveries of farm products to the government according to instructions centrally prepared.

On March 5, 1956, the Central Committee of the Party and the Council of Ministers of the USSR passed a resolution to encourage the collectives to depart from the pattern and adapt their charters to local conditions. After the Twenty-first Party Congress, the Supreme Court of the Soviet Union followed this resolution with a ruling (March 26, 1960) which instructed the courts that charters of the collective farms had to be considered as the basic source of law in legal disputes:

[W]hile adjudicating in civil matters pertaining to agricultural collectives, the courts should take into account that members of the collectives make decision as regards the disposal of the products and of the property of the collective, and direct its activities in accordance with the laws of the Soviet authority, decisions of the Party and of the Government . . . and that a collective's charter with its supplements and amendments which were registered by the executive committee of the region represents the basic law for its activities.[24]

24 Bardin, "Novoe postanovlenie plenuma Verkhovnogo Suda SSSR 'O Sudebnoi praktike po grazhdanskim kolkhoznym delam,'" SGP 12 (No. 6, 1960).

Self-government of agricultural collectives has also been upheld by the Supreme Court in connection with the administration of criminal statutes. Thus, the court quashed the case against three members of a collective, who were charged with a theft of social property, stating:

It is not correct to initiate criminal prosecution of the members of an agricultural collective for offenses connected with the economic activities of the collective, without a prior decision in this respect by the general meeting of the collective. If the injured party is a collective farm, then the problem regarding making good the losses, application of correctional measures to the offenders should be in the first place decided by the general meeting of the members of the collective.[25]

The Chairman of the Supreme Court of the Union, in an article published in the leading legal periodical, approvingly described the situation in one of the agricultural collectives with a membership of some six thousand. This collective gives no business to the criminal courts. It is admitted that criminal offenses are committed in this exemplary association of Soviet citizens. The chairman of the collective explained this situation by the fact that, owing to the organization of work, not the slightest transgression of the law escapes attention. Transgressions are dealt with on all of the levels of the organization of the collective, in the working brigade, by the party committee, and by the administration, as well as in the general meeting. The results of this method are said to be most satisfactory, particularly in regard to moral rehabilitation of the offenders.[26]

A somewhat analogous development took place in the industrial sector of the national economy. The decree of the Presidium of the Supreme Soviet of July 15, 1958, gave additional jurisdiction to the factory and local trade union committee regarding participation in the management of industrial enterprise or a working institution, in all those aspects which concern the interests and the rights of the factory crew, enforcement of the labor law, and matters affecting the fulfillment of the economic plan. Expansion of administrative responsibilities was combined with expansion of judicial powers. Thus, the factory and trade union committee deal locally with all matters of discipline, with appeals from the labor disputes boards, and render

25 Gorkin, "O zadatchakh sovetskogo suda v period razvernutogo stroitelstva kommunizma," SGP 17 (No. 3, 1960); *cf.* Pravda, July 29, 1959.
26 *Ibid.*

decisions on the dismissal of workers. In this particular field their decisions are final, and their powers resemble very much the powers of an umpire. The factory committee may modify the decision to dismiss a worker and impose another disciplinary measure, with a warning to the culprit. It may also order steps designed to instill in the member of the crew a correct attitude toward work and performance of his duties, including social supervision by the members of his working brigade or team, as well as investigation of his personal circumstances.[27]

As compared with the situation in the agricultural collectives, the operation of group government in the industrial environment of socialist society is narrow in scope, and certainly the urban environment restricts the degree of the factory committee's control over individual workers. However, the expansion of factory housing projects and of welfare services and the amenities of factory life tend to increase the effectiveness of collective control over individual members of the factory crew.

NEW FORMS OF ADMINISTRATIVE JUSTICE

The outline of principles to provide a guide for the reform of criminal codes in the Soviet republics states that

... administration of justice in criminal matters belongs exclusively to the court. Nobody may be declared guilty of committing a crime and be subjected to penalty except by court sentence.

Article 7 of the General Principles of Criminal Legislation was read in the context of the abolition in 1955 of the Special Board in the Ministry of the Interior which exercised vast punitive powers, generally without trial, and which at one time was the most important instrument of criminal repression.[28]

---

27 Akhverdian, "Zakreplenie vazhneishykh dostizhenii sovetskogo naroda," SGP 97 (No. 11, 1959): "... in those enterprises, where the factory committee of the trade union under the leadership of the party organization fully exercises the rights which it has under the statute, all basic problems of production, of work and living conditions are decided by the management of the enterprise only in cooperation with the trade union organization."

28 Gsovski & Grzybowski, Government, Law and Courts in the Soviet Union and Eastern Europe 578 (1959).

The significance of Article 7 was somewhat weakened by the fact that in a number of Soviet Republics a law against parasites was adopted. It provided that a meeting of neighbors could exile for two to five years of forced labor persons who carry on "a parasitic mode of life . . . as well as those living on unearned income." The only formality required, in addition to the popular vote, was that the decision to impose a sentence was subject to confirmation by the executive of the district soviet. There was no appeal to a court.

However, at that particular moment this method of criminal repression of the enemies of the socialist mode of life was somewhat in doubt. Its adoption was discussed in other republics but was rejected in RSFSR, which somewhat checked its progress. In the absence of the regime's clear position, it seemed that this law would not significantly detract from the judicial monopoly for the administration of criminal statutes.

The situation changed materially after the Twenty-first Party Congress. Khrushchev declared himself in favor of the exercise of governmental functions by social organizations:

Problems of security in our social order, and enforcement of the rules of socialist coexistence should, to an ever increasing degree, become the business of social organizations. . . . Socialist society forms such voluntary agencies of enforcement of the social order as people's militia, comradely courts, and similar institutions. They will discharge in new manner . . . social functions. . . .

According to Khrushchev, this new approach to law enforcement was dictated by the serious restriction of the powers of the security police.[29] The proposal soon became adopted in the RSFSR and in a number of other republics, reflecting a change in the general attitude of the legislatures of the various republics toward the law on parasites.

In the debate which followed, the administration of serious penalties by nonjudicial bodies was declared to be typical for the period of transition to communism. Administrative regulation of certain relationships is being replaced by the institutes of civil law and *kolkhoz* law. Similar changes occur in the field of the administration

29 Pravda, Jan. 29, 1959.

of justice, where judicial functions and court action are replaced by administrative forms of criminal responsibility:

In conditions of transferring separate functions of the governmental agencies to social conditions, the tendency in this group of relations is to tie it directly to the expansion of autonomous and creative participation of the broad working masses in the maintenance of social order and of rules of socialist coexistence.[30]

The inference is that the broad working masses may provide administrative action but cannot be a source of judicial process.

In the past, the functions of the comradely courts were primarily concerned with the internal discipline of the social groups which they served. As a party resolution stated:

Disciplinary courts should . . . raise the discipline of labor and cultural forms of the struggle for the higher productivity of labor not interfering with the functions of the people's courts and governmental functions.[31]

The main duties of the comradely courts were in the re-education of the workers, with a view to advancing the interests of production. Their social significance consisted in the specific purposes of the group, as defined by its economic function. But, in addition, the comradely courts dealt with immoral behavior of the factory crew, rowdiness, indecent behavior, cursing, minor thefts, etc.[32]

The resolution of the Executive Committee of the Council of National Economy of the RSFSR of August 27, 1928, added to the jurisdiction of the comradely courts cases of insults and lies.[33] A year later, they were instructed to deal with cases of bodily harm, minor larceny of materials and tools, and civil disputes involving small value.[34]

Comradely courts were instructed to proceed in an informal and simple manner. However, their duty was always to give an opportunity to the accused party to be heard. Their action included

---

30 Aleksieiev, *supra* note 1, at 17.
31 Decision of the Central Committee of the Party of January 12, 1922, Savitskii & Keyzerov, *supra* note 22, at 38.
32 *Ibid.*
33 Sob. uzak. No. 114/707 (1928).
34 Sob. uzak. No. 67/62; Savitskii & Keyzerov, *supra* note 22, at 39.

conciliation, arbitration, arrangements for the restitution of damages, as well as simple judicial functions.

Post-Stalin developments have contributed significantly to the expansion of their function, although the technicalities of their action have remained practically unchanged.

At the Twenty-first Party Congress, Khrushchev postulated expansion of their activity outside the immediate social group they serve.[35] This was duly reflected in Article 1 of Model Act of the Comradely Courts, stating that their duty consists in

... educating Soviet citizens in the spirit of communist attitude to work, socialist property, observance of the rules of socialist coexistence, promoting with the Soviet people the spirit of collectivism, comradely help, respect for dignity and honor of the citizens.

Their duties were no longer confined to the framework of a social group, but were to extend to everybody within their territorial jurisdiction.

Following the Twenty-first Party Congress decision, No. 3 of the Plenary Session of the Soviet Supreme Court (June 19, 1959) and Order No. 43 of the Procurator General of July 20, 1959, the courts and subordinate prosecutors were instructed to restrict judicial action to cases which called for the action of courts. Minor cases which could be sucessfully dealt with by social organizations and comradely courts should be transmitted to them for informal disposal without resorting to formal criminal procedures.

Both the Supreme Court and the Procurator General resorted to an unusual legal argumentation. They referred to Article 7, part 2, of the Principles of Criminal Legislation enacted in December 1958. Article 7, part 1, contains the definition of the crime. Part 2 of Article 7 states that:

An act of commission or omission shall not be deemed a crime; if although formally containing the elements of an act specified by the criminal statute, it nevertheless does not represent social danger, because of its insignificance.[36]

35 Khrushchev, O kontrolnikh tsyfrakh razvitia narodnogo khoziaistva SSSR na 1959–1965 gody 122 (1959).
36 Sots. zak. 13–19 (No. 9, 1959).

The jurisdiction of the comradely courts was regulated in detail by the Model Act of the Comradely Courts, which was to serve as the basis for the adoption by the individual republics. The Model Act appeared in *Izvestia* on October 23, 1959.

Comradely courts are competent to deal with minor civil cases, breaches of the discipline of labor or factory rules, misuse of materials, tools, instruments, or means of transport which are social or government property, failure to provide proper education for children, refusal to accept respectable employment and carrying on of a parasitic mode of life, small thefts, minor assault, violation of the government monopoly of trade, speculation, breaches of peace, violation of rules in living quarters, and in all those matters which are transmitted by the prosecution or courts. Comradely courts may apply various forms of censure, impose fines, put an offender on probation, obligate his immediate collective to exercise supervision during a certain period, and impose on him the obligation to make up the damages caused by his action.

The primary purpose of the comradely courts is to relieve courts of general jurisdiction from dealing with minor criminal and civil cases. As an editorial in a Soviet periodical revealed, people's courts dispose yearly of more than four million civil cases, quite frequently of great simplicity and concerning small value.[37]

Moreover, their purpose is to combine the protection of social interests with preventive action. The law states:

The main task of the comradely courts is to prevent violations of the law and all actions which harm society, education of the people by means of crime prevention and social influence, creation of an atmosphere of intolerance for anti-social behavior of any kind. Comradely courts are clad in the confidence of the collective and express its will.

The broad aims of the quasi-judicial action of the comradely courts are made realistic by the fact that their action is supported by the general mobilization of social organizations in the enforcement of the rules of life in socialist society. Simultaneously with the Model Act of the Comradely Courts, two additional model acts, one dealing with raising the Role of Social Organizations in the Struggle

37 SGP 4–5 (No. 2, 1959).

with the Violations of Soviet Laws and Rules of Soviet Society, and the other on the creation of committees for the Affairs of the Juveniles (*Izvestia,* October 23 and 24, 1959), were published. The comradely courts thus became a center of a vast mechanism which is to deal with antisocial manifestations in Soviet life, beginning with the affairs of children without proper care, and affecting the behavior of Soviet citizens in public places and at work, their general attitude toward one another, family relations, manners in public places, and even at home.

The leading idea in this scheme of things is that not all violations of codes of social behavior need to be dealt with through judicial channels.[38]

The action of the social courts and social organizations is strengthened by the formation of the so-called people's detachments, which strengthen police action and work on a part-time basis to provide security and safety in public places. They participate as a supporting arm for the regular police in the investigation of crimes and intervene on the spot in all situations which would threaten disturbance of the peace. Their obvious advantage is the presence of members of the detachments everywhere—in streets, houses, dwellings, at work, and in recreational institutions—in numbers greatly exceeding manpower possibilities of the regular police.[39]

Article 38 of the Principles of Criminal Legislation gave social organizations the right to intervene in a criminal case, thereby assuming direct responsibility for the rehabilitation of the offender:

Taking into consideration the circumstances of the case, the character of the guilty person, as well as the petition for suspension of sentence presented by a social organization, or a collective farm, where the guilty person is employed, the court may impose upon these organizations the duty of re-educating and reforming the person whose sentence is suspended.

38 Utevskii, "Voprosy ugolovnogo prava v projekte zakona," SGP 116–19 (No. 1, 1960). The leading principle in this connection is that judicial punishment is necessary only for those who cannot be reformed by means of social influence.

39 "Nekotorye voprosy sudoustroistva," SGP 72–83 (No. 7, 1959); Barsukov, "Ob uchastii trudiashchikhsia v okhranie obshchestvennogo poriadka," SGP 51–55 (No. 8, 1959).

The close collaboration of the courts with the various forms of crime prevention is further assured by the institution of the social prosecutors and social counsels who, by court order, may be called upon to participate for the defense (Article 41 of the Principles of Criminal Procedure).

The purpose of these provisions was to further the idea that only some forms of actions and some types of duties may be discharged satisfactorily by the institutions of the state. The functions of rehabilitation and re-education are thought to be the proper province of social organizations. Some of the drafts of the criminal codes for the individual republics have rules that convicts with suspended sentences will be placed in the charge of local and village Soviets, which report to the courts on the rehabilitation and re-educational procedures in each individual case. Some of the other drafts have demonstrated rather poor understanding of the new approach. Although it was clear that a suspended sentence precluded execution and that educational and supervisory methods did not constitute a penalty, it was specified that in such cases procedures provided for in the legislation on correctional labor should apply. Correctional labor is conceived as a form of penalty which consists in performing labor at a selected place of work, without deprivation of freedom and at reduced wages (Article 21 and 25 of the Principles of Criminal Legislation).[40]

The new order of things, which in this respect differs little from the practices of the Stalinist period, aims at exploiting the administration of criminal justice for the education of the populace at large.

40 Durmanov, "Ugolovnoe zakonodatelstvo Soiuza SSR i ugolovnoe zakonodatelstvo soiuznykh respublik," SGP 87–95 (No. 7, 1959).

Direct participation of social organizations in the administration of justice has a long tradition in the Soviet administration of justice. Basic principles of criminal procedure of 1924 provided that "deprivation of freedom as a preventive measure may be replaced by the guarantee of the professional, and other workers, peasant, and social organizations" (art. 10). Similarly, art. 142 of the Code of Criminal Procedure of the USSR ruled that in addition to the individual guarantee that the suspect will not evade justice, such a guarantee may be given by social organizations of which the suspect is a member. However, codes of the Union republics have not included this provision. Baginskii, "Institut obshchestvennogo poruchitelstva kak miera preduprezhdenia pravonarushenii i perevospitania pravonarushytelei," SGP 71 (No. 10, 1959).

Thus, great attention is being paid to the idea that some trials should be held in the factories or collective farms which made up the scene of the crime or involved their members.[41]

Another idea was that a social group or a locality which was involved in some manner in the commission of the crime should, preliminary to the hearing and the trial of the case itself, be the scene of the public investigation of the crime. The proposal was to effect this desire at a public meeting in the presence of all those possessing some knowledge of the circumstances of the case or at least of the actors of the judicial drama. The only objection to this treatment of the procedural aspects of criminal proceedings was that it could hardly satisfy the need for the secrecy of the pretrial investigation.[42]

These various schemes and proposals demonstrate the new concept of the judicial process, which differs in form from direct social action only in the feeling of a need for a higher expertise in the practical handling of the case. The chief element of formal justice—the absence of the influence of the local environment on the minds of the judges—has been eliminated and replaced by the idea of collective responsibility for the behavior of the individual. This is to become the cornerstone of the social order in which the coercive role of the state and of public authority is to play an ever diminishing role.

SOCIAL ACTION AND LAW ENFORCEMENT

There is a good deal of confusion in the minds of Soviet jurists concerning the question of to what extent social organizations called upon to perform governmental functions are to be bound by the rule of law. It is certain that their action will be different as to form, but at the same time members of the legal profession point out that all governmental functions must conform with the principles of the Constitution and of the Soviet statutes.[43] The same impression is gained from the provisions of the law on the Increasing the Role of Society in the Protection of Social Order. Its basic idea is to make the entire

41 Sovetskaia obshchestvennost, reshaiushchaia sila v borbe za ukreplenie sotsialisticheskogo pravoporiadka, SGP 20 (No. 10, 1959).

42 Mitrichev, "Privlechenie obshchestvennosti k rassledovanii prestuplenii," Sots. zak. 84 (No. 10, 1960).

43 Mitskievitch, *supra* note 12, at 32.

society responsible for the maintenance of law and order. It postulates that each Soviet citizen shall not only follow the rules of law, but shall act as a law enforcement officer and demand that others conform to the rules of socialist legal order (Article 1).

Moreover, the Resolution of the Twenty-first Congress of the Party indicated that some form of lawmaking will still be preserved, even after the higher form of social organization is reached. The change will affect the form of legal rule, but not its content.[44]

Characteristically enough, if there is apprehension as to the competence of social organizations to deal with the legal problems of modern life, there is a good deal of evidence that, on the whole, social organizations are inclined to adopt at least formal aspects of governmental action. They are sternly warned, however, that this is not what is needed. Informality and direct action should be guiding principles in their operations.

Nevertheless, the quest for informality does not dispense with a need for some expertise in the field of law. The very fact that social organizations have been given a role in the preservation of law and order and in the administration of justice calls for some familiarity with its rules and with certain refined legal techniques. Only then may the distinction be made between those cases which are fit for social treatment and those which still need to be handled with reference to the strict rules of the Codes. A high government official (Procurator General of Kazakhstan) was greatly concerned with the level of legal education of those members of Soviet officialdom who were responsible for the application of Soviet statutes. Many violations of the rights of citizens could be traced to the lack of legal education, and this problem becomes even more acute as social organizations are called to discharge public functions:

Now that participation of society in the strengthening of socialist legality and protection of citizens' rights expands, popularization of Soviet laws among the population has an even greater significance in order to prevent the violation of social order.[45]

A great obstacle in the preparation of the vast social strata for proper functioning in their new role is also a generally low level of

44 *Cf. supra* at 245; Aleksieiev, *supra* note 1.
45 Nabatov, "Strogo okhraniat prava grazhdan," Sots. zak. (No. 2, 1960).

studies and scholarly research in certain areas, which must involve broad ranks of the public if the new order is to function as designed. This is especially true in regard to the study of some basic concepts of criminal law:

Can it be said that the study of criminology and of the causes of crimes is properly organized in our country? Unfortunately this work is still of departmental nature. The public, including the scientific community, has not been drawn into this work. True, of late the study of criminology has received some treatment in the general and specialized legal literature. Scientific and practical conferences devoted to the study of crime and its causes have been held in Moscow.... But these conferences were of an episodic nature and did not result in programs of systematic studies with the participation of the public... for the purpose of eradicating crime in our country. Because of this, highly primitive methods of criminological studies and of the causes of crimes are locally employed.... The tasks consist in... popularizing the experience in this matter, in working out a method of instruction... and in making available to the offices of the procuratura, of the militia, to the courts, and also to the social organizations, information as regards fundamental and at the same time totally effective methods of crime detection and prevention.[46]

It is easy to see that, without proper guidance and instruction in methods of justice, the comradely courts would reach that degree of simplicity and informality which characterized the courts of revolutionary Russia during the chaotic years of the Civil War.

In the beginning of 1960, the Law Institute of Sverdlovsk, with the approval of the Party authorities, decided to establish a university of legal knowledge to provide a basic legal education to all those needing some familiarity with the Soviet legal system. It will consist of three faculties. A faculty of Soviet work is intended for economic and trade union officers, executive officers of Soviet institutions,

... activists of the Party, of the Communist Youth Organizations and of the local Soviets. Another faculty will give instruction in all those subjects useful to the commanders of voluntary people's detachments, and a third will cover all aspects required by the chairmen of the people's courts.[47]

46 Gertsenson, "Ob izuchenii i preduprezhdenii prestupnosti," SGP 85 (No. 7, 1960).
47 Semenov i Yakushev, Sov. iust. 14–17 (No. 4, 1960).

Some consolation is offered by those who insist that the transition to higher forms of social organizations will also simplify the forms of social action.

According to this pattern, labor relations, affairs of the agricultural collective, and business relations are governed by the general institutions of the proper branches of law, labor, *kolkhoz,* and civil. Individual life is increasingly coming under the rule of administrative law and of administrative action.[48]

Irrespective of the problem of the dialectics of transition to higher forms of social organization, it seems that the prediction that greater opportunities for social action in the maintenance of public order will emphasize administrative rather than judicial action is well founded. As an arm of formal justice, social organizations represent an inferior and ill-equipped instrument. As instruments for social regimentation, they are far superior to any other form of social action, and the enforcement of individual rights and adjudication of disputes will have to take second place.

Quite a different tendency may be observed in business relations. Here it has been realized that higher forms of economic organizations call for individual initiative and transactional forms of economic cooperation.

Thus, each economic institution, which is at the same time a basis for the coordination of human participation in economic processes, represents a complex of relations run according to conflicting principles. Internal relations of the factory crews and of farming communities in the agricultural collectives are handled according to the flexible rules of administrative action. In the socialist business world, rights and duties are gaining expression, and their social role, a wider recognition.

Max Weber observed, in connection with the social function of formal justice, that:

[T]he bourgeois strata have generally tended to be intensely interested in rational procedural systems and therefore in a systematized and unambiguously formal and purposefully constructed substantive law which eliminates both obsolete traditions and arbitrariness and in which rights can have their source exclusively in general objective norms.[49]

48 Aleksieiev, *supra* note 1.
49 Weber, On Law in Economy and Society 229 (1954).

It seems that the general tendency of the Soviet legal order is to shift the rule of law almost exclusively into the service of its economic operations.

PROPERTY REGIME AND SOCIAL CONTROL

The central aim of the social reforms launched by the Twenty-first Party Congress is a higher degree of equality for all members of the Soviet polity. This is to be achieved through the reform of property relations:

The building of communism, transforming of all aspects of social and personal life on a higher social basis, also introduces substantial changes in the problem of personal property. The establishment of communism is the objective basis for the intensification of tendencies toward complete equality on the basis of creation of an abundance of material and spiritual wealth.

Socialism, Soviet scholars claim, achieved the first condition of human equality by monopolizing in the hands of the State the ownership of the means of production (socialist property). It left a good deal of inequality in the category of consumer goods (personal property). This was due primarily to the fact that the state of the national economy was such that equal satisfaction of everybody's needs was impossible. Communism, it is argued, will remove that last aspect of inequality by increasing the ability of social institutions to meet individual needs beyond bare existence. The increasing ability of social production to satisfy the needs of society is eventually to result in a fundamental revision of the concept of property.

In order to achieve this new dimension of equality, a new attitude and a new legal basis must be created regarding the use of the so-called durable consumer goods. Under socialism, those who earned higher incomes, owing to their contribution to social life, were able to acquire legally a greater share of durable consumer goods, private homes, cars, pleasure boats, etc. than the rest of society. This attitude and legal form, as expressed in personal ownership, was correct as long as these articles were in short supply. Now that their production is assuming mass proportions, personal ownership is no longer a correct solution. The ideal solution would be to establish a situation where the use of certain consumer goods would be made available to the public without turning them into the personal property of individuals.[50]

The first hint of the new approach in this matter came from Khrushchev at the Twenty-first Party Congress:

Satisfaction of individual needs of each citizen must take place in the measure of the growth of the material and cultural welfare of the society. It should take place not only in the form of raising wages, but also through the so-called funds, the role and function of which will constantly increase.

As an illustration of what he meant in this connection, Khrushchev referred to the expanding production of automobiles in the Soviet Union, which will serve society not according to the American pattern but will be used to establish taxi pools. Rather than own individual cars, people will rent them as they need them.[51]

In June of 1960, *Pravda* began to publish letters from its readers concerning abuses in connection with the distribution of plots from the so-called collective gardens, which were established on government lands allotted to individual factories for the use of their members. It appears that these collective gardens, divided into small plots, were then used by the individual workers to build small *dachas*. Furthermore, vegetables grown in these small plots were disposed of at a handsome profit, thus causing a good deal of jealousy and anguish among those who were unable to secure such plots. It also appears that these gardens were given to those who occupied higher positions in the factory's hierarchy, and generally to those who were able to use some influence. This again caused indignation among the lower ranks of Soviet society. In this manner, members of the Party and those holding executive positions in the factories were accused of succumbing too easily to the lures of capitalism. Moreover, it was reported that in some localities (in Sverdlovsk) a real black market in the garden plots developed.[52]

50 Stepanyan, "Kommunizm i sobstvennost," Oktiabr (No. 9, 1960).
51 Khrushchev, *supra* note 35, at 53.
52 Pravda, June 16, July 3, August 31, 1960; the Decree of the Presidium of the Supreme Soviet of the Tadzhik Republic of August 21, 1960, declared punishable all concealed transfer of land allotted for construction of private housing, unauthorized construction of houses, and illegal ac-

The sale of vegetables from private gardens was not the only form of obtaining a profit from objects which were primarily designed to serve the person of the owners. Owners of automobiles were paid for hiring them to others, or for renting their houses, *dachas,* and garages. Thus, they were turned into the private property of the means of production and a source of unearned income.[53]

In consequence, a further restriction on the scope of objects capable of personal ownership became imperative. As a first step toward communism, it would be necessary to liquidate all those situations which represented a differentiation as to source of income in the Soviet society:

The complete liquidation of private property and its anti-socialist tendencies is a task of the first stage of communism.... The existing garden plots and dachas personally owned by workers, employees, scientists and writers must be voluntarily placed under a cooperative system. The cooperative system, as one of socialist property, strengthens the socialist nature of personal property and makes it possible through the common efforts ... to stop abuses....[54]

The proposed reform of property relations will also affect the forms of legal relations. Legal commerce concerned with private life will shift from the contract of sale to contracts of lease, rent, and hire between individuals and social institutions controlling and administering social funds. Such will "promote the development of new relations and will lead to the liquidation of all proprietary concepts of 'mine' and 'yours,' to be replaced by a truly communist concept that all this is 'ours.' "[55]

THE CROSSCURRENTS

At present the growth of Soviet law and its institutions is influenced by two conflicting tendencies. In the first place, one may clearly discern a tendency toward expansion of the rule of law. After long years, the Soviet leadership has finally realized that continuation of administrative regulation of economic activity represents serious

quisition of building materials. Kommunist Tadzhikistana, Aug. 21, 1961.

53 Stepanyan, note 50.

54 *Ibid.;* XXI sjczd KPSS, *supra* note 4, at 7.

55 *Ibid.*

drawbacks and adversely affects economic progress. While the state may intervene locally and adjust the flow of capital, while it may plan investment according to social needs, the end result in terms of the national product depends equally upon the individual initiative of those who manage production, distribute, and serve. As a result, a legal system combining administrative action with transactional forms of economic cooperation has been developed.

This tendency favors codification as the method of social ordering. Business activity calls for the presence of general rules of law to which partners in legal commerce could readily refer without involving official action, except in the form of expert solution of their disputes by the courts.

In contrast, methods of social ordering affecting individual life reveal a different tendency. Here, the function of the abstract legal precept and of the general rule of law is on the decline. It is replaced by social discipline, by collective action, and by the intervention of public authority. And these latter are deeply and intimately concerned with all aspects of individual existence.

Extensive reforms feature deeper involvement of social organizations and individual representatives of society in the affairs of government. The human being is submerged in the social mass and appears only as a carrier of higher authority, as a representative of the people, as a social activist and social organizer. Social pressure and mass control become important instruments of social and even legal reforms.[56]

The characteristic feature of social and governmental reforms is the transfer of vast judicial powers to social organizations which dispose of private litigations and minor conflicts in a nonjudicial manner. Legal development stresses social harmony—composition rather than litigation.

To seek an analogy with these developments of the Soviet legal order, one must leave the world of the Western European tradition.

---

56 "The complete liquidation of private property and its antisocial tendencies is a task of the first stage of communism. By force of the law, which expressed the will of a united and monolithic Soviet people, it is necessary to close all the loopholes through which private owners crawl.... Obviously, this will be done not through a legislative action, but by the pressure of public opinion, by mass action." Stepanyan, *supra* note 50.

As one of the keen observers of the rule of law in Chinese civilization stated:

The peoples of Western civilization have all lived under the Graeco-Roman conception of law. In the West the law has always been revered as something more or less sacrosanct, the queen of gods and men, imposing itself on everyone like a categorical imperative, defining and regulating, in an abstract way, the effects and conditions of all forms of social activity. In the West there have been tribunals, the role of which has not only been to apply the law, but often to interpret it in the light of debates where all contradictory interests are represented and defended.... But as one passes to the East, this picture fades away. At the other end of Asia, China has felt able to give to law and jurisprudence but an inferior place in that powerful body of spiritual and moral values which she created and for so long diffused over so many neighboring cultures....[57]

In this conception there is no place for law in the Latin sense of the term. Not even rights of individuals are guaranteed by law. There are only duties and mutual compromises governed by the ideas of order, responsibility, hierarchy, and harmony.... The supreme idea of the Chun-tzu is to demonstrate in all circumstances a just measure, a ritual of moderation; as is shown in the Chinese taste for arbitration and reciprocal concessions. To take advantage of one's position, to invoke one's rights, has always been looked at askance in China.[58]

It is a moot question whether modern tendencies in the development of the Soviet legal order are due to the national characteristics of the peoples of Russia, the absence of a legal tradition in the Russian culture, or to its transitional character as a bridge between the East and the West. Nor is it important to establish the relationship between Soviet policies and the political doctrines of Marxism.[59] Social and legal reforms which followed the demise of Stalin were a response to the needs of the Soviet economy. Further progress was

57 Escarra, Le droit chinois 3 (1936).
58 *Id.* at 17; "Lao Tzu advocated a government of men who might possess all powers but would not use them. This idea of government of men was fully developed by Confucius...." Tseng Yu-Hao, Modern Chinese Legal and Political Philosophy 8–9 (1930); *cf.* van der Valk, An Outline of Modern Chinese Family Law 10, 12 (1939); 1 Wigmore, Panorama of the World's Legal Systems, ch. 4 (1928); Hu Shi, The Development of the Logical Method in Ancient China (1922); Wu, The Art of Law (1936).
59 *Cf.* Guins, Soviet Law and Soviet Society 382 (1954).

predicated by greater opportunity for business initiative and a further strengthening of the discipline of labor.

There is no doubt that Soviet leadership was convinced that Soviet workers would be capable of greater effort if social discipline would also involve the Soviet citizens' life outside the boundaries of the institution in which he works. Constant concern with the disorganizing effect of industrial economy and the urban conditions of life suggests that they are considered a serious obstacle in economic progress. The model law on Raising the Role of Society in the Struggle with the Violations of Soviet Legality and Rules of Socialist Coexistence points out that:

Soviet citizens devotedly work on all sectors of communist construction, honorably discharge their social duties, abide by Soviet statutes and respect the rules of socialist coexistence. At the same time there are still among us people who live an undignified life, commit crimes and other antisocial offenses. By their doings they make it impossible for Soviet people to live quietly and to work, and they harm society.[60]

A proper style of life corresponding to the dignity of the Soviet man—stressing the duty to work—will result in great economies both in terms of costs of maintaining social discipline and order and greater discipline of labor.

The need for greater social discipline in modern mass society is not less keenly felt in open societies. The Western response was a system of rules and social organizations which emphasized the accommodation of conflicting situations, individual rights, collective action, administrative intervention of public authority, and economic initiative within a framework of abstract legal institutions and judicial controls. The polycentric social mechanism of the Western type provided room for individual existence. A process of delegation of power in the Soviet social order brought an even tighter control of individual life. In the Soviet system, it is exposed to several tyrannies, which are petty and local but nonetheless erosive to human dignity.

60 Izvestia, Oct. 23, 1959.

BIBLIOGRAPHY

Akhverdian. "Zakreplenie vazhneishykh dostizhenii sovetskogo naroda," SGP, No. 11, 1959.

Aksenenok and Ruskol. "Neobkhodimo dalneisheie sovershenstvovanie pravovogo regulirovania khoziaistvennoi deiatelnosti kolkhozov," SGP, No. 1, 1959.

Aleksandrov. O moralnom oblike sovetskogo cheloveka, 1948.

Aleksandrov. Sovetskoe trudovoe pravo, 1954.

Aleksandrov and Pasherstnik. Sovetskoe trudovoe pravo, 1952.

Aleksieiev. "Differentsiatsia grazhdanskogo pravovogo regulirovania v sotsialisticheskom obshchestve," SGP, No. 2, 1960.

Aleksieiev. "O teoreticheskikh osnovakh klasifikatsii otraslei sovetskogo prava," SGP, No. 11, 1958.

Aleksieiev. "O zakonomernostiakh razvitia sovetskogo prava v period razvernutogo stroitelstva kommunizma," SGP, No. 9, 1960.

Alibert. Le contrôle jurisdictionnel de l'administration au moyen du recours pour excès de pouvoir, 1926.

Amfiteatrov. Osnovnye cherty zakonoproekta o dogovorakh, 1934.

Antimonov and Fleishits. Avtorskoe pravo, 1957.

Antimonov and Fleishits. "Avtorstvo i trudovoe pravootnoshenie," SGP, No. 5, 1956.

Appleton. Traité élémentaire du conténtieux administratif, 1927.

Aumann. The Changing American Legal System: Some Selected Phases, 1940.

Baginski. "Institut obshchestvennogo poruchitelstva kak mera preduprezhdenia pravonarushenii i perevospitania pravonarushitelei," SGP, No. 10, 1959.

Bahr. Der Rechtsstaat, eine publizistische Skizze, 1864.

Bardin. "Novoe postanovlenie plenuma Verkhovnogo Suda SSSR 'O

Sudebnoi praktike po grazhdanskim kolkhoznym delam,' " SGP, No. 6, 1960.

Barsukov. "Ob uchastii trudiashchikhsia v okhrane obshchestvennogo poriadka," SGP, No. 8, 1959.

Barton. "The Current Status of the Soviet Worker," 9 Problems of Communism, July 1960.

Bauer. The New Man in Soviet Psychology, 1952.

Berle and Means. The Modern Corporation and Private Property, 1933.

Berman. "Commercial Contracts in Soviet Law," 35 Calif. L. Rev., 1947.

Bernatzik. Rechtssprechung und materielle Rechtskraft, 1886.

Beurdeley. Le détournement de pouvoir dans l'interêt financier ou patrimonial de l'administration, 1928.

Biber. "Reevaluation of Money Claims in Hungary," 2 Highlights, 1954.

Bolgár. "The Concept of Public Welfare," 8 Am. J. Comp. L., 1959.

Bolgár. "The Magic of Property and Public Welfare," 2 Inter-Amer. L. Rev., 1960.

Bouère. Le droit de grève, 1958.

Bratus. "Khoziaistvennyi dogovor kak grazhdansko-pravovaia forma planovogo razpredelenia produktsii," SGP, No. 2–3, 1953.

Bratus. "O nekotorykh chertakh istorii sovetskogo grazhdanskogo prava," SGP, No. 11, 1957.

Bratus. "O normowaniu prawnym stosunków majątkowych w ZSRR," PiP, No. 4–5, 1960.

Bratus and Lunts. Voprosy khoziaistvennogo dogovora, 1954.

Brus. Prawo wartości a problematyka bodźców ekonomicznych, 1956.

Buczkowski. "O właściwą rolę prawa cywilnego w gospodarce uspołecznionej," PiP, No. 8–9, 1956.

Bury. The Idea of Progress, An Inquiry Into Its Origin and Growth, 1932.

Cardozo. The Nature of the Judicial Process, 1921.

Chkhikvadze. Sovetskoe ugolovnoe pravo, obshchaia chast, 1952.

Cohen. "The Place of Logic in the Law," 29 Harv. L. Rev., 1916.

Denisov. "O sootnoshenii gosudarstva i obshchestva v perekhodnyi ot kapitalizma do kommunizma period," SGP, No. 4, 1960.

Denisov and Bernstein. "Osnovy grazhdanskogo zakonodatelstva i 'khoziaistvennoe pravo,' " SGP, No. 5, 1959.

Denning. The Changing Law, 1953.

Deutscher. Soviet Trade Unions, 1950.

Dicey. Relation Between Law and Public Opinion in England During the Nineteenth Century, 1952 reprint of 1905 edition.

Dogadov. "Etapy razvitia sovetskogo kolektivnogo dogovora," Izvestia Akademii Nauk SSSR, Otdelenie ekonomiki i prava, No. 2, 1948.

Dogadov. "Istoria razvitia sovetskogo trudovogo prava," Uchonye Zapiski, Leningradskogo Universiteta, No. 2, 1949.

Donnedieu de Vabres. La crise moderne du Droit pénal, la politique criminelle des États autoritaires, 1938.

Duguit. Traité de droit constitutionnel, 1927.

Durand. "Les fonctions publiques de l'enterprise privée," 8 Droit Social, 1945.

Durmanov. "Ugolovnoe zakonodatelstvo Soiuza SSR i ugolovnoe zakonodatelstvo soiuznykh respublik," SGP, No. 7, 1959.

Eason. "Population and Labor Force," in Soviet Economic Growth, Bergson ed., 1953.

Ehrlich. Fundamental Principles of the Sociology of Law, 1936.

Ehrlich. "Uwagi o praworządności socjalistycznej," PiP, No. 8–9, 1958.

Engelman et al. A History of Continental Civil Procedure, 1927.

Escarra. Le droit chinois, 1936.

Fedkin. "O rukovodiashchei roli VKP(b) v razvitii sovetskogo sotsialisticheskogo prava," SGP, No. 6, 1950.

Fenet. Recueil complet des travaux préparatoires du Code Civil, 15 vols., 1827.

Fleiner. Über die Umbildung zivilrechtlicher Institute durch das öffentliche Recht, 1906.

Fleishits. Lichnye prava v grazhdanskom prave SSSR i kapitalicheskikh stran, 1941.

Fleishits. Obiazatelstva iz prichinenia vreda i neosnovatelnogo obogashchenia, 1951.

Frank. Law and the Modern Mind, 1930.

Friedmann. Law in a Changing Society, 1959.

Friedmann. Legal Theory, 1953.

Friedmann ed. The Public Corporation, A Comparative Symposium, 1954.

Fuller. "Pashukanis and Vyshinsky: A Study in the Development of Marxian Legal Theory," 47 Mich. L. Rev., 1949.

Genkin. "K voprosu o sisteme sovetskogo sotsialisticheskogo prava," SGP, No. 9, 1956.

Genkin. "Predmet i sistema sovetskogo trudovogo prava," SGP, No. 2, 1949.

Genkin, Bratus, Lunts, and Novitskii. Sovetskoe grazhdanskoe pravo, 2 vols., 1956.

Geny. Méthode d'interprétation et sources en droit privé positif, 1899.

Geny. Science et technique en droit privé positif, 1927.

Gerskovic. "On the Basic Institutes of Property Law," The New Yugoslav Law, January–June 1955.

Gertsenson. "Ob izuchenii i preduprezhdenii prestupnosti," SGP, No. 7, 1960.

Gertsenson *et al.* Istoria sovetskogo ugolovnogo prava, 1948.

Ginsburg. "Voprosy sovetskogo khoziaistvennogo prava na dannom etape," in Voprosy sovetskogo khoziaistvennogo prava, 1943.

Gliksman. "Recent Trends in Soviet Labor Policy," 79 Monthly Labor Rev., July 1956.

Gneist. Der Rechtsstaat, 1872.

Gneist. Self-government; Kommunalverfassung und Verwaltungsgerichte in England, 1871.

Gneist. Zur Verwaltungsreform und Verwaltungsrechtspflege in Preussen, 1881.

Goikhbarg. Khoziaistvennoe pravo RSFSR, 1 Grazhdanskii kodeks, 1924.

Goldstajn. "The Economic Courts," The New Yugoslav Law, July–December, 1954.

Gordon. "Poniatie sovetskogo avtorskogo prava," Uchonye Zapiski Kharkovskogo Iuridicheskogo Instituta, No. 1, 1939.

Goricar. "Worker's Self-Government in the Light of the Scientific Socialism," The New Yugoslav Law, April–December, 1957.

Gorkin. "O zadatchakh sovetskogo suda v period razvernutogo stroitelstva kommunizma," SGP, No. 3, 1960.

Green. Judge and Jury, 1930.

Gruenbaum-Ballin and Pettit. Les conflits collectifs du travail et leur réglement dans le monde contemporain (grèves, procédures de conciliation et d'arbitrage). Travaux et récherches de l'Institut de droit comparé de l'Université de Paris, 1954.

Grzybowski. "La continuité légale dans les démocraties populaires," 54 Revue politique et parlementaire, July 1952.

Grzybowski. "Continuity of Law in Eastern Europe," 6 Am. J. Comp. L., 1957.

Grzybowski. "The Criminal Law of France," in Essays on French Law, 1958.

Grzybowski. "Directive Rulings of the Supreme Court in Criminal Matters," 6 Highlights, 1958.

Grzybowski. "Evolution of the Polish Labor Law 1945–1955," in Legal Problems under Soviet Domination, 1956.

Grzybowski. "From Contract to Status, Some Aspects of the Reception of Soviet Law in Eastern Europe," 2 Seminar, 1953.

Grzybowski. "Fundamental Rights of Persons and Social Groups," in Mémoires de l'Académie Internationale de Droit Comparé, Vol. III, Part 6, 1957.

Grzybowski. "New Trends in the Administration of Penal Justice in Poland (Offenses of Public Officials)," 2 Highlights, 1954.

Grzybowski. "Polish Workers' Councils," 17 Journal of Central European Affairs, 1957.

Grzybowski. "The Powers Trial and the 1958 Reform of Soviet Criminal Law," 9 Am. J. Comp. L., 1960.

Grzybowski. "Reform and Codification of Polish Laws," 7 Am. J. Comp. L., 1958.

Grzybowski. "Soviet Criminal Law Reform of 1958," 35 Ind. L.J., 1960.

Grzybowski. "Trade Unions in Communist Poland," Problems of Communism, No. 5, 1956.

Gsovski. Elements of Soviet Labor Law, Bulletin, No. 1026 of the U.S. Dept. of Labor, 1951.

Gsovski. Soviet Civil Law, 2 vols., 1948.

Gsovski and Grzybowski. Government, Law and Courts in the Soviet Union and Eastern Europe, 2 vols., 1959.

Guins. Soviet Law and Soviet Society, 1954.

Gurvich. L'expérience juridique et la philosophie pluraliste du droit, 1934.

Gurvich. Sociology of Law, 1942.

Gwiazdomorski. Prawo spadkowe, 1959.

Halévy. Essai sur l'accéleration de l'histoire, 1948.

Hall. "Nulla Poena sine Lege," 47 Yale Law J., 1937.

Harper and James. The Law of Torts, 3 vols., 1956.

Hauriou. Précis de droit administratif, 1927.

Hazard. "Le droit soviétique et le dépérissement de l'État," in 8 Travaux et conférences, Université Libre de Bruxelles, 1960.

Hazard. Law and Social Change in the USSR, 1953.

Hazard. Settling Disputes in Soviet Society, The Formative Years of Legal Institutions, 1960.

Holmes. Common Law, 1881.

Hu Shi. The Development of the Logical Method in Ancient China, 1928.

Ilyin and Mironov. "O forme i stile pravovykh aktov," SGP, No. 12, 1960.

Isayev. Obshchaia chast ugolovnogo prava, 1925.

Jaroszynski, Zimmerman, and Brzezinski. Polskie prawo administracyjne, część ogólna, 1956.

Jellinek. Ausgewählte Schriften und Reden, 1911.

Jellinek. L'état moderne et son droit, 1904.

Jellinek. Gesetz, Gesetzanwendung und Zweckmassigkeitserwagung, 1913.

Jellinek. Der Kampf des alten mit dem neuen Recht, 1907.

Jhering. The Struggle for Law, Lalor transl., 2d ed., 1915.

Jhering. Der Zweck in Recht, 2 vols., 4th ed., 1904.

Jones. "The Rule of Law and the Welfare State," 55 Colum. L. Rev., 1958.

Kaminskaia. "V chem znachenie protsessualnikh garantii v sovetskom ugolovnom protsesse," SGP, No. 5, 1950.

Karev. "Dalnieishee sovershenstvovanie sovetskoi pravovoi sistemy," SGP, No. 2, 1959.

Karev. "The Forthcoming Reform of USSR Criminal Law," Harv. L. Record, May 1, 1958.

Karev. Sovetskoe sudoustrojstvo, 1951.

Kareva. Pravo i nrastvennost v sotsialisticheskon obshchestve, 1952.

Kelsen. General Theory of Law and State, Wedberg transl., 1945.

Khrushchev. O kontrolnikh tsyfrakh razvitia narodnogo khoziaistva SSSR na 1959–1965 gody, 1959.

Kirichenko. Vidy dolzhnostnikh prestuplenii po sovetskomu ugolovnomu pravu, 1959.

Kiselev. "O pravovom polozhenii profsoiuznykh organizatsii v SSSR, SGP, No. 4, 1956.

Komarov. "K voprosu ob unichtozhenii klassov," SGP, No. 3, 1936.

Kozak. "Otvestvennost za zaniatie zapreshchonymi promyslami," Sots. zak., No. 3, 1958.

Kozyr. "Aktualnye problemi kolkhoznoi sobstvennosti na sovremennom etape," SGP, No. 8, 1960.

Krylenko. "Sudebnaia sistema i Gosarbitrazh," SGP, No. 7–8, 1932.

Kryvickas. "Illustration of the Rule of Law in Lithuania," 6 Highlights, 1958.

Kucherov. Courts, Lawyers and Trials Under the Last Three Tsars, 1953.

Kulski. The Soviet Regime, 1954.

Kurskii. "Novoe ugolovnoe pravo," Proletarskaia Revolutsia i Pravo, No. 2–3, 1919.

Laferrière. Traité de la juridiction administrative et des recours conténtieux, 2d ed., 1896.

Laptev. "K voprosu o khoziaistvennom prave," Voprosy Ekonomiki, No. 12, 1959.

Laun. Das freie Ermesse und seine Grenzen, 1910.

Lemkin and McDermott, translators. The Polish Penal Code of 1932 and the Law of Minor Offenses, 1939.

Lenin. Sochinenia, 4th ed., 1949–51.

Lenin. The State and Revolution, 1935.

Leroy. La loi, essai sur la théorie de l'autorité dans la démocratie, 1908.

Lundstedt. Legal Thinking Revised, 1956.

Lys, Lesnik, and Borzova. "Struktura dogovornykh sviazei i nekotorye voprosy ulutshenia organizatsii materialno-tekhnicheskogo snabzhenia," SGP, No. 2, 1960.

Maksimovich. "Experiments in Legislative Technique in Yugoslavia," 2 Highlights, 1954.

Mankowski. "Zasady radzieckiej praworządności socialistycznej," PiP, No. 1, 1950.

Marx and Engels. Selected Works, 2 vols., 1950.

Materialy Narkomyusta, 1918–22.

Mayzel. "O umowach dostawy pomiędzy jednostkami gospodarki uspołecznionej," PiP, No. 8, 1956.

Mead. Soviet Attitude Towards Authority, An Interdisciplinary Approach to Problems of Soviet Character, 1951.

Mendelssohn-Bartholdy. Das Imperium des Richters, 1908.

Merz. "A jednak zgodnie z ustawa," PiZ, Aug. 23, 1959.

Merz. "O dobrą wiarę," PiZ, June 30, 1959.

Michoud. La théorie de la personalité morale et son application en droit français, 1906–9.

Mitrichev. "Privlechenie obshchestvennosti k rassledovanii prestuplenii," Sots. zak., No. 10, 1960.

Mitskevitch. "Razshirenie roli obshchestvennikh organizatsii v period razvernutogo stroitelstva kommunizma," SGP, No. 9, 1959.

Młyńczyk. "Rzecz o grzechach administracji," PiZ, Dec. 13, 1959.

Mohl. "Gesellschaftswissenschaft und Staatswissenschaft," 7 Zeitschrift für die gesammte Staatswissenschaft, 1851.

Morel. Traité élémentaire de procédure civile, 1949.

Motovilovker. "Dokazatelstvennoe znachenie dannykh o lichnosti obviniaemogo," Sots. zak., No. 9, 1959.

Nabatov. "Strogo okhraniat prava grazhdan," Sots. zak., No. 2, 1960.

Nabatov. "Strogo okhraniat prava grazhdan," SGP, No. 1, 1956.

Nagórski. "Draft of the New Civil Code for Poland," in Studies of the Polish Lawyers in Exile in the U.S., 1956.

Olivecrona. Law as Fact, 1939.

Opałek and Zakrzewski. Z zagadnień praworządności socjalistycznej, 1958.

Orlovskii. "Zadatchi pravovoi nauki v svete reshenii XX siezda KPSS," 26 Vestnik Akademii Nauk, No. 8, 1956.

Ostrovitianov. "Tovarnoe proizvodstvo i zakon stoimosti pri sotsializme," Kommunist, No. 13, 1958.

"Osuzhdenie voprosov sistemy sovetskogo prava i sotsialisticheskoi zakonnosti," SGP, No. 11, 1958.

Papierkowski. "A jednak contra legem," PiZ, Aug. 23, 1959.

Papierkowski. "Niebezpieczne prawo," PiZ, April 19, 1959.

Pasherstnik. Teoreticheskie voprosy kodifikatsii obshchesoiuznogo zakonodatelstva o trude, 1955.

Pashukanis. Allgemeine Rechtslehre und Marxismus, 1929.

Pashukanis. "The General Theory of Law and Marxism," in Soviet Legal Philosophy, 1951.

Pavlov. "K voprosu kodifikatsii sovetskogo grazhdanskogo zakonodatelstva," SGP, No. 8, 1959.

Pietek. "W imieniu ryb," PiZ, Jan. 11, 1959.

Piotrowski. "The Great Importance of Commercial Law for Peaceful Economic Collaboration of All Nations," The New Yugoslav Law, July–December, 1958.

Piotrowski. "Na marginesie proponowanych zmian w polskim prawie rodzinnym," PiP, 1960.

Pollock. A First Book of Jurisprudence for Students of the Common Law, 2d ed., 1904.

Portalis. Discours préliminaire, Projèt de Code Civil présenté par la Commission nommée par le Gouvernement, Le 24 Thermidor an 8, 1801.

Pound. Fashions in Juristic Thinking, 1938.

Pound. "Individualization of Justice," 7 Fordham L. Rev., 1938.

Pound. Jurisprudence, 5 vols., 1959.

Pound. "The Need of a Sociological Jurisprudence," 19 The Green Bag, 1907.

Pound. The Spirit of the Common Law, 1921.

"Property and Inheritance Rights of Peasant Members of the Collective Farms in Romania," 2 Highlights, 1954.

Pyontkovskii. "K voprosu o vzaimootnoshenii obiektivnogo i subiektivnogo prava," SGP, No. 5, 1958.

Reisner. "Law, Our Law, Foreign Law, General Law," in Soviet Legal Theory, Babb transl., 1951.

Renard. Le droit, la logique et le bons sens, 1925.

Renard. Propriété privé et propriété humaine, 1926.

Renard. La théorie de l'institution, essai d'ontologie juridique, 1930.

Renner. The Institutions of Private Law and Their Social Functions, Schwarzchild transl., 1949.

Ripert. Le déclin du droit, 1949.

Rivero. "Les droits de l'homme dans le droit constitutionnel français d'aujourd'hui," in Memoires de l'Académie Internationale de Droit Comparé, Vol. III, Part 6, 1957.

Robson. Justice and Administrative Law, 2d ed., 1947.

Romashkin. "Razvitie funktsii sovetskogo gosudarstva v protsesse postroienia kommunizma," SGP, No. 10, 1958.

Rommen. Die evige Wiederkehr des Naturrechts, 1947.

Rommen. The Natural Law, A Study in Legal and Social History and Philosophy, 1947.

Ross. On Law and Justice, 1959.

Roubier. Théorie générale du droit, 1946.

Rummelin. Metodisches über juristische personen, 1891.

Rusis. "Law Enforcement in Soviet Latvia," 6 Highlights, 1958.

Saleilles. De la personalité juridique, 1922.

Savatier. Du droit civil au droit public, 1950.

Savatier. Métamorphoses économiques et sociales du droit civil d'aujourd'hui, 1948, Series 2 and 3, 1959.

Savitskii and Keyzerov. "Razvitie pravovykh form organizatsii i dejatelnosti tovarishcheskikh sudov," SGP, No. 4, 1961.

Sawicki. "Dobra wiara a zniesławienie w projekcie prawa prasowego," PiZ, January 25, 1959.

Schmied. "Das Familienrecht der Volksdemokratien 1945–1951," 17 Zeitschrift für ausländisches und internationales Privatrecht, 1952.

Schultz. History of Roman Legal Science, 1946.

Schwarz. Labor in the Soviet Union, 1952.

Serick. Rechtsform und Realitet juristischer Personen, 1955.

Shargorodskii. "Tolkovanie ugolovnogo zakona," Uchonye zapiski Leningradskogo Gosudarstvennogo Universiteta, No. 1, 1948.

Shargorodskii and Joffe. "O sisteme sovetskogo prava," SGP, No. 6, 1957.

Shkundin. "Gosudarstvennyi arbitrazh i arbitrazhnyi protsess," in Arbitrazh v Sovetskom Khoziaistve, 1938.

Sipkov. "The Bulgarian Supreme Court and Its Directive Rulings," 6 Highlights, 1958.

Sipkov. "The Concept of Public Official and Offense in Public Office," 2 Highlights, 1954.

Social Security in the Soviet Union, Draft of the report by the U.S. team that visited the USSR, 1959.

Solnar. "Maintien ou abandon de la règle nulla poena sine lege," 17 Revue de droit pénal et de criminologie, 1937.

Sorok let sovetskogo prava 1917–1957, Vol. 1, Period stroitelstva sotsializma; Vol. 2, Period sotsializma, 1957.

Sovetskoe Grazhdanskoe Pravo, 2 vols., Vol. 1, Genkin ed., Vol. II, Bratus ed., 1950–51.

Stalgievitch. Puti razvitia sovetskoi pravovoi mysli, 1928.

Stammler. "Fundamental Tendencies in Modern Jurisprudence," 21 Mich. L. Rev., 1923.

Stammler. Theorie der Rechtswissenschaft, 1911.

Starosolskyj. The Principle of Analogy in Criminal Law: An Aspect of Soviet Legal Thinking, 1954.

Stein. Der Begriff der Gesellshaft, 1855.

Stein. System der Staatswissenschaft, 1856.

Stepanyan. "Kommunism i sobstvennoost," Oktiabr, No. 9, 1960.

Stier-Somlo. Politique, 4th French ed., 1919.

Strogovitch. "Nekotorye voprosy sudoustroistva," SGP, No. 7, 1959.

Stuchka. Introduction à la théorie du droit civil, 1926.

Stuchka. Kurs sovetskogo grazhdanskogo prava, 1931.

Stuchka. "Otchet Narodnago Komissara Iustitsii," Proletarskaia Revolutsia i Pravo, No. 1, 1918.

Tadevosyan. "Nekotorye voprosy sistemy sovetskogo prava," SGP, No. 8, 1958.

Tezner. Das Oesterreichische Administrativverfahren, 1925.

Tikhomirov. "Nekotorye voprosy dalneishego razvitia miestnykh organov gosudarstvennoi vlasti SSSR," SGP, No. 1, 1960.

Timasheff. "The Impact of the Penal Law of Imperial Russia on Soviet Penal Law," 12 American Slavic and East European Rev., 1953.

Trainin. "Gosudarstvo stroiushchegosia kommunizma," Izvestia Akademii Nauk SSSR, Otdelenie Ekonomiki i Prava, No. 5, 1945.

Trainin. "Nekotorye vivody dla nauki prava iz diskussii po voprosam biologii," SGP, No. 2, 1949.

Trestní právo hmotné (Čast obecná), 1955.

Trotsky. Moia Zhizn, 1930.

Tseng Yu-Hao. Modern Chinese Legal and Political Philosophy, 1930.

Unesco. Copyright Laws and Treaties of the World, 1956.

Urakov. "Povisyt kulturu sledstva," Sots. zak., No. 7, 1960.

Utevskii. "Novye formy i metody borby z prestupnostiu i lichnost prestupnika," Sots. zak., No. 2, 1960.

Utevskii. "Voprosy ugolovnogo prava v projekte zakona," SGP, No. 1, 1960.

Valk, van der. An Outline of Modern Chinese Family Law, 1939.

Vasiliev. Generalni dogovori, 1958.

Vasiliev. Grazdanskoe pravo narodnoi Respubliki Bolgarii, obshchaia chast, 1956.

Venediktov. Gosudarstvennaia sotsialisticheskaia sobstvennost, 1948.

Verdross. Abendländische Rechtsphilosophie, 1958.

Vlasov and Studenikin. Sovetskoe administrativnoe pravo, 1959.

Vyshinskii. The Law of the Soviet State, Babb transl., 1948.

Vyshinskii. Materialy pervoi konferentsii nauchnykh rabotnikov prava, May 16–19, 1938.

Vyshinskii. Osnovnye zadatchi nauki sovetskogo sotsialisticheskogo prava, 1938.

Vyshinskii. Teoria gosudarstva i prava, 1945.

Vyshinskii. Teoria sudebynkh dokazatelstv v sovetskom prave, 1950.

Vyshinskii. Voprosy teorii gosudarstva i prava, 1949.

Waline. Traité élémentaire de droit administratif, 1957.

Weber. On Law in Economy and Society, Rheinstein ed., 1954.

Welter. Le contrôle jurisdictionnel de la moralité administrative, 1929.

Willoughby. The Ethical Bases of Political Authority, 1940.

Wolter. Prawo cywilne, częśċ ogólna, 1955.

Woywod. Practical Commentary on the Code of Canon Law, 1948.

Wu. The Art of Law, 1936.

Yntema. The Crossroads of Justice, 1957.

Yudin. "Socialism and Law," in Soviet Legal Philosophy, Babb transl., 1951.

"Za povishenie roli pravovoi nauki v kodifikatsii sovetskogo zakonodatelstva," Sots. zak., No. 2, 1960.

Zhdanov. Voprosy Filosofii, No. 1, 1947.

Zimin. "Novoe polozhenie o selskom sovete deputatov trudiashchykhsia RSFSR," SGP, No. 1, 1958.

INDEX